The Art of Sergio Leone's
*Once Upon a Time in the West*

# The Art of Sergio Leone's *Once Upon a Time in the West*

## A CRITICAL APPRECIATION

*by* John Fawell

McFarland & Company, Inc., Publishers

*Jefferson, North Carolina, and London*

All of the photographs are from Photofest.

LIBRARY OF CONGRESS CATALOGUING-IN-PUBLICATION DATA

Fawell, John, 1959–
    The art of Sergio Leone's Once upon a time in the West : a critical
appreciation / by John Fawell.
       p.     cm.
    Includes bibliographical references and index.
    **ISBN-13: 978-0-7864-2092-6**
    softcover : 50# alkaline paper ∞

    1. C'era una volta il west (Motion picture)   I. Title.
PN1997.C3748F38   2005
791.43'72 — dc22                       2005004750

British Library cataloguing data are available

Cover photograph: An evocative shot illustrating Leone's gift for dramatic
composition.

Manufactured in the United States of America

*McFarland & Company, Inc., Publishers*
  *Box 611, Jefferson, North Carolina 28640*
  *www.mcfarlandpub.com*

To Yvette

# Table of Contents

# Preface

There are a good many of us who cannot get enough of Sergio Leone's epic Western *Once Upon a Time in the West*. We play the highly choreographed showpiece sequences of the film over and over again as though they were favorite musical recordings. We memorize the film's concise, aphoristic dialogue. And we find that the film stands up quite well to repeated viewings because, with its solemn, majestic gestures and allusive script, it never quite yields its full meaning. In this book, I will delve into the intriguing mystery of the film, read between the lines of Leone's script, but even more study the meaning inherent in the way the film is shot, the meaning inherent in Leone's musical and ceremonial aesthetic.

The book, however, represents more than the study of a single film. I mean it also as a study of Leone's filmmaking in general. Few directors in the history of film can match Leone for experience and expertise in film craft. The son of a film director and film actress, he was born into the movie world and had apprenticed on over fifty motion pictures, under Italian and American masters, before turning his hand to his own films. Leone had a marked genius for almost all aspects of the process and so this book represents an examination, not only of the film, but of Leone's approach, in general, to cinematography, *mise-en-scène*, set and costume design, editing, the mixing of sound and the direction of actors. It is Leone's meticulous approach to each in the making of *Once Upon a Time*\* that warrants a book-length study of the film.

I am obviously taking an "auteurist" approach to Leone's films—in other words, looking at Leone as the artful progenitor of the film. I am not sure how it can be otherwise. Leone worked with the most talented

---

\**Repeated references to this film may be shortened, as here; there is another Leone film, Once Upon a Time in America, which will always be given in full when mentioned herein.*

1

people in their fields but they all conceded that Leone was in control of their input. At the same time, I hope the book gives full representation to the collaborative nature of filmmaking.

For example, the significance of Ennio Morricone's music in this film is arguably as important a contribution as any composer has ever made to a film. Carlo Simi's skills as an architect and his inherently elegant taste are a large part of Leone's success in set design. Leone's collaborators on the film's original story, Bernardo Bertolucci and Dario Argento, bring an intellectual spark to this screenplay that is missing in Leone's other work. On the other hand, it is screenwriter Sergio Donati's gift for verbal economy that makes the final version of the script the strongest in Leone's oeuvre. This book then is also a study in the kind of talent to which Leone was drawn and how a good film is born from a fortuitous assemblage of talent. And I have placed as much emphasis on the testimony of Leone's co-workers as I have on the critical and academic response to the film.

While analyzing the artful filmmaking represented by *Once Upon a Time in the West*, I also hope to challenge, or at least complicate, some of the myths and criticisms about Leone that I think are ill-considered, particularly that Leone was characterized by a childish cynicism that disqualifies him as a legitimate heir to the great tradition of the Western and, even more seriously, that he was a kind of Mannerist, a grand stylist and director of gestures, who, in the end, had little to say.

Leone could tolerate a great deal of evil in his world view but he had a deep faith in the Western, something that is best expressed in the careful structure of his film. The bias against Leone has always come from the literary segment of the film world. It is his screenwriters who have most often scratched their head at his success. But, a child of Cinecittà studios, the Roman Hollywood, Leone was, above all, a studio director. And like the Hollywood masters under whom he apprenticed at Cinecittà, he revered the genre as much as he disdained films that expressed their meaning in obvious platitudes.

It is in his sense of the American Western as a kind of sacred ritual that Leone expresses himself most personally. The script of *Once Upon a Time* is a masterpiece of concise aphorisms and deft allusiveness. But to appreciate the film, one needs to study its musical thrust and its adherence to the rhythm and ritual of the American Western. Flaubert felt that the writer had no right to express an opinion. "Has God ever expressed his opinion?" he demanded. Like Flaubert, Leone was studiously uninterested in expressing his ideas verbally, preferring to sublimate them into his style. It is the significance of Leone's style — his sure rhythm and strong sense of ritual and ceremony — that is, above all, the subject of this book.

# The Chapters in This Book

The first two chapters of this book deal with the relationship between *Once Upon a Time in the West* and the Western films that preceded it, and which are so often quoted, or referred to, in the film. I argue against the notion that the many references to previous Westerns which appear in *Once* represent an arid game or intellectual tendency on Leone's part to show off his film knowledge, as critics like Bogdanovich have suggested. I contend instead that Leone was careful to avoid "citation for citation's sake," always taking the gestures and rituals of the Hollywood Western and expanding them and according them new meaning.

The second chapter of the book deals specifically with the relationship between Leone's films and those of John Ford. Leone was a cinematic heir to Ford and *Once Upon a Time* represents a textbook of references to Ford's Westerns. But Leone's relationship to Ford's films is complex, characterized by equal measures of reverence and rebelliousness. In general, though, critics have tended to remark more on those scenes where Leone darkly satirizes Ford, and to underestimate how moved Leone was by Ford's honesty and idealism. As dark and elegiac a film *Once Upon a Time* is, it is deeply imbued with Ford's sense of the beauty and majesty of the American West.

The third, fourth and fifth chapters concentrate on the central characters. The third chapter deals with Charles Bronson's "Harmonica" and how he represents a kind of force of destiny as much as he does a human character, an organizing principle for everything that happens in the film. This chapter also addresses Harmonica's relationship to Cheyenne which, in its gruff male camaraderie and allusive code language, reminds us of Leone's debt to Howard Hawks as well as John Ford.

The fourth chapter discusses the character of Jill, Leone's first female protagonist, and some of the criticisms sent her way. I argue that, ultimately, she represents a surprisingly strong and successful character for a filmmaker reputed to be a misogynist. In the end, Leone proves not to be uninterested in women characters, only in *superficial* women characters. Jill is a rich character, central to almost everything that happens in the film and accorded a kind of existential solitude and strength normally reserved for the men in Westerns.

The fifth chapter deals with the railroad baron Morton and his relationship to the gunslinger Frank. Morton's character introduces a discussion of Leone's politics because it is in Morton's story that Leone reveals his Italian Socialist roots and expresses his criticism of American capitalism. Morton's character also brings to the forefront the rich argument in Leone's films between his love of American cinema and mythology and his disdain for the reality of American politics and economics.

The sixth, seventh and eighth chapters are on Leone's visual style. Chapter Six discusses Leone's meticulous attention to, and cult of authenticity in, his set design, and his unique ability to register a fairy tale–type of story in a documentary or neo–Realist fashion. Chapter Seven is devoted to his approach to shot composition, which represented a unique fusion of Hollywood classicism and elegance and a more modernist style, influenced by Italian Surrealism and the French New Wave, and characterized by ruptures in image and rhythm and strange hallucinatory effect.

Chapter Eight deals specifically with Leone's penchant for extraordinarily tight close-ups. Critics have tended to disparage Leone's close-ups as an eccentricity, characteristic of a kitschy '60s style. But it is in his close-ups that Leone pulls off some of his greatest cinematic miracles, capturing the quietest of meanings, the subtlest of psychological nuances.

Chapters Nine through Eleven deal with the rhythm of *Once Upon a Time,* perhaps the most important facet of the films of this director whose approach to film is, above all, musical.

Chapter Nine discusses Leone's editing process and his penchant for slow, deeply articulated rhythms; more than any other aspect of his films, these point to his Romanticism, his tendency to slow time down, to capture it in its greatest leisure and significance. Chapters Ten and Eleven explore the way Leone's soundtrack contribute to the film's rhythms. Chapter Ten discusses not only Leone's famous ballets characterized by elaborate *mise-en-scène* and the choreography of cowboys to Ennio Morricone's scores, but also his tendency to film his actors in close-up with musical accompaniment, his "stared arias" where eyes rather than bodies move in accompaniment to music. Chapter Eleven discusses the way Leone finds rhythm in non-musical sources. In that chapter, I analyze scenes, such as the one that opens the film, that represent veritable exercises in "musique concret" and scenes where dialogue, as well as natural sound, are woven into the musical soundtrack, registering their own musical or rhythmic effect.

# ONE

# Defending Leone

One critic has written that even the better studies of Sergio Leone are characterized by "a defensive tone," when they should have been written with a "liberating laugh" and in a "spirit of euphoria."[1] This is a thought worth emphasizing as I introduce this book, the principal goal of which is to sharpen our appreciation of Sergio Leone and his Western *Once Upon a Time in the West*, rather than to engage in negative scholarly debate.

That said, it must be admitted that a defensive tone is hard to escape in making a case that Leone's filmmaking should be taken seriously. There are few directors who marry such extraordinary film craft with such a reputation for lowbrow films. One of the first obstacles American audiences confront in taking Leone seriously is that his films (typical of most Italian films at that time) have entirely post-synchronized soundtracks and dubbed dialogue. American audiences are so hostile to post-dubbed voices that even those who recognize the visual sweep and glory of Leone's films still dismiss the movies because of what they perceive as cheesy dubbing and a soundtrack on a par with Japanese Godzilla films.

This is probably the easiest criticism to refute. Dubbing was the accepted method of the time. To fault Leone's cinema for being dubbed is a little like faulting a silent film for having no sound. Moreover, notions of realism are relativistic. Leone and his generation were constantly astounded by what they saw as the American obsession with invisible dubbing when they found Americans so accepting of other non-realistic traditions in filmmaking. This contradiction in the American audience is as true today as it was then. The same contemporary audience that finds dubbing ludicrous is happy to accept patently artificial sound techniques such as the noises used to communicate a fistfight in a typical American action film.

Moreover, even the most cursory examination of Leone's soundtracks reveals that he labored mightily over them. The very artificiality of Leone's soundtrack freed his spirit of invention. The attention to, and careful arrangement of, sound in this film puts to shame the majority of films that record with "realistic" and direct sound. In fact, there is a correspondence between the visual glory of Leone's films and the artificiality of their sound. Freedom from direct sound allowed Leone to conceive of his images with the abandon of a silent film director. It is interesting to note that in the one film (*Once Upon a Time in America*) where he logged substantial time with direct sound, the images shrink. As the early talkies showed us, gains in aural authenticity come hand in hand with losses in visual creativity.

But Leone's reputation as "lowbrow" is not just due to his films being dubbed. Certain critics have judged Leone's films vulgar and visually squalid. One of Leone's directorial heroes, Anthony Mann, complained of the "ugliness" of Leone's close-ups in *For a Few Dollars More*. "My God, what faces! One or two is all right, but 24 — no, it's too much!" Mann also felt that Leone depended too heavily on scenes of violence ("shoot-outs every five minutes or so") to hold his audience's interest.[2] Phillipe Haudriquet too, in *Image et Son*, finds *Once Upon a Time in the West* "heavy and complacent in its depiction of vice and violence, in a word profoundly unhealthy."[3]

Those who would criticize Leone for being vulgar tend to find a moral, as well as visual ugliness, to his films. They find Leone's universe unduly pessimistic. They are troubled by his heroes' cynicism and evident lack of morality. Peter Bogdanovich spits at the notion of Leone as the heir to the Western traditions of Hollywood master John Ford, finding Leone's films "cynical, which Ford never was."[4] Mann agrees. "We," he says, referring to the great Hollywood practitioners of the Western, "tell the story of simple men, not professional assassins."[5]

Another recurrent criticism of Leone (probably the most serious) is often voiced by those who worked with him and even those who respect him generally: that he is a Mannerist. In other words, his films are characterized by a great deal of style and technical savvy but in the end have little substance. He is all style, no content, a "poor man's Visconti," as Frayling puts it. What is interesting about this criticism is not only that it gets repeated fairly often but that it gets mixed up with a kind of personal invective against Leone himself. Over and over again, some of Leone's co-workers (particularly his writers) seem hell-bent on conveying to their interviewers that Leone was not an intellectual. His craftsmanship is never called into question by friend or foe alike, but these critics feel compelled to emphasize that there are no ideas in Leone's cinema. "He hadn't read anything," said Tonino Valerii, "Tolstoy, Dostoevsky, Kafka — and if you don't read you don't know how to tell a story."[6]

Mickey Knox, who translated the script for *Once Upon a Time*, disagrees with Valerii about Leone as a storyteller ("He was a great storyteller") but agrees that Leone was not scholarly. He was, Knox told Frayling, "shallow as hell; he was bereft of profound ideas. But nobody topped him in the technique of making films"[7] In another interview, he describes Leone as a "brilliant technician" but "a rather shallow man." He did not, Knox says, "have any ideas that he wanted to convey."[8]

Bertolucci, in his comments on Leone, always seemed to aim for appreciation but usually finished with a dismissal not unlike Leone's sharper critics. He said that Leone's movies "are good directly at the surface level." Leone "was stronger as a pure talent of *mise-en-scène* — the relationship between the camera, the bodies of the people in front of it, and the landscape — than as a philosopher."[9]

Leone's most vociferous critic is screenwriter Luciano Vincenzoni, the principal writer of *The Good, the Bad and the Ugly*. Of all of Leone's collaborators, Vincenzoni is the most affronted by critics who take Leone seriously. "Do you imagine Sergio Leone with a philosophy? Come on!" he chides one interviewer. To the question of whether he would consider Leone an intellectual, Vincenzoni responds, "Absolutely not! He was a great director on the set. That's all."[10]

Criticisms that Leone's cinema is coarse or crude coincide easily with criticisms that it is too mannered. In both cases, critics take Leone to task for a lack of intellectual content. Leone's cinema, these critics seem to agree, often dazzles and often packs a punch but ultimately it is "bereft of profound ideas."

## Once Upon a Time in the West and Leone's Other Films

*Once Upon a Time in the West* is Leone's greatest film and the one that best refutes the criticisms that Leone's cinema is coarse and operates only "at the surface level." Leone's first two Westerns (*Fistful of Dollars, For a Few Dollars More*) were a delightful shock to the film world and the genre of the Western, but Leone had not, in those two films, assembled the crew that would allow him to express his vision of the West in its greatest scope. They are thinner films than *Once Upon a Time*, both in script and *mise-en-scène*, though we see in *For a Few Dollars More* many of the key ingredients of Leone's best Westerns coming into play.

For example, in *Few Dollars* Leone arrives at his first experiment in a three-pronged arrangement of protagonists—his first "good, bad and ugly" scenario—in the characters of Monko, Mortimer and Indio. Monko and Mortimer represent Leone's first foray into the Howard Hawks–like world of gruff male comradery, with friendship expressed in a dignified, allusive short-hand dialogue that is both competitive and affectionate. The flashback aspect of the narrative anticipates that in *Once Upon a Time in the West,* though the flashbacks are not as carefully doled out as they will be in the later film. And in this film, as in *Once Upon a Time,* Leone finds a material object on which to focus his film's mystery, Mortimer's watch, which occupies the same role in *Few Dollars* that Harmonica's harmonica does in *Once.* In both films, too, that object has a musical dimension that allows Leone to root his central musical theme within the action of the film.

*The Good, the Bad, and the Ugly* is Leone nearly at his best. By this time, he had assembled the team with whom he would do his greatest work: set designer Carlo Simi, an architect who, like Leone himself, had a sophisticated sense of history and plastics; cinematographer Tonino Delli Colli, whose visual sense was so sympathetic to his own and who would provide a rich texture to Leone's later work; editor Nino Baragli, who understood Leone's desire to shoot a great deal of footage so that he could play with it in the editing room; and of course composer Ennio Morricone, whose soundtracks are so close to the heart of Leone's films that he almost seems to qualify as a co-director of sorts.

But the script of *The Good, the Bad* also is thinner than that of *Once Upon a Time in the West.* It seems never to have quite recovered from the misguided contributions of the comic screenwriters Agenore Incrocci and Furio Scarpelli who originally worked on it. And Luchino Vincenzoni, who is credited with its final screenplay, was not as fruitful a collaborator as screenwriter Serge Donati was on *Once Upon a Time.* Donati understood better Leone's open-ended way of filming, providing him with a variety of alternatives in each scene; Donati had a gift for the allusive and aphoristic language Leone prized. Nor does *The Good, the Bad and the Ugly* represent a vast commentary on the West in the manner of *Once Upon a Time,* Leone's melancholy farewell to the genre. And despite its extraordinary finale, there are not as many scenes in *The Good,* as there are in *Once,* in which Leone's gift for luxurious, operatic *mise-en-scène* gets extended play.

Few would nominate *Fistful of Dynamite*[11] as Leone's greatest film, though many might herald it as his most underrated. Leone did not intend to direct it and did not bring the same concentration to the film that he

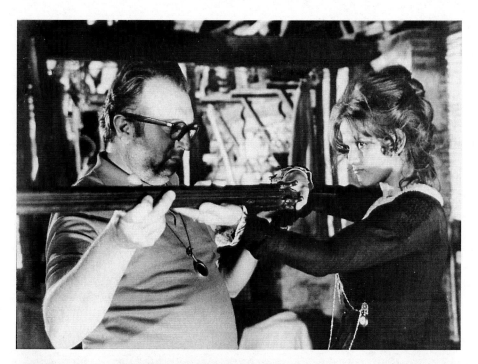

Leone instructs Claudia Cardinale (top) and Jason Robards (bottom) in one of his favorite aspects of Westerns: gunplay.

did his others. By this time, Leone had entered the last phase of his career, a 20-year Puccini-like period of vacillation during which he found it very difficult to settle on a project and pursue it with confidence and efficiency. Serge Donati has complained that the film's final script does not resemble the one he wrote and, indeed, it does suffer the very symptoms Donati was best at curing. It tends to be heavy-handed in its political rhetoric and clumsy in its articulation of the buddy theme, so important to Leone (as it was to Howard Hawks) and so deftly handled by Donati and Leone in *Once Upon a Time in the West* and by Donati, Leone and Vincenzoni in *The Good, the Bad and the Ugly.*

Leone's last film, *Once Upon a Time in America*, has probably received the greatest critical attention; some declare it his finest work. But it probably should be noted that this film was released after Leone's critical acclaim had solidified and he had become recognized, finally, in some quarters, as a film "master." There is a kind of impulsive genuflection to this last film that increasingly, as time passes, seems inconsistent with its glaring insufficiencies. *Once Upon a Time in the West* has a greater musical force and rhythm and greater visual clarity than *Once Upon a Time in America*, which does not seem to express nearly as forcefully the confidence and bravado of Leone's style. Despite the magnificence of the shots of the Williamsburg bridge in *Once Upon a Time in America* and despite its ambitious and epic time frame, it seems a smaller film than *...in the West*. Leone's touch does not seem as assured. And the film's parts, though often representative of Leone at his best, do not add up to the coherent whole that *...in the West* does. Moreover, though Leone's attitude to women in his films is always problematic, there are scenes involving women in *Once Upon a Time in America*, as there are in *Fistful of Dynamite,* that even a critic struggling mightily to avoid political correctness would have difficulty explaining, much less admiring.

# A Film for Myself

*Once Upon a Time in the West* represents Leone at the height of his powers, before the indecision and lack of confidence that would plague the latter part of his career, including the filming of *Once Upon a Time in America.* Coming on the heels of three Westerns, it shows him sure in his technique and confident in his genre. It is a more ambitious and personal film than any of the three Westerns that preceded it, a "a film for myself rather than for the public, a reaction to my previous work." And, if it was his most personal film, it was also his most professional. In this film, Leone aimed for a more classical polish. He wanted it to bear, as little as possible, the stamp of the Cinecittà studios, the highly commercial film studios at which he had apprenticed and still worked. It would be a more contemplative film and more reflective of the Western genre and of Leone's particular contribution to the Western. Leone saw ... *in the West* as his farewell to the Western and so it was to have the scope of a summary statement on the West and the melancholy of a farewell.

So *Once Upon a Time in the West* is Leone's first and only Western to find itself with an actual American setting. And not just *any* location, but *the* location of the American Western: Monument Valley, where John Ford had set nine of his films, among those some of his most important, both to his general public and Leone: *Stagecoach*, *My Darling Clementine*, *Fort Apache*, *She Wore a Yellow Ribbon* and *Cheyenne Autumn*. Leone further invoked Ford's presence by using Ford regulars Henry Fonda and Woody Strode, Fonda in a principal role, Strode in a striking opening-scene cameo. Leone consciously drew out the Fordian iconography in these actors. His camera is as attentive as Ford's was to the strength and elegance of these actors, although Leone cast them in evil roles they never would have been given by Ford. In addition, Leone packs the film with shots and pictorial compositions that are references and homages to Ford, many of them inspired by the Ford landscape.

*Once Upon a Time* is Leone's strongest effort to situate himself in the Western tradition, to engage in dialogue with the great Western directors of the past. As has often been noted, it is packed with countless references to other Westerns besides Ford's, to the point where its represents a veritable visual encyclopedia of the American Western. The references are so thick that the film has been criticized for being too much of an insider's game. But it is this contemplation of the Western tradition and its meaning that lends the film a greater depth than Leone's earlier films. There is an elegiac mood to this film. Leone's determination to finish with Westerns coincided with his own melancholy sense that Westerns were about loss, about the passing of an era of great mythic power to one characterized by pettiness and greed, and also his sense that the Western, as a film genre, was dying.

The elegiac tone that Leone sought to strike in this film brought him and Morricone into new musical terrain. As Christopher Frayling has noted, Morricone's score is more serious and ambitious than those of his earlier Leone films, statelier and with a slower tempo. Morricone's previous scores were more comical in tone, more playful, more concerned with sending up, or challenging, Western traditions. In *Once Upon a Time*, Morricone's soaring and majestic score is suggestive of classical Hollywood soundtracks like Bernard Herrmann's. It takes the Western more seriously, putting less emphasis on teasing the conventions of the genre than in giving them their fullest expression.

By this time, the Morricone-Leone collaboration had reached its creative peak. For the first time, Leone had the full recorded score available to him before production so that he could play it in its entirety for his crew as he filmed. It was important to Leone that his entire crews (actors, cameramen, crane operators, and others) work in such a way as to synchronize their craft to the music he played. The device of the harmonica within the narrative allowed Morricone and Leone even more possibilities for planting their soundtrack within the actual action of the film. And Leone and Morricone were never more experimental in their mixture of dialogue and music or in their investigations into the musical quality of natural sound.

Leone's desire to escape the low-comedy and "assembly-line" Cinecittà feel of his earlier films in *Once Upon a Time* is also reflected in his original choice of screenwriters Bernardo Bertolucci and Dario Argento, both destined to become renowned film directors themselves. The two ended up abandoning the film for their own projects but not before they had created, with Leone, a kind of story treatment that he never would have achieved with old stalwarts like Serge Donati and Luchino Vinncenzoni (both of whom felt betrayed by not being asked to participate in the project).

Donati would come to be rightfully frustrated at how much credit Bertolucci and Argento have been given for the screenplay (particularly Bertolucci, due to his later fame) when it was he, Donati, who (with Leone) actually wrote it and hammered it into its spare and solid shape. Nevertheless, the writing contributions of Bertolucci and Argento are a big reason why this screenplay and film have deeper emotional resonance and wider thematic reach than Leone's earlier screenplays. By all accounts (and the accounts of all three differ wildly in other details), Bertolucci, Argento and Leone enjoyed a fruitful collaboration as they laid the groundwork for this meta–Western — watching, talking about and using past Westerns, creating the dialogue between this Western and the ones that preceded it that would be a central part of the final work's identity. In the end, Leone seems as blessed by their excited contributions as he was by Donati's willingness to shake off his anger and step in and finish the project, with his typically unerring sense of what Leone needed. The screenplay represents a nice marriage of the "young intellectuals'" energy and Donati's professional aplomb.

The screenplay is notable for strengths that, in the end, are impossible to assign to any one writer. First, it manages to invest a political content into the film, through the story of Morton and Frank and the oncoming railroad, a critique of American capitalism that avoids clichés and heavy-handed rhetoric. The script is also notable for its clean spareness. In its simple, allusive language and brief aphorisms, it suggest Howard Hawks' films. Indeed, it seems to be imbued with many of the important Hawks themes: There are two men, Cheyenne and Harmonica, both disreputable on the outside, sound as gold within, who speak a kind of code language of moral imperatives. The mutual respect between Harmonica and Frank as they head off to their duel is reminiscent of the ambiguity of good and evil in Hawks' films where the bad and good guys share a common dignity and grandeur. In Leone's film, as in Hawks', there is an emphasis on dignity in the face of death and a strong nod to the Existentialist idea that even if the world is meaningless, the Western hero brings meaning to the world through the dignity he exhibits in the face of that meaningless-ness.

## Jill

Bertolucci, it seems, can also take credit for persuading Leone to do something in the film that Leone had not done in any of his previous Westerns, and something that went a long way to giving this film a greater emotional depth than his previous Westerns. Bertolucci convinced Leone to award a principal role in the film to a woman. Leone had always taken great pride in having de-feminized the Western, in having taken away the superfluous love stories that had bored Leone as a child and which he felt were not a significant part of the organic power of the Western myth.

Bertolucci says that he worked hard at convincing Leone to bring a woman into the film. He claims to have introduced Leone to Nicholas Ray's *Johnny Guitar* (though it is difficult to believe that the cinephile Leone had not seen that film already), a Western that claims not only a female lead, but a female villain as well. There is no doubt that, whether Leone saw this film for the first time, or revisited it during the writing of *Once Upon a Time*, *Johnny Guitar* had an impact on the making of the film.

Despite being Leone's first experiment with a lead female character, Jill is a remarkably strong one and crucial to the action and meaning of the film. Her character was not tacked on as (Leone felt) women's roles in Westerns often were. (Rhonda Fleming's role in John Sturges' *Gunfight at the O.K. Corral* was his favorite example of a woman character who he felt

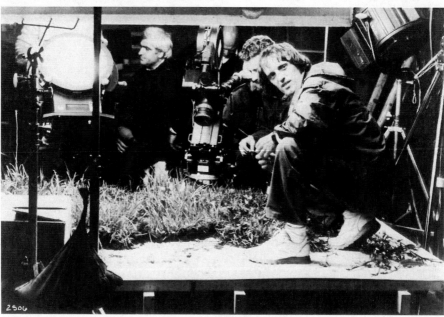

*Top:* Bernardo Bertolucci, one of the two young, up-and-coming writers Leone enlisted to collaborate with him on the original story of *Once Upon a Time in the West. Bottom:* The other now famous co-writer of the original story, Dario Argento. His lush, operatic horror films are sometimes strongly reminiscent of Leone, from whom he says he learned that "films are time, rhythm."

got in the film's way.) Jill is pivotal to all the stories in *Once Upon a Time.* All four of the principal male leads are fascinated by her. McBain falls head over heels in love with her. The dreamy Irishman wants to save her from a life of prostitution and make her the mother of his children. Cheyenne falls in love with her too, though he sees her more as a mother figure. At first Frank wants to kill her, but falls for her enough to lose sight of that goal. His feelings for her are his eventual undoing. Harmonica wants to kill Frank but he equally wants to protect Jill and the dream she represents (inherited from McBain) of building a railroad that is outside the clutches of the evil Morton.

In the end, all four men have died or disappeared, and only Jill is left — the water bearer for a new, more feminine West, one that is not unlike the more feminine, civilized West that exists at the end of John Ford's *The Man Who Shot Liberty Valance.* Leone was right to criticize certain Westerns for tacking on romance conventions that cluttered the Western landscape. But the presence of Jill in this film contributes to a deeper view of the West. Jill saves the film from being just about the camaraderie and grudging respect between men. And her presence reintroduces the complexity of tones that we see in Ford's *Liberty Valance,* a film that, like *Once Upon a Time in the West,* laments the passing of a mythic, masculine West, but at the same time cannot help but eulogize the feminine, civilized West that replaces it. Ford and Leone's vocabulary is not the same. Ford loves the churches, schoolrooms and gardens that his women demand. Leone finds beauty in the bare shoulders of Claudia Cardinale and her good-natured endurance of the men slapping her behind. You might call it "Ford Italianized." But Jill, like Vera Miles' Hallie in *Liberty Valance,* both represent a feminine grace that offsets or balances their director's passion for the violence of the mythic West.

## Romanticism Sublimated into Style

The more somber, elegiac tone Leone aimed at in this Western that is about the passing of the West also allowed this most musical of directors to arrive at some of his slowest rhythms and most deliberate and extended *mise-en-scène.* The opening sequence, in which three gunslingers meet Harmonica at the train station (in a reversal of the scenario from *High Noon*), the massacre of the McBains, Jill's arrival in Flagstone, the duel between Harmonica and Frank, and Harmonica's flashback, represent some of the slowest, most deliberate, carefully articulated filmmaking, not only in Leone's film career in but in all of film history. Leone specialized in taking the ritualized gestures and scenes of Hollywood films and slowing them down, extending and embellishing them, translating them into his own highly personal rhythm, a rhythm that was as slow and ritualistic as church ceremony. The approach, in its slow rhythms, also resulted also in some of Leone's most subtly communicative close-ups (an underestimated aspect of Leone's craft) and most careful attention to, and experiments with, isolated sounds.

In general, the film is characterized by a slowing down or dilation of time. This is only fitting in a film that is so much thematically about time in general. Harmonica and Frank's story, for example, is about time catching up with someone, about the inescapability of the past. The entire film is imbued with a melancholy sense of the passing from one time, the mythic time of the old West, to another, the modern West of trains and telegraphs. The film recurrently contrasts the immense leisure of time in the old West, to the new frenzied approach to time, characterized by the Capitalist Morton (and his protégé, Frank) who are in a deathly hurry, and for whom time is money. It is these themes that led D. Nichols to describe Leone as a Romantic. So many of the grand Romantic themes are here: the mythic sense of the beauty and power of the past; a corresponding sense of the puniness and sordid materialism of the present; and, finally, a sense of the inescapability of the past — its haunting presence in our present-day lives.

But Nichols also emphasizes also that Leone's Romanticism is sublimated into his style.[12] Leone's very way of shooting this film is Romantic. Many critics have noted as a trademark Leone's tendency to play with time, to extend it in long bouts of reflection or drama, where time seems to stop and we embark on a frozen inward journey within the characters' consciousness, only to be jerked out of this quiet reflection by some loud and abrasive sound (the quick report of gunfire, for example) back into external time. This external time moves with a murderous speed that contrasts sharply with the slow rhythms of internal time we have just experienced. There is a Romanticism implied in this trademark tendency — in its sense of the relativity of time, the way time changes in speed according to the drama or quiet of a scene, in its fascination with the luxurious movements of interior time, and in its suggestion of the superiority of inner time to external time, which Tennyson characterized as "a maniac scattering dust." Leone's Romanticism is not just a question of themes. It is built into the rhythm of his filmmaking, in its very sense of time.

The fact that so much of Leone's point of view is "sublimated into style" and finds expression in his films' rhythms rather than their words may explain why he has been so often accused of being a Mannerist and his films criticized for their paucity of ideas, for being, as Bertolucci said, good only "on a surface level." Anyone who has ever been stirred by the deep rhythms of *Once Upon a Time* is struck by the injustice of remarks like these. The film is characterized by a great gravity, but one that owes itself not to the explicit expression of ideas, but rather to the film's uniquely musical translation of the Western genre.

## Leone vs. the Writers

It is worth noting that Leone's most astringent critics were writers who, though superior to Leone in literary skill, may not have been as astute as he in their understanding of the grammar of the Western. Leone, like so many great directors before him, did not have the gift for maintaining good relationships with his writers. His writers, visitors from a more exalted art form, tended to evince a superiority to the Western genre, certainly to Leone's brand of the genre. They were affronted when, as time passed, Leone came to be exalted as a something of an artist. This conventional tension between the intellectual writers and the vulgar director was, in this case, further exacerbated by the fact that many of Leone's co-writers (like Vincenzoni or Bertolucci) were from Northern Italy and felt, inherently, the age-old condescension of the Northern Italian for the Southern Italian. The North-South distinction was particularly felt in the film world, since the bastion of cheap commercial cinema, Cinecittà studios, was located in the South of Italy, in Rome. Pasolini (a Northern intellectual, like Vincenzoni and Bertolucci) described Cinecittà as "the belching stomach of Italy."[13]

One can sense, for example, Vincenzoni's frustration with the fact that, despite his own writing career, he was increasingly approached for interviews, and their sole purpose was to cull his observations on Leone, a man he deemed his intellectual inferior. "I don't understand why you people take seriously what he meant to say," he says of Leone. "No," he snaps at one interviewer, "you try to find philosophical significations out of nothing."[14] There is nothing new in this tendency of intellectual writers to be shocked at how little their contribution is valued in a medium that they often mistake for the stage, but which in reality deals with sounds and image as well as words.

To be fair, Leone brought upon himself some of the frustration that his literary cohorts felt for him. Though he emphasized throughout his career that, "I don't want to be remembered as a philosopher,"[15] as Leone grew more successful with film critics, he warmed to the role of intellectual sage. Bertolucci gently expresses a frustration with how Leone's intellectual pretension increased with his fame. Leone would at times, Bertolucci wrote, "talk like a supercritic, almost a philosopher of the cinema. That was the weaker part of him."[16] Vincenzoni's comments are more vitriolic. "Leone was surprised to be successful and he started to take himself too seriously. And, there was a moment in which he supposed himself to be something in between Bernard Shaw and Karl Marx."[17] Leone particularly irked Donati and Vincenzoni by waving about copies of Celine's *Journey to the End of Night* at press conferences and referring to it as the central text of his life. Both writers were certain that Leone had never read the book and only knew of it what Vincenzoni had told him when they were working on *The Good, the Bad and the Ugly.*

Nevertheless, there may have been a kind of literary bias against Leone. Leone, it seems, was not well-read. But no one calls into question his encyclopedic knowledge of film. He was the son of a silent film director and a silent film actress, raised on studio back lots, and worked as an assistant on some 58 films, including De Sica's *Bicycle Thief* (where he can be spied as one of the German priests in the rain scene). Even Vincenzoni has to admit that Leone had "started to eat film when he was just about one year old."[18] Frayling emphasizes that Leone had a Buster Keaton–like knowledge of the mechanics of the craft, noting that Leone was the first in Italy to use a simultaneous video screen (which permitted a shot to be seen on a video screen while it was being filmed). As an assistant director on *Ben-Hur*, Leone was responsible for constructing a special camera apparatus, which was attached to the front of the chariot, making all the shots behind the horses at a very low angle. "That was Leone's invention," Frayling notes. "He invented the arm that you put the camera on. He loved the machines, and that came out of his long career of apprenticeship as a filmmaker."[19]

Moreover, all accounts are that his knowledge of film was part of a larger sensibility in the plastic and visual arts. Leone was knowledgeable in art history and Frayling does a good job in showing how painters like Goya, Dalí, Degas and De Chirico directly influenced the visual feel of Leone's films. Frayling also documents the subtlety of Leone's taste in his collection of antiques. A great part of Leone's success was in finding collaborators like cinematographer Tonino Delli Colli and set designer Carlo Simi who shared his sophisticated visual sense. It is probably more fair to describe Leone, not as unintellectual, but as an aesthete of sorts, someone whose intelligence expressed itself more easily in the visual and plastic, rather than literary, arts.

That said, it is important not to undervalue Leone's skill as a screenwriter. One of the principal goals of Leone's filmmaking was to de-clutter the Western of dialogue with its tendency to over-explain things and detract from the quiet grandeur of the Western story. John Boorman felt this "de-psychologizing" of the Western was one of Leone's great gifts to the genre. "The Western," Boorman writes, "went into decline when writers and directors became self-conscious and introduced psychological elements. John Ford and others worked from the blood. Sergio Leone's 'spaghetti' Westerns revitalized the form because he consciously reverted to mythic stories, making the texture and detail real, but ruthlessly shearing away the recent accretions of the 'real' West and its psychological motivation."[20]

Boorman's comments express how Leone could be more faithful to the technique of Ford's cinema than other directors who shared more closely Ford's optimistic world view. Leone spoke often of freeing the Western of dialogue so that the audience could appreciate the texture of the genre. For Leone, the sounds of the West, the gunshots and hoof-beats, are more important than dialogue: "I have always limited the use of dialogue so that spectators can use their own imagination while they observe the slow and ritual gestures of the heroes of the West."[21] Leone's business was not with an analysis of the West but with a recording of its liturgy. Few directors can match Leone in his reverence for genre. His goal was to cleanse the Western, free it from, among other things, verbal clutter, to let the genre breathe again. He had immense respect for the meanings inherent in the genre itself, its "mythic stories," its "texture and detail," the hoof-beats and gunshots, its "slow and ritual gestures."

## A Rhythm He Believed In

Donati came about as close as one can to summing up the significance of Leone's craft when he said that, for Leone, "the Western was a kind of religion; he invented a rhythm, a world in which he believed. To believe deeply in something always bears fruit."[22] Donati describes Leone's films as hymns or prayers in a religion in which he (despite his reputation as a cynic for cynic's sake) devoutly believes. Time and time again, critics who label Leone a pessimist underestimate how palpably his devout faith in American films is manifested in his own movies. Inherent in Donati's description of Leone's cinema is the notion that if we gain understanding from Leone's films, we do it in the same way we gain understanding through church ceremony. We apprehend meaning by attending to the details of the ritual as closely, with as much concentration as possible. In this sense, the understanding is emotive, not rational. But this understanding is no more superficial than the wisdom that comes through prayer or meditation. And it comes not by a lazy yielding to an emotional manipulation, but by a concentration of attention, both on Leone's part, in his slow, deliberate, hyper-aware filmmaking technique, and on ours, as we concentrate on his carefully arranged details with him.

Leone also used religious terms in describing his passion for Westerns. "I came to the cinema with a sense of vocation that was stronger than a religion," he told *Cahiers du Cinéma*.[23] This notion of Leone's set as characterized by a religious intensity is echoed by Claudia Cardinale, who described Leone's set, during the filming of *Once Upon a Time in the West*, as a "serious set" where the technicians rarely spoke of anything but the film. There was, Cardinale said, a "religious atmosphere" on Leone's set, which, she said, was notable for its periods of great silence and concentration.[24] Leone was as open to psychology and explanatory language in his Westerns as an orthodox Catholic would be to New Age rants replacing church ritual. For Leone, the significance of the Western was in the structure of the genre itself, in the rhythm of the genre that he perceived. As Donati notes, Leone believes fervently in the Western, but as a story or ceremony, an unfolding of ritualistic elements and gestures, not as a collection of ideas.

Leone was particularly disgusted with the tendency to sanitize or lighten Westerns through language. Contemporary Westerns had "superimposed the most positive and reassuring values of the day on to a brief period of American history which was in reality amazingly violent. But you wouldn't know that from the films, 'talk, talk, talk.'"[25] Again, we hear the Neo-Orthodox Leone, who feels the story of the West has been softened, diluted by language that seeks to talk away the inherent violence and immorality of the age. Another significant goal in Leone's cinema is to portray violence and evil without judging or explaining that violence. When Frank murders the McBains, Leone plays the scene to music that can only be described as majestic or awe-inspiring. It is almost as if he finds beauty in this atrocity, as if he were regarding from it such a distant, neutral, God-like point of view, from which the slaughter can only be seen as part of the much larger mechanics of fate, mechanics that *are* in their nature beautiful. "There is no message of morality behind the action of my characters," Leone wrote in *Cahiers du Cinéma*. "I do not like to bring pedantic or definitive judgments to my films or to dictate rules of conduct. I like to think that the mythic masks of fables are able to express what belongs to their nature most powerfully through allusion."[26] One critic apprehended this studied neutrality of Leone's in an early review of the film. Leone, he wrote, "had a very personal way of telling a story, of expressing violence and cruelty without seeming to judge or complain about them. The Western was, for him, a ceremony that excludes all vulgarity."[27]

It is easy to see why Leone is judged severely by writers who find his films lacking in ideas and moralists who find his films unduly cynical. He prefers to express himself through the ceremony of genre and he often records events that might be perceived as good or evil with a disturbing neutrality. When he does find recourse to language, it tends not to be to clarify his point of view or our understanding but to express, through words, his respect for the power and mystery of the Western story, the way hymns might punctuate a church service. Donati emphasizes that writing a script for Leone meant packing it with "allusive dialogues." Leone described his scripts as "purely aphoristic" and filled with "maxims" that were written to be repeated and memorized. Sarris refers to *Once Upon a Time* as a "silent film with aphorisms for dialogue."[28] Leone is as ritualistic and highly ceremonial in his language as he is in *mise-en-scène*. For example, Harmonica tells Cheyenne, "I came across three dusters like that today. Inside the dusters were three men. Inside the men were three bullets." This is not what you would call naturalistic dialogue. Leone felt the Western could express itself if it was left to breathe, if it was allowed to unfurl, in a careful, appreciative, patient way. To that end, he freed it of the verbal language that he felt trivialized the powerful textures, gestures and rituals of the genre. When Leone's cowboys speak, they do so in chiseled epigrams, almost mathematical in clarity, in little aphorisms and prayers that dramatize rather than explain the role they play in the story.

## Leone, the Professional

It is interesting to note that if Leone's greatest critics were intellectuals, writers and directors, his greatest supporters were his crew, the wide variety of technicians and actors who worked on his set. Child of Cinecittà studios, veteran of over 50 movie productions even before he began his own directorial career, Leone seemed to be comfortable on a set, and to exhibit an authority there that he could not match in other circumstances, for example when he was interviewed about the meaning of his films. Throughout his biography, testimonies tumble out from editors, cinematographers, production managers, actors and musicians about Leone's great command over the materials of cinema. Over and over Leone's crew refer to the seriousness of purpose on Leone's set. Fulvio Morsella speaks of Leone's talent for mobilizing a "high-commitment purposeful set."[29] Mickey Knox said that "no director I have ever worked with before him ever worked so hard, so concentrated. The picture was in his mind for 24 hours a day."[30] Nino Baragli, editor on *Once Upon a Time in the West,* said that when he worked for Leone he did not think of the film just when he was at work but all day long, even "when I am watching television at night."[31]

Of all the European directors of the '60s and '70s—and this was a period singular in its devotion to American film — Leone is closest in spirit to the classic American director. Like Ford or Hawks, Leone (despite some late in the career intellectual primping for the press) consciously disparaged himself as a philosopher. Like them, he refused to let his films get too philosophical or message-oriented. Like them, he recognized the power of genre and subordinated himself to that genre. There was a similar proportional relationship between how little credence he gave "ideas" and how seriously he took craft. And despite his conscious desire to strip his films of explicit ideas and over-explanatory dialogue, his films, like those of Ford and Hawks, are rich fodder for interpretation. As Luc Moullet noted, Leone's "genre films" have turned out "to be even more personal and artistic than the films of auteur cinema."[32] Leone stamped a personality on the West, found rhythms to the Western that are uniquely his own.

At the same time, Leone's accomplishments are as much restorative as creative. It is easy to see Leone's approach to the Western as a logical extension of his hobby of restoring antiques. Leone was a kind of a restorer of the Western, who scraped away accretions and residue that had accumulated on the Western genre until he had managed to liberate the genre. He again allowed the Western to express itself with a leisure and solemnity, a breadth and power that it had never enjoyed before. *Once Upon a Time* represents Leone's greatest expression of the ceremony or spectacle of the American Western, "a gift," as John Boorman has said, "to America of its lost fairy stories."[33]

# TWO

# Once Upon a Time in the West: The Meta-Western

## A Postmodernist Work

One of the great paradoxes and strengths of *Once Upon a Time in the West* (and one of the things that makes it a difficult film to categorize) is that it is at once immensely popular with a general audience and the darling of academics and critics. It appeals to those who want to reflect on its many references to film and the Western genre and to those who do not. It is certainly a strange hybrid, criticized from one quarter for its vulgarity and from another for its intellectual pretension. But no one would argue with the assertion that it exhibits many of the complexities of a postmodernist work. De Fornari describes *Once Upon a Time* as a "meta–Western, a deconstructionist Western" and an example of the "cinema reflecting upon itself."[1] The French philosopher Jean Baudrillard referred to Leone as "the first postmodernist director," and praised Leone for creating a Western within the contemporary "culture of quotations.'"[2] Umberto Eco called Leone's films a "cinema of frozen archetypes," "sublime" because the "archetypes begin to talk among themselves."[3] How Leone gets the number one spot in post-modernism, with the likes of Jean-Luc Godard around, may be a mystery, and one can feel Leone's Northern Intellectual peers wincing at this kind of intellectual aggrandizement of Leone, to whom they steadfastly refused to concede this kind of intellectual ground. But the comment of De Fornari and Baudrillard testify to the considerable depth of self-consciousness and self-reflexivity in the film.

*Once Upon a Time in the West* exhibits the classic traits of a postmodernist work. It eschews realism and psychological depth in favor of archetypical characters and familiar generic conventions. It is replete with self-reflexive scenes: Characters refer to themselves as literary and filmic devices rather than representations of real people. And it is teeming with references to other films and other Westerns. It seems to gather its very substance from the bin of past films. Leone repeatedly emphasized that his characters were straight out of the most familiar Western conventions: the lone gunslinger defending women and family, the hooker with the heart of gold, the sniveling train man come to capitalize on Western expansion, the final duel between the good guy and the bad, the grudging friendship and gradual bonding of cowboys on different sides of the law. The list is endless. The vendetta plot ("You killed my brother") is particularly familiar, as is the story of the old West meeting the new in the form of the train's arrival. Leone had no intention of telling a new story. All of his characters were archetypes, all his storylines familiar. In fact, Leone's goal seemed to be to strip away all elements that he felt were extraneous to the Western myth, to offer as pure a representation of the genre as possible.

It is interesting how often critics turn to stripping metaphors to describe Leone's approach to genre. Producer Damiano Damiani noted, "Leone really loves the formulaic aspects of genre and strips them of all possible content." Boorman writes of Leone's "sheering away the recent accretions of the 'real' West and its psychological motivations."[4] Leone was an enemy to much of what we normally accord positive virtue in our art: content, psychology, depth of character. Leone aimed at a Western that was simple and pure and found meaning in its own style and structure, not in what it had to say. Leone's characters in particular, writes Sylvie Pierre, "obey only the dictates of the fictional machine and never those of ideology. Their motivations and their dreams have only a poetic value."[5]

The characters in the film themselves often seem to recognize that they are only archetypes with poetic value. Jill caustically refers to herself as "the poor defenseless widow" and Harmonica as the "protector of poor defenseless widows." Frank and Harmonica's final conversation makes little sense in terms of the action at hand but is rich with a mutual consciousness of their role as literary types or mythic figures. "Other Mortons will be along and they'll kill us off," says Frank, referring to Harmonica and himself less as men than as vanishing archetypes, mythic figures of the old West. "Before they even come on to the scene," writes Frayling, "these stereotypical characters know themselves to be dying in every sense, morally and physically."[6] Frank, Cheyenne and Harmonica all carry around with them a sense of their fate as literary archetypes and this consciousness lends a pathos to their dialogue. When Jill tells Cheyenne that he's "sort of a handsome man" and Cheyenne responds, "But I'm not the right man," he does not just mean that he notices that she loves Harmonica more than she loves him. He also means that he knows his spot in this literary universe and that that spot is vanishing. He understands the role his character plays in this film.

Harmonica, in particular, strides through the film with an author's sense of what is going to happen and when, less a character in the film than a kind of pseudo-author of the work. He seems to know everything that will and should happen: when Jill should go home, when it is time for Frank to die, what McBain was up to and how to realize McBain's dream, what the onset of the railroad means to gunslingers like him and Cheyenne and Frank. The character of Harmonica goes a long way towards explaining why one finds recourse to religious terms such as ritual, ceremony and pageantry in describing Leone's cinema rather than fictional terms. The film adheres so closely to generic conventions, laws and formulas that it seems to represent a religious liturgy, and acting out of antique rituals as much as it does a fictional creation. Even the film's characters are conscious of the rituals they enact, and not at all surprised with what happens to them.

Leone, of course, was cinematically "raised" in the Cinecittà studio, the Italian Hollywood, a hotbed of generic conventions. He was also a lover of antiquity, who often compared his films to Homer and had a passion for the old and antique in his personal life. And so he was comfortable with his films being seen as celebrations of ancient ritual. It is as clear in his set design, as it is in his respect for generic convention, that Leone loved that which had been tested by time. He was as drawn to antique plotlines as he was to those costumes that he found (in the basement of Western Costume in Hollywood) that were creased, torn and tattered, but of better material than contemporary costumes and which had been worn by the Gods of classic Hollywood Westerns.

## Leone's Storytelling: A Cinema of Pleasure

Leone's penchant for cut-out generic characters and conventions has, however, opened him up to criticisms of an arid and self-indulgent postmodernist technique. Leone is often criticized in *Once Upon a Time* for being too intellectual, for playing dry, referential games within the film, for sapping the blood out of the Western and turning it into a postmodernist exercise of generic conventions, self-reflexivity and cinephilia.

Certain critics have accused *Once Upon a Time in the West* of stripping the Western so far down to the essentials of the genre that the film represents nothing more than, as Eco put it, "archetypes talking among themselves." David Thomson goes the furthest in this line of criticism in his essentially negative review of Leone's career, "Leonesque," published in *American Film*. Thomson echoes the criticisms he has made of other directors whose films are distinguished by meticulous, highly orchestrated *mise-en-scène* (Hitchcock, for example). He complains about the excessively "ordained" (a nasty word in Thomson's lexicon if there ever was one) quality of Leone's work. He finds in *Once Upon a Time* "less a feeling of action than of narrative echo and obligatory fulfillment." He acknowledges the "majesty of Leone's eye — the fateful arrangements of figures and space" but he finds these arrangements stifling and static. "The very air feels as statuesque as the pillars and posing. The figures are not human or vulnerable; they are gargoyles of scrutiny or malice, yet as flimsy as cardboard cut-outs." Thomson feels that "the power of the story is undermined by this commitment to style and eternity.... When everything contributes to the perfection of the composition, there is no room for narrative suspense. Why should we care who wins? What choice exists?" Thomson finds, in Leone's static compositions and his strict adherence to genre guidelines, a suffocating stillness.[7]

German director Wim Wenders' criticisms of the film correspond with Thomson's. Watching it, Wenders said, made him feel "like a tourist in a Western." He saw the film as "the end of the genre" and felt it turned the Western into an "abstraction where the images no longer signify themselves." Wenders sees the film as marking the point where Westerns can no longer be made sincerely, only contemplated from the point of view of archetypes and genres, that while perhaps sophisticated, are lifeless and purely intellectual.[8]

Others are rankled by the film's endless references to other films, which they see as representative of a sterile postmodern cinephelia. Gilbert Salachas finds in *Once Upon a Time* "nothing but a folkloric festival and an anthology filled with hackneyed pieces borrowed from other Westerns."[9] Peter Bogdanovich, who conceived a lifelong distaste for Leone after their misfired partnership in the making of *Fistful of Dynamite*, was annoyed by all the references in *Once Upon a Time in the West*: "It's completely arid. It's like critics talking to each other. And the film buffs don't make much of an audience."[10] All of these critics are rankled by the film's intellectual approach to the Western, the way it views the Western through a prism of familiar motifs and film references.

And yet there are, it seems to me, answers to these criticisms. Thom-

Peter Bogdanovich. Because of his failed collaboration with Leone on the film *Fistful of Dynamite*, Bogdanovich would be one of Leone's harshest critics. He found *Once Upon a Time in the West* "completely arid."

son's frustration with the film's static, formulaic nature does not take into account that many of the criticisms he levels at *Once Upon a Time* could be leveled at any Greek tragedy, wherein the pleasure lies, not in being surprised, but in slowly being gathered towards a fate we see coming all too well.

Also, the film does surprise. Most devotees first respond to it simply on an entertainment level. Few have had to work hard to enjoy it. Leone had, despite his predilection for an air of fatalism, a gift for narrative twists and turns, a gift for the shaggy dog story. Leone's popular success suggests he knows how to draw in an audience despite the slowness of his tempo and the ritualistic nature of his story. Even his most disparaging colleagues grant that he was an ingenious storyteller who loved to mesmerize friends with his latest cinematic party pieces that he would act out emphatically. Leone's wife Carla lists his storytelling as one of the qualities of Leone that first drew her towards him.[11] True to his roots in commercial cinema, Leone always operated under the assumption that he had a responsibility for holding an audience's attention. "I'm always looking for the element of surprise," he told Noel Simsolo. "I work hard to sustain people's curiosity…. On first viewing, people experience the aggression of the images. They like what they see, without necessarily understanding everything. And the sheer abundance of baroque images privileges surprise over comprehension. On second viewing, they grasp more fully the discourse which underlies the images."[12] Leone describes here one of the great aspects of his art: to make a film that entertains, even when it is not fully explaining itself. Leone is elliptical and allusive enough in the way he communicates his ideas, even his narrative information, that audiences are not exactly sure of all that has happened on a first viewing. But the audience is willing to tolerate confusion or mystery in a Leone film because of, as he says, the "privilege" of the "Baroque images," the visual surprise, originality and vitality of his scenes.

There is much that is predestined in *Once Upon a Time*. We have little doubt that Harmonica will kill Frank. Harmonica knows it, we know it, even Frank knows it. We know that Frank is evil and that evil will get its reward. We know that the railway will conquer the old West. In this sense, the film move along iron grooves, as Thomson notes. But Leone's great talent is in his decoration of these ancient plotlines, the care he puts into, and the glee he takes in, Harmonica's story and Frank's punishment. We are curious here, as we were in *For a Few Dollars More*, as to the motive for revenge, and what part in that motive the mysterious object (in *Once*, the harmonica, in *Few Dollars*, the watch) plays. The mystery of Frank's crime is carefully doled out in flashbacks that intrigue us as the mysterious blurred figure walking towards the screen slowly assumes the shape of the young Frank. Leone takes his time in solving his mystery. He teases us slowly.

Moreover, when Leone finally reveals his mystery, we are not likely to feel let down, as we do in so many films that move to a plot revelation in the end. Why not? Because Leone the storyteller comes up with a striking crime — not just a brutal crime, but an ingeniously sadistic one. Frank has killed Harmonica's brother, the oldest plotline in the book. But there is nothing clichéd about how Frank has killed him. This murder is so fantastic and ingenious as to intrigue us by its very mechanics. By putting Harmonica's brother on the child Harmonica's shoulders, Frank is, like Leone, taking time with his murder, luxuriating in it. By making Harmonica complicit in the crime (his brother can stay alive as long as he has the strength to stand), Frank has found a way for his crime to have a lasting mark on someone. When Frank puts the final touch on his masterpiece and crams his harmonica into Harmonica's mouth, the meaning of the music we have been hearing throughout the film is finally explained. We knew it was the music of fate and vengeance; now we know what crime the vengeance is rooted in. So much of the pleasure here is in delayed pleasure, in the satisfaction of finally understanding something of which we have had only vague intuitions. Moreover, Leone has rendered all this through means that are distinctly cinematic. He does not just describe a crime, he translates it into a concrete symbol, the harmonica and its wailing sound, and one that has been central to the entire film. We have been hearing that sound from the beginning of the film. It is the very name of the lead character.

And the crime is not just diabolical, it is also visually striking. The image of the brother perched on his brother's shoulder, framed by the Spanish arch and flanked by Frank's henchmen who stretch out with the languor of Renaissance angels, is not one we have seen before or will likely forget. To suggest that "the power of the story is undermined" in scripts like these is to fly in the face of the film's popular success. It would be more accurate to say, that, yes, Leone's great skill in *Once Upon a Time* is to take the measure of fate, and, in this way the film is greatly characterized by a pre-ordained ceremonial and ritualistic feel. But, due to Leone's great ability as a storyteller, the skill with which he withholds information from his audience and the power with which he finally delivers that information, fate comes in the film (as it often does in real life) in the form of a walloping surprise.

Frayling writes that Leone's talent was "to take visual moments from the classic Hollywood Western and film them in a deliberately expansive way."[13] Leone's great originality is not in his basic storylines, which are all too familiar, but in the way he plays with these storylines, the way he slows them down, fills them out and decorates them, the infinite care and patience and leisure he brings to Western motifs. And the care and fascination he brings to Western conventions testifies to his love of those conventions— it testifies, in short, to a sincerity in his approach, a love of the Western that those who disparage him for a postmodernist aridity and cynicism often miss. "This cinema," writes Michel Madore of *Once Upon a Time*, "is one of pleasure. [Leone] entertains himself by inventing, discovering a gag for each shot. Each of Leone's images reveal a formidable appetite. He loves what he creates, he can't get enough, he astonishes himself like a child."[14] Madore stresses Leone's "formidable appetite" as Frayling stresses Leone's "expansiveness." Leone respected Ozu's ability to get a great deal out of the silent and the immobile, and Leone has a similarly quality of being able to dig deeply in one place, of taking the slimmest plot, the thinnest archetype and giving them depth and amplitude.

Madore also touches on one of the most significant aspects of Leone's cinema, and one that is not that often discussed, especially by those who see Leone as the punk antagonist of the West, accentuating the violence and grotesque in his films. Madore stresses the joy in creation one senses palpably in Leone's films, the "pleasure" he takes, like a child, in cinematic invention, in making something of every scene, in making every scene expressive. Here, as so often with Leone, the parallel is to Buster Keaton, in whose films also we sense continually the delight of invention. It is this quality of Leone's cinema that Fellini touched on at Leone's funeral. "I have the impression," said Fellini, "of a colleague who worked joyfully at something that made him happy: a presence and a voice, full of love for the cinema."[15] These are words ("joy" and "love") not typically bandied about in discussion of Leone's dark take on the West but that is because critics persevere in judging Leone's films by their content more than their form. Harmonica, Frank, Cheyenne and Jill are not particularly happy creatures. The West they inhabit is rather frighteningly gruesome. But the way in which Leone goes about telling his story is light-hearted and characterized by constant invention, a child-like glee, a hungry desire to arrive, as Madore says, at a memorable "gag" or idea in every shot. The film is a somber, elegiac work but also one that expresses great joy in, and love for, the Hollywood Western and cinema in general.

## A Formal Mask for a Subjective Need

Bogdanovich's criticism that the multiple references to other films and other Westerns in *Once Upon a Time* is evidence of an arid modernity, an intellectual gamesmanship interesting only to film aficionados does also not quite hold water. This criticism might be more fairly applied to Bernardo Bertolucci who, with Dario Argento, helped Leone conceive the film's story but who was not involved with the actual writing of the final script, which Leone accomplished with Sergio Donati. Bertolucci emphasizes that he and Leone shared a love for the Hollywood cinema and Western and that, when they watched these films, "the fever in our eyes must have been at the same temperature." But he also emphasizes that they came to this passion by separate paths. Bertolucci's love of Hollywood came from "having read Bazin and French film theorists" and Leone's path to the Western was "more direct," by which Bertolucci means Leone grew to love the conventions of Hollywood through his experience growing up and working in the environs of the Italian film industry. Leone's film education was much more a hands-on one than Bertolucci's. And, for Bertolucci, stuffing *Once Upon a Time* with references to other Westerns and American films was much more of an intellectual game. He often bragged about slipping references to films by Leone, though Leone always insisted that he recognized any reference to another film in his movie. And Bertolucci admitted that his referencing to American film was much more self-conscious than Leone's: "I put them rather more in quotation marks. For me, movie-making has always meant making movies that ask just what movies are. So, unfortunately, for me the allusions are more conscious."[16]

No one ever underestimates Leone's own encyclopedic knowledge of American film. Even his most vociferous detractors like Vincenzoni cede to Leone an awe-inspiring lexicon of film references, but Leone's sense of American film was much more that of the craftsman, not the intellectual. It came from being raised in the Hollywood tradition of Cinecittà and from his experience working with great American directors during their sojourns through the Italian film industry. Leone's head was not crammed with intellectual references, but with the tricks of the trade, the shots and ideas of the American Western. Over and over again, his peers (Dario Argente, Tonino Delli Colli, Mickey Knox) praise Leone for having "shots in his head," shots from great films, shots he planned to use in his films. Delli Colli recalls visiting Monument Valley with Leone in preparation for filming and Leon excitedly describing to him all the shots and camera placements that he recognized from Ford's movies.

"And it was all in his head," Delli Colli said in disbelief.[17] This is not the cinephilia of the intellectual, even the aficionado; this is the knowledge of the craftsman, steeped deeply in the ideas and techniques of a tradition. All of these films and these shots mixed together in his head to create what Leone often described as a "mosaic" or "kaleidoscope view of all American Westerns." He really was incapable of conceiving of the West except in the striking images of the American Western tradition his mind had been steeped in.

But Leone was always adamant that he put this mixture of references to the past to his own use, that he never cited other films "for citation's sake." "It wasn't done in that spirit at all," he told Frayling. "The 'references' aren't calculated in a programmed kind of way." Leone's intent was to use the conventions of the American Western "to tell my version of the story of the birth of a Nation."[18] In short, from the rich mixture of previous Westerns that few filmmakers had acquainted themselves with as well as he, Leone developed his own language. "Westerns have been made over and over again," Japanese director Akira Kurosawa said. "And in the process a kind of grammar has evolved. I have learned from this grammar of the Western."[19] Leone learned to speak "the grammar of the Western" as fluently as any director since Ford, so fluently that he was able to arrive at new forms of communication with that language. Bill Krohn writes that in *Once Upon a Time*, "the grammar and lexicon of the Western is systematically perverted for the sole pleasure of discovering narrative laws until now undiscovered." By using the word "perverted," Krohn emphasizes Leone's tendency not to simply genuflect before the grammar of the West, but to play with it some, to satirize and challenge its conventions, make something new of it."[20]

There are no moments in *Once Upon a Time in the West* like the one in Jean-Luc Godard's *Contempt* when Michel Piccoli explains that he is wearing his hat in the bathtub because he wants to be like Dean Martin in *Some Came Running*—that is, moments where you need to have seen the film to know what a character is talking about or what is happening or moments where the reference is given with a smug wink to the knowing. All of Leone's references are subterranean, buried within the organism of the film. They are never casual, throw-away or "intellectual." When Leone does refer to past Westerns, and Ford in particular, he does so in deeply felt ways. The only films in which Monument Valley is shot as dramatically as it is in *Once Upon a Time* are Ford's. Leone is careful to use the tomb-like monuments for scenes of greatest emotional intensity— Harmonica's memory of his brother's death, for example, or Jill's lonely arrival to the West. They are never just scenic backdrop. And if Leone chose Henry Fonda for his association with Ford, he nevertheless develops and challenges those associations in interesting ways. Leone accentuates Fonda's lanky carriage as no one has since Ford, while at the same time putting Fonda's great elegance into the service of the film's greatest evil.

Serge Patry insists that what Jean Mitry says about John Ford also applies to Leone's work on *Once Upon a Time*. "Is not creative genius," wrote Mitry, "collecting all the most common premises, all the clichés, all that have been most used and worn, mixing them all together and creating from them something new, original and personal?"[21] The new, the original and personal is all that loving ceremony and detail Leone brings to the generic conventions of the past, the deep faith he displays in those conventions by studying them so carefully and amplifying them so richly, even when he is challenging them or satirizing them. It is hard to credit Wenders' summary of the film as "tourism" because the metaphor of tourism seems inconsistent with such rich, native knowledge of the terrain. As Leone repeatedly emphasized, he felt he had a right to the Western, despite being Italian, that even American directors did not have and that right came from his love and knowledge of the genre.

It is interesting to note that Bertolucci lost interest in this project, jumping ship at the first chance to get his own directorial career started again. It had been a diversion from Leone's normal technique to work with young intellectuals of Bertolucci's ilk. Working with them was part of his desire to separate himself from his Eastwood trilogy and Cinecittà, to (somewhat) join the ranks of the more serious, *Cahiers du Cinéma*–type film directors. But he found, oddly enough, that his "intellectual" collaborators did not take his project as seriously as he did. When they left him, he called on an old stalwart, Sergio Donati, to save the day. "The two intellectuals, they abandoned work," Donati recalls Leone saying. "How can we go and make a movie?"[22] Leone's turning to Donati suggests Leone's roots in the dependable professionalism of a Cinecittà style ran deeper than his dabbling with the young *Cahiers du Cinéma* crowd. His reference to Bertolucci and Argento as "the intellectuals" suggests that this "kaleidoscope of American Westerns" was more of a game for them than it was for Leone.

Argento went on to work in a generic convention, the horror film, and that propensity for working in genre may explain why he remained one of Leone's greatest fans and students. Bertolucci's praise of Leone was always more muted. He was part of the chorus of Northern Italian intellectuals and screenwriters who tended to see Leone as a great craftsman, not a great artist. That lesser appreciation of Leone may stem from Bertolucci's lesser appreciation of genre filmmaking. The conventions and references in which Leone trafficked were not a game to Leone, but quite a personal business, hence his astonishment when "the intellectuals" abandoned him. Luc Moullet, as we have seen, emphasizes that Leone was of that breed of filmmaker whose "genre films often turn out to be even more personal and artistic than the films of auteur cinema," which is to say films like Bertolucci's.[23] Westerns provided Leone with, he said, "a formal mask for a more subjective need to express myself."[24] Leone saw the possibility of saying something "personal" and "subjective" through the grammar of the Western, his own distinct, complex, melancholic take on the myth of the American West and the grandeur of the Western film.

Moreover, for every intellectual who approaches the film as a cinephile's game, there are probably a hundred or so fans of the film, encountering the film on television, for example, who love the film for itself, who do not have the precise film literacy to appreciate it for anything *but* itself. It is not necessary to know all of Leone's directorial ancestors to deeply appreciate the movie. If it was, it would not have the broad base of popularity that it does.

What viewers do often experience is the feeling that they are watching some kind of emblematic Western. There is a familiarity to the film that makes them feel as though they are on firm ground as they watch it. Leone wanted that feeling of a "kaleidoscopic view of all American Westerns put together," Leone said. The references "are there to give the feeling of all that background of the American Western to help this particular fairy tale."[25] Leone emphasizes the emotional, rather than intellectual, impact of the references to other Westerns. They are there to create a "feeling," to establish a dream-like "fairy tale" effect. Leone wanted to convey the dream of the American Western film, not cite its index.

In the end, whether you respond to the references to film history in this film in an instinctual way as part of a kind of presentation of a dream or meta–Western, or whether you are conscious of the dialogues in the film with the Western tradition or with John Ford, it is hard to argue against the notion that this film's sharp sense of its own tradition is what gives it greater depth and stature than other Westerns, including Leone's other Westerns. *Once Upon a Time* is that rare film, like Hitchcock's *Rear Window* or Polanski's *Chinatown*, that reflects on the filmic traditions from which it derives and at the same time, effortlessly, and entertainingly, fulfills those film traditions. It is a film that delights aficionados and novices alike.

# References

Coming up with a complete survey of the references to other Westerns in *Once Upon a Time in the West* is a tricky (if not impossible) business. A review of the Leone bibliography for references to other films suggests approximately 40 to 50 films. But this list is very fluid. Some references are very precise and corroborated by Leone and his screenwriting collaborators. For example, when Frank asks Wobbles how he can trust a man who wears both a belt and suspenders, Leone is lifting the line almost verbatim from Billy Wilder's *Ace in the Hole*. Leone is on record referring to the opening shootout (where three gunmen wait at the train station for the hero) as a reversal of *High Noon* and of referring to both *Shane* (the scenes with the boy hunting) and *The Searchers* (the slaughter of the family) in the McBain massacre. Of certain references there can be no doubt. The long raincoats of Cheyenne's gang were inspired by the garb of Walter Brennan's gang in Ford's *My Darling Clementine*. Charles Bronson plays a harmonica in *Once*, just as he did in *Vera Cruz*, and whittles, just as he did in *The Magnificent Seven*. Henry Fonda kicked out a paralytic's crutches from underneath him in *Warlock*, just as he would kick out Morton's crutches in *Once Upon a Time*.

Other times, critics stretch the connections. In Cheyenne's notable line about Harmonica, "people like that have something inside, something to do with death," Frayling hears echoes of Doc Banton in *High Sierra* when he says, "Remember what Johnny Dillinger said about guys like you and him — he said you were just rushing towards death. Yeah, that's it. Just rushing towards death."[26] If the criteria for a "reference" is that slight, we can probably come up with more than fifty.

And, indeed, it is hard to watch any high-profile American Western without seeing or suspecting a reference to it in *Once Upon a Time in the West.* I would be hard-pressed to find an image of the Western town closer to Leone's than that in Ford's *Cheyenne Autumn* and Cheyenne's devotion to Jill has always, for me, carried with it associations of the outlaw Ringo's devotion to the prostitute in *Stagecoach* and yet I have not come across reference to either of these parallels in Leone criticism. Bertolucci says the name of McBain's ranch, "Sweetwater," was selected randomly from a map of Arizona.[27] But in the opening minutes of *My Darling Clementine*, Henry Fonda's Wyatt Earp points vaguely to a spot in Monument Valley where you can find "sweet water" and Robert Cumbrow has noted that a town named "Sweetwater" appears briefly in Michael Curtiz's 1961 *The Comancheros.* (John Wayne goes briefly under the name of McBain in this films as well.)[28] The whole reference-gathering game seems rather pointless when dealing with Leone, who was so steeped in American Westerns, whose cinematic language was so infused with past American Westerns, that it was probably impossible for him to shoot a scene or come up with a name without reference to past films.

That said, there are a few films that are singularly important to *Once Upon a Time.* The spirit of *Shane*, with, as Frayling says, "its self-consciously mythic qualities," seems to pervade the film. The McBain hunting and funeral scenes directly refer to the film. The texture and visual sweep of Henry King's *The Bravados* is very close to *Once Upon a Time.* The two films share the motif of the villains mystified by the man who tracks them down in the name of vengeance. But the films are even closer in their images: shots of Gunmen from below, with the sky in the background; scattered horsemen dramatically toppling down hills. King shot his Westerns like Ford, but a little more expressively, less classically. Leone saw something very close to his vision of the West in this film.

*Johnny Guitar* is often cited as the film that most influenced *Once Upon a Time.* I have even seen Leone's film referred to as a remake of *Johnny Guitar.* Bertolucci claims to have introduced Leone to *Johnny Guitar* in an effort to show Leone the relevance of a female protagonist in a Western. Vienna, in *Johnny Guitar,* and Jill, in *Once*, do have a great deal in common: Both are prostitutes trying to make the transfer to business-women. Both have the assistance of gunslingers who adore them. Each has a dream of a town that will be built (though Jill's dream is inherited from McBain). And both possess a literal model of that town, a strong visual symbol of their dreams. Both films have a broad operatic quality. Berto-lucci referred to it as "the first of the Baroque Westerns."

But to call *Johnny Guitar* the primary influence on Leone's master-piece would be a gross exaggeration. If one were to argue for the primary influences on the film, it would be hard to turn to just one. Rather, I think the entire work of two filmmakers lie at the heart of Leone's approach to the Western: Howard Hawks and John Ford. Ford's influence on *Once Upon a Time* is so dramatic and pervasive that I have reserved discussion of Ford and Leone for a chapter in itself, which follows this one.

## Hawks and Leone

Ford's influence on Leone has been well-celebrated, Hawks' less so, though it has often been noted that the *deguello*, the slow Mexican death march in trumpets that was at the heart of *Rio Bravo*'s soundtrack, was the genesis for the rich musical themes produced by Ennio Morricone that represent the showpieces of Leone's films. Stuart Kaminsky, writing years before he would work as a screenwriter for Leone, finds Leone "very like Howard Hawks" in his emphasis on "male style in the face of world hor-ror." In Leone's film, Kaminsky writes, "a man's death is less important than how he faces it." At the end of the film, Frank's stately ride up to Har-monica, his relinquishment of his base capitalist enterprises, his desire to die "just a man" and to face up to Harmonica's judgment represents the Hawksian "male style before death."[29] Cheyenne also conducts himself with great calm and dignity at the end of the film, even though he suffers from a mortal wound, insisting on one final shave and cup of coffee and a few parting words of advice for Jill, before he goes off and dies in soli-tude.

There is also, in Leone, a great emphasis on friendship, particularly between men, as there is in Hawks' films. Leone usually recognized that his particular brand of musical filmmaking did not translate easily into ideas you could talk about in interviews. He was at his best when he would assert "I don't want to be remembered as a philosopher." But friendship was one of the few "themes" that Leone was willing to allow existed in his films. In his interviews, he repeatedly described "the friendship that can spring up between two men" as his "theme." A male rivalry that develops into mutual respect and friendship is central to *For a Few Dollars More,* *The Good, the Bad and the Ugly* and *Once Upon a Time in the West.* These friendships give some warmer shading to Leone's austere protagonists, as they do Hawks'. They allow us to see some humanity in characters who, without these friendships, might seem too cruel and cynical. And yet, even in these friendships, the protagonists only express their humanity in a gruff, teasing, roundabout way. Leone was drawn to the allusive nature of Hawksian dialogue, where affections were implied but where it was also considered bad form to state them outright.

Leone adopts Hawks' code language of male camaraderie. As in a Hawks film, the good guys, the ones who understand each other, tend to have nicknames. In Hawks' films, nicknames like Frenchy and Cricket are almost always clues that the character is "one of us." It is WASPy names like Johnson that mark you as suspicious in Hawks' world. Similarly, Leone gives his two good cowboys, Harmonica and Cheyenne, nicknames. Frank, titan from the past that he is, is a little too nasty to enter into the Hawksian fraternity of gruff camaraderie. Someone like Wobbles, who is on the wrong end of the moral conflict in this film, is still, in his messy crudeness, enough a part of the ancient world for which Leone has a fondness to get a nickname. Morton, railway baron, is not even given a first name, much less a nickname.

And, as in Hawks' films, the heroes, careful never to embarrass themselves by explicitly expressing affection for someone or a belief in something, develop a kind of code language that can only be understood by a kind of club of the "right sort." As I discuss in more detail in Chapter Four, which deals in part with the Harmonica-Cheyenne relationship, Harmonica and Cheyenne's dialogue, with its elliptical references to knowing how to "play," is distinctly Hawksian. It is a code language that they alone understand, like the nonsense banter about dead bees between Humphrey Bogart and Walter Brennan in *To Have and Have Not.* It does not take Cheyenne long to learn that Harmonica "knows how to play" but that the nervous city slicker who draws on him from behind does not.

Like Hawks, Leone also finds poignancy and drama in the friendship or mutual respect between two enemies, as well as between two friends. In Leone's films, Kaminsky notes, the "bad guy appears to have all the skills and style of the good guy, but he is totally immoral, willing to serve anyone for money and to do anything for it." Still, even though he does evil he "must retain his dignity while doing so." And this villain often sees in the hero "another character who lives by the code of style."

Frank is, in a sense, the mirror image of Harmonica (hence all the images in the final duel of Frank and Harmonica as doubles of each other).

Frank and Harmonica are equally skilled and exhibit a similarly superior style and sense of dignity in the midst of trouble. The two only differ in their morals. And they are interested in each other, not only because they share a similar style, or approach to life, but because they know they are on a collision course with one another. They share an intimacy known only to competitors who know that one will inevitably vanquish the other. The good and bad guys in a Leone film, Kaminsky emphasizes, like those in a Hawks film (he cites the John Wayne and Christopher George characters in *El Dorado*), "respect each other, see the possibilities of alternate existence in each other, and recognize early that their styles demand that they eventually shoot it out in a morality combat."[30]

The scene in which Frank rides up to Harmonica and presents himself for the duel is moving because of the mutual respect between the two gunslingers. In Harmonica's unswerving pursuit of him, Frank sees the truth of the ancient West, a truth he has been repressing in his awkward attempt to become a modern businessman. Harmonica sees in Frank an epic figure from the old West, a man who, however evil, is worth a hundred Mortons. The two come together in, to use one of Leone's favorite terms in speaking of *Once Upon a Time*, "a dance of death" that is as much an embrace as it is a duel. "In my films," Leone wrote, "the positive and negative are complementary. My characters are neither bad, nor good. Love and hate are two moments of equal intensity."[31] In a sense, the "mortality combat," or final duel, in the film is even more deeply felt than in other Westerns. The action of this film moves in such well-worn archetypal grooves that Frank seems to understand his own destiny, to know that he is going to die. Frank does not so much approach Harmonica for a duel as he does relinquish himself to his executor. There is a "story of Isaac" quality to this scene as Frank puts his head on the executioner's block so that the new West can replace the old.

Leone's interest in the vocabulary of Hawks' world is part and parcel of his determination to tell a story in his Westerns that does not make explicit moral statements, that tries to hold itself back from judgments about what is good and what is evil, that aims, like the Neo-Realist films on which Leone worked in the early stages of his career, at a studiously neutral tone. "My characters are not guided by a moral message," Leone wrote in *Cahiers du Cinéma*.[32] It is this neutrality of tone that make his films seem, to many, morally indifferent when they are, actually, just very careful in the way they deal with morality. "I had always thought that the 'good' and the 'bad' and the 'violent' did not exist in any absolute, essential sense," Leone said. "It seemed to me interesting to demystify these adjectives in the setting of a Western. An assassin can display a sublime altruism while a good man can kill with total indifference."[33] Harmonica is capable of stunning cruelty (in his beating of Wobbles, for example), while we cannot help but appreciate the elegance and stature that Henry Fonda brings to Frank's evil.

Leone had a penchant for locating goodness in surprising places, hence the nickname of "Angel Eyes" for Eastwood's ruthless bounty hunter in *The Good, the Bad and the Ugly*. When Lee Van Cleef refers to Tuco's "guardian angel," Leone gives us a shot of Eastwood with the suggestion of a halo around his head to the accompaniment of choral voices meant to suggest an angelic choir. We are supposed to laugh because we know this man is a bounty hunter, a con man and, at times, as with Tuco, a ruthless double crosser — in short, that he is far from angelic. But we also laugh because we know the title is accurate. We sense, and our suspicions are confirmed at the end of the film, that this is a man who operates according to his own personal code of ethics, and who will, when it comes down to essential matters, do the right thing, as he does when he shoots Tuco loose from his noose at the end of the film.

Harmonica is another guardian angel (for Jill) encased in a criminal exterior. Leone had Hawks' taste for the hard-bitten hero, the man who likes to cast himself as disbelieving and remorseless but cannot stop himself, in the pinch, from doing good, the hero who seems almost aggravated by his lingering sense of morality. The scene in which Harmonica is content to have Jill think he intends to rape her, when in actuality he is plotting to save her life, is typical of the way the heroes in Hawks and Leone films like to court ill opinion, as though they only feel free to do good when everyone thinks they are bad. There is an existentialist notion operating in both directors' films that good actions shine more powerfully against a black background, that the less nobility their heroes claim for themselves, the more deeply resonate their noble actions.

We do not want to make the mistake of too simplistically associating this kind of male camaraderie and quiet morality just with Hawks. Hawks was the director who most fully articulated an ethos of gruff male camaraderie and reluctant morality that permeated not only the Western but the best of Hollywood's action films in general. In Anthony Mann's *The Far Country*, for example, the relationship between hero Jimmy Stewart and the heavy, played by John McIntire, is complicated by a strong affection for each other. Frayling's own reference point for Leone's gruff morality is not Hawks but Budd Boetticher. Leone, Frayling notes, admired the mixture of pessimism and humor in Boetticher's films. Frayling finds that in Leone's films, as in Boetticher's, "life goes on with no meaning other than the sense of worth and purpose that strong individuals bring to it."[34]

Leone's cowboys, Frayling suggests, like Boetticher's, are not willing to admit there is any meaning to life, but they are willing to act as if there is. A morality in which they make no effort to profess belief is inscribed in their actions. This is the kind of ethos, most typified by Hawks' films, with which Leone felt most comfortable.

# THREE

# Ford and
# *Once Upon a Time in the West*

Leone's references to John Ford's Westerns in *Once Upon a Time* represent a dialogue between a student and his teacher. Ford is everywhere in this film. Leone set the film in the most famous of all Ford and Western locations: Monument Valley. Henry Fonda and Woody Strode bring to the film rich, iconographic presences, earned to a great extent through their work with Ford. The film is replete with specific references to Ford films. The careful appreciation of Fonda's physical grace and the dramatic use of weathered dusters links the film to *My Darling Clementine*. Leone described his casting of Fonda as a bad guy in *Once Upon a Time in the West* as a "carrying forth" of Ford's intuition when he cast Fonda as the brittle martinet of a colonel in *Fort Apache*.[1] *Once Upon a Time* also represents a response to Ford's own story of the train's arrival out West, *The Iron Horse*. And in its melancholy depiction of the passing away of the mythic West, it is close to the spirit of *The Man Who Shot Liberty Valance*, the film Leone seems to have had most in mind when he made *Once*.

The massacre of the McBains is an example of how closely allied certain of Leone's scenes are to Ford's. Like the McBains, the family in *The Searchers* nervously sets the table for a feast while sensing an imminent attack. Her nerves strained, the mother snaps angrily at her daughter, as McBain does at his son and daughter. The rustle of bird wings, as a bevy of game birds rise to the sky, alerts the families in both scenes to their impending doom. The first-person shot, in which Timmy McBain races to the door to find his family dead outside, strongly echoes the backlit doorways that lend such drama to the opening scenes of *The Searchers*. The silent "stare down" of the little girl and the Indian who will kidnap her in *The Searchers* is echoed in the silent exchange of first-person shots

The kind of shot from a Ford film (*My Darling Clementine*) that Leone often mimics: figures composed around doorways with Renaissance elegance. Henry Fonda is framed in the doorway.

between Frank and Timmy McBain, who he will kill. In the openings of both films, doom approaches quietly.

Ford shots are all over the film as well. As we have seen, Leone's cinematographer Tonino Delli Colli was astonished, during his visit to Monument Valley with Leone, by Leone's photographic memory for all the shots of Monument Valley in Ford's films. Ford's filmic language was an

*Three. Ford and* Once Upon a Time in the West

43

intrinsic part of Leone's filmic language. In *Once Upon a Time*, as in Ford's films, shots of landscapes dominated by vast skies abound. Leone exhibits the same penchant Ford did for far shots in which men riding horses are dwarfed by their massive Western landscape. In these shots, the men are little more than tiny specks of movement in an otherwise static shot that conveys the power and leisure of nature. Leone often shoots his characters with Ford's trademark low-angle shot that makes the figures tower above the camera, according them a mythic power, and emphasizing the vastness of the sky behind them. In Leone's films, as in Ford's, interior shots from below accentuate ceilings and cramped interiors that are more historically accurate renderings of the cramped and badly lit interiors of the actual West than we usually find in Westerns. The power of the West to overwhelm us with its vastness is accentuated by shots of that vastness through the windows and doorways of these cramped interiors. Heroes pose in backlit doorways and villains pile through doorways with the richness and balance of Renaissance compositions, as they do in Ford's films. And Leone, of course, follows the Ford dictum that he quoted appreciatively in the essay on Ford that he wrote for *Cahiers du Cinéma,* "The best cinema is that where the action is long and the dialogue is short."[2]

Leone admired the realism Ford brought to the Western. "He was," Leone wrote, "the first to show us that real Western cowboys did not walk around dressed in clean black on white plucking banjos and batting their eyelashes like gigolos, in the manner of Tom Mix and Hopalong Cassidy." Leone cites the mud-caked duster in *My Darling Clementine,* the movements of white clouds over blue cavalries, the image of a dust-covered John Wayne halting the stage coach in *Stagecoach,* as images that "sacrificed nothing for postcard effects." Ford was the one, Leone wrote, "who tried most carefully to find a true visual image to stand for the West," one of "the most authentic pioneers of modern realistic cinematography. And in this respect I declare myself his student." Leone was close to Ford in his fascination with archival photographs of the past and his desire to recreate these photos, and in his fascination with the archaeology of the West.[3]

Leone was also fond of a romanticism he found in Ford's Westerns, a melancholy consciousness of the passing of a time that was greater than the one we live in now. That is why the Ford film to which *Once Upon a Time* is most strongly linked is *The Man Who Shot Liberty Valance.* Both *Liberty Valance* and *Once Upon a Time* venerate the old West that is giving way to the new. And Tom Donovan in *Liberty Valance* is a precursor to Harmonica, the archetypal fast gun who selflessly effaces himself so that a West in which he has no place can appear. Leone's only mistake *vis-a-vis Liberty Valance* was to sometimes speak as if it were the first film in which

Ford expressed a cynicism about the building of the West. In *Liberty Valance*, Leone said, "Ford finally, at the age of almost sixty-five, understood what pessimism is all about. In fact, with that film Ford succeeded in eating up all his previous words about the West—the entire discourse he had been promoting from the very beginning of his career."[4] This is a pretty large overstatement. Most critics would find a complex mixture of pessimism and optimism in the best of Ford's films, early or late, and not for the first time in *Liberty Valance*.

Leone's sensitivity to Ford's melancholy also explains in part why Leone wanted to set *Once Upon a Time* in Monument Valley. As usual, Leone's citing of Ford is not a case of citation for citation's sake. Setting this film in that panoramic 30-mile strip was appropriate in a way it would not have been for Leone's earlier Western trilogy. *Once Upon a Time* is an elegiac film and therefore fits nicely in a locale which, as Jean-Louis Leutrat and Suzanne Liandrat-Guiges have noted, has an elegiac quality. "The most remarkable feature of Monument Valley," write Leutrat and Liandrat-Guiges, "is the architectural metaphor contained in its name, which Ford exemplifies in his use of both the frieze (the skyline) and the stele, which are linked in so far as the monuments rise like steles in relation to a horizontal space." In other words, Monument Valley, both in name and form, suggests monuments, friezes, steles, tombstones—rock solid testimonies of the past. Ford saw in Monument Valley "a place of memory, or more exactly a theater of memory," an atmosphere evocative or redolent of the past. From *My Darling Clementine* on, Leutrat and Liandrat-Gigues note, "Ford's perception of Monument Valley is as a place of funerals."[5] The burial of Wyatt Earp's brother in *Clementine*, the demise of Owen Wilson and his men in *Fort Apache* and the women's graves in *The Searchers* are all scenes where Ford emphasized and took advantage of the funereal quality of Monument Valley.

John Ford. The guiding spirit behind *Once Upon a Time in the West*, the director with whom Leone carries on a sort of filmic dialogue in this movie.

*Three. Ford and* Once Upon a Time in the West

45

Similarly, in *Once Upon a Time,* Jill will pass the monuments on her way to her new family's funeral. And, in what represents the seminal crime of the film, Harmonica's brother will be killed with the monuments in the background. But more generally, the monuments represent the proper backing for this film that is, overall, so concerned with death — the death of the McBains, the death of titans from the past like Frank and Cheyenne, the death of the old West, and the death of the Western genre and film.

By placing *Once* against the backdrop of Monument Valley, Leone found a setting, as he found actors, that came replete with rich associations for viewers who are sensitive to the majesty of Ford's Westerns. Like Woody Strode and Henry Fonda, Monument Valley comes with its own grandeur. And Leone understood that this grandeur was a melancholy one, that Monument Valley had a symbolic import in Ford's film that was consistent with the feel of the film.

## Anti-Ford Elements in Leone

But if Leone revered and emulated Ford, he was also very clear where he differed from Ford. He could not share Ford's optimism about America, an optimism which he thought was distinct to an Irish immigrant grateful to America for the opportunities it had offered him. Ford's America, Leone wrote, "was a utopia, but an Irish utopia. Which is to say, profoundly Catholic," not a recommendation for someone like Leone, with deep roots in Italian Socialism.[6] For the most part, Leone was as cynical about the real America as he was adoring of the mythic America. At times, he responds to Ford's personal mythology with the edginess and rancor of a rebellious son. For example, the Union captain in *The Good, the Bad and the Ugly* gives a speech about how whisky is "the most potent weapon in the war — the fighting spirit is in this bottle" during the battle of the bridge, because Leone had been annoyed by a scene in Ford's *The Horse Soldiers* where John Wayne refused a slug of whisky during an equivalent scene describing a battle over a bridge. Leone's homage to Ford was often a corrective one and could veer into irritation and mockery.

Frayling sees the massacre at the McBain ranch in *Once Upon a Time* as Leone's satire on Ford's utopian vision of the Western community.[7] This scene is a bit of a send-up, not only of Ford, but of idealistic Westerns in general. The scenes leading up to the massacre are a kind of Ford-like celebration of family, dreams and bounty. The sequence begins with a father and son hunting together and is meant to evoke the scenes with Joey Starret and his father in George Stevens' *Shane.* Only, as Frayling points out, instead of a blond hero emerging from the sagebrush, as in *Shane,* this time a gang of murderers appears out of nowhere. We learn in this sequence that Brett McBain is a loving dreamer who plans on showering his daughter with wealth. We also learn that he has fallen deeply in love with Jill, whom he plans to save from the bordellos of New Orleans and introduce to the life of a lady. He is a good man with a profound dedication to marriage and family.

These scenes are characterized by a Ford-like peace, quiet and bounty, with McBain's daughter putting the finishing touches on several tables laden with a feast, while peacefully humming "Danny Boy" to herself. (The Irishness of this family represents its closest link to Ford's world.) Her final gesture in the film is to watch the birds that have stirred and flown away (frightened by Frank's men) with a kind of beatific appreciation of nature's quiet beauty. Then a shot rings out and the entire family is massacred. Soon they are neatly laid out on the tables they were to feast on, like the birds they had planned to consume. In Ford's films, farm families like this were the cultivators of a new, roughly hewn paradise. In Leone's film, they are literally run over by greedy capitalists looking to take this land. They are as vulnerable to these malevolent forces of greed as the wild fowl were to their own guns, a parallel that reinforces Leone's sense of the West, not as a burgeoning paradise, but a Hobbesian world where the strong consume the weak and life is nasty, brutish and short.

This is Leone having his macabre fun with Ford. This is the cynical European gleefully stating that he cannot share Ford's vision of a West of increased culture, beauty, bounty and femininity. When pushed to describe what he did believe in, Leone would often mention friendship and, if pushed even further, family, "my final archetype, handed down to us from pre-history."[8] (He never mentions community.) But Leone's picture of the family, like most of the archetypes he deals with, is not a sunny one. McBain's family is slaughtered, as is Juan's in *Giu la testa* and the family Lee Van Cleef dispatches in *The Good, the Bad and the Ugly.* "With John Ford, people look out the window with hope. Me, I show people who are scared even to open the door. And if they do they tend to get a bullet right between the eyes."[9] There is an Existentialist quality in Leone's films. He respects certain values, like family and friendship, but he is, at the same time, cynical about the chances these concepts have of surviving in the real world.

Jill, for example, arrives in the West cherishing McBain's dream of family. She innocently, and naively as it turns out, hopes to put her years of prostitution behind her and to give McBain "a half dozen kids," as she tells Cheyenne. But she quickly learns that such visions are impossible to

*Three. Ford and* Once Upon a Time in the West

47

realize in a Leone film. A Leone character is not allowed a life of peace and ease. Jill loses McBain, and finds no replacement in Harmonica and Cheyenne. She is left to realize McBain's vision of Sweetwater on her own. "Have you ever noticed," writes Leone, "that Ford's heroes are never individualists or solitary? On the contrary, they are always men who are profoundly rooted in their community, exactly like Irish immigrants, satisfied with their new condition."[10] Leone's heroes, though — Jill, Harmonica, Frank, Cheyenne — are individualist and solitary. Friendship and family offer consolation along the way but for the most part they are on their own. They exist much more in a Hawksian ethical universe than a Fordsian one, where their challenge will be to meet their fate, usually a dark one, with humor and dignity — and on their own.

## The Reverence for Ford

That said, and this is crucial, one should not make the mistake of interpreting Leone's films as simple oppositions to, or mockeries of, Ford's optimism. Fierce defenders of Ford's legacy, like Bogdanovich, often make this mistake in discussing Leone's work. These critics underestimate how appreciative Leone can be of Ford's optimism, both in his writings and interviews and in *Once Upon a Time*. Leone could be very articulate in his appreciation of Ford's "cinema, so simple and open, so humane and dignified." He never mistook Ford's optimism for sentimentality. He recognized that Ford had accomplished the most difficult task of all, building films around a faith in goodness, without (most of the time) falling into treacly clichés. And Leone insisted that even though he saw a different side to America than Ford did, "a side corrupted by the dollar, hidden rather than apparent," it was still "this solar and humanistic West of Ford that has guided my route" through the making of Westerns.[11] "I was very influenced by Ford's honesty and directness," he told Frayling.[12] It is important to keep in mind that Leone's films can be "solar and humanistic," like Ford's films, that they can approach certain of the Western myths with Ford's honesty and directness, while trampling on others with anarchistic glee.

In fact, a strong current of optimism runs through the admittedly hard-bitten and elegiac *Once Upon a Time* that is rarely acknowledged and that is distinctly Ford-like in its nature. Brett McBain's family may be wiped out in this film but his dream of Sweetwater is not. Harmonica, Jill and Cheyenne will all pick up that dream and make it a reality. The goal of realizing McBain's dream becomes the driving moral force of the film and the element that provides a moral counterbalance to the violence and self-interest of these characters.

Leone tells us a lot about McBain in the few minutes we see him. It is apparent that McBain is one of the few good guys in this film. In the quiet dialogue with his daughter, it is achingly apparent that he wants to make her life better and at the same time that he is afraid he will not be able to do so. After bragging about the prospect of wealth to her, he looks away nervously when she asks quite innocently, "We gonna be rich, Pa?" The scenes before the massacre make it clear that he is a Romantic. He can barely read Jill's letter without falling into reverie over the straw hat she wore when they first met. He seems unfazed by the fact that she is a prostitute, and in fact aims to fulfill two dreams: to build a town and to redeem Jill, giving to her the life of a lady. Even Frank grudgingly nods to McBain's kind and dreamy nature when he asks Jill, "Tell me, did old McBain know?," referring to her past as a prostitute. "Yeah," he concludes, "I bet he did. He's just the type to marry a whore."

McBain's goodness seems closely tied to his Irishness. "That crazy Irishman," cackles Jill's coach driver when he hears McBain has idealistically named his dusty patch of land "Sweetwater." The very name of the community McBain envisions is a dream. Jill describes to Cheyenne how McBain aimed to redeem her and then sums up McBain's ideal view of their life together in two words: "an Irishman." Then she offers a typical Irish eulogy for McBain: "God rest your soul, Brett McBain. Even if he's gonna have a job pulling you out of the Devil's grip." McBain is the Ford character *par excellence* in this film. He is Irish for better and for worse. He has a fiery temper (hence the scene where he strikes his son one moment and coos softly to him the next) and he is tempted by the Devil (hence New Orleans) but he is also a poet (his dreamy response to Jill's letter describing her clothes) and a dreamer (Sweetwater). And the dream is Ford's dream of the West, centered around femininity, marriage, family, development and bounty.

When McBain dies, Harmonica and Cheyenne pick up his dual dream of giving Jill a better life and of building Sweetwater. Cheyenne seems motivated by a love of Jill and perhaps even a desire to settle down with her, though Morton's bullet will end that fantasy. Harmonica too wants to help Jill but he also exhibits an intuitive understanding and appreciation for the dead Irishman's hopes and aspirations. At first, Cheyenne can only understand McBain's venture as a moneymaking scheme and wonders why McBain did not simply sell his property when it became valuable. But Harmonica understands that "you don't sell the dream of a lifetime." Perhaps thinking of his own, darker dream of a lifetime (to kill Frank), he under-

*Three. Ford and* Once Upon a Time in the West

**49**

stands the importance of something you plan to do for a long time. Perhaps he appreciates McBain's dream because it is a constructive dream while his is destructive. In this sense, Harmonica's appreciation for McBain's dream parallels Leone's appreciation for Ford's, one he respects but cannot accomplish himself. Whatever the reason, Harmonica's determination to improve Jill's life and realize McBain's dream becomes as big a part of his and the film's purpose as does the killing of Frank.

This central element of *Once Upon a Time*, McBain's dream, so close to Ford in its Irish optimism, its faith in the civilizing virtues of women and the beauty of developing the West, puts the lie to critics like Bogdanovich who tend to dismiss Leone as a crass cynic trampling the more honorable territory of Ford. Frayling says that Bogdanovich felt Leone's films "suffer from a total absence of Ford's concern for the maintenance and protection of family, home, tradition and future." In Leone's pictures, Bogdanovich says, "there is no future; it's just killing."[13]

But Leone did believe in the family ("my final archetype"). It is just that the family Leone believes in is a ghost family, the dream of the family rather than the real thing. Leone's take on the family may be more melancholy than Ford's, more Romantic, but it is just as deeply felt. Robert Cumbow recognizes this when he writes, in comparing Leone to Ford, that for Leone family "is equally important but distinctly less visible."[14] Many of the characters in *Once Upon a Time* feel deeply about family, but about a family that is lost. Jill loses her family the day she gets it, proving (more than any of the other characters) that Leone finds family happiness touching in its fleetingness. Cheyenne soliloquizes appreciatively about his dead mother. Harmonica's mission, like Mortimer's in *For a Few Dollars More,* is to avenge the murder of his brother. Cumbow notes that "even the garrulous barman (played by Lionel Stander) in the first tavern speaks of a distant sister." Leone's West is packed with loners who seek each other out as temporary or provisional family, but who carry within them, as a lodestar of sorts, memories, or hopes, of family life.

It is too simple, then, to oppose a cynical Leone to an optimist Ford, as Bogdanovich does. Leone revered Ford's films and participated in their view of the West as far as he could. Sometimes, his appreciation of the West is so simple and direct as to be a replica of Ford. Other times, as in his evocations of family life, he seems to heed the distant echo of Ford. And still other times, as in the McBain massacre, he rebelliously sends up or satirizes Ford. Leone was as mindful of his duty to honor Ford as he was determined to not to blandly worship him.

# Henry Fonda

Leone's use of Henry Fonda is a good example of how he uses the language of Ford's Westerns for his own purposes, at once taking advantage of the iconic power and drama this language brings to his film and, at the same time, playing with that language and drawing new meanings from it. Leone's first intention in using Fonda, whom he had been seeking for several films, was to tap into in his huge iconic significance as a Hollywood star, a Ford actor and, by consequence of his Ford films, a symbol of calm, steady American wisdom and kindness. Leone was conscious of working with Hollywood royalty and tried to capture that royalty in his films. He joked about how hard it was to even make Fonda look like a regular man. "No matter what I put on him — even the most worn-out old rags— he always seemed a prince, with his noble walk and aristocratic bearing ... his way of placing one foot in front of the other has an unequaled aesthetic effect."[15] (Claudia Cardinale too noted that Fonda "had a beautiful way of moving; I don't think anyone could ride a horse like him; he seemed a part of the horse.")[16] Leone saw Fonda's lanky elegance, the long legs that Ford put to such good visual use in such scenes as the dances in *Young Mr. Lincoln* and *My Darling Clementine*, or the famous porch scene from *Clementine* where Earp plays the game of balancing on his chair with his legs perched on the porch beam before him. Leone instinctively understood and took advantage of Fonda's physical elegance.

Leone was acutely conscious of working with Hollywood royalty while shooting with Fonda. "No matter what I put on him — even the most worn-out rags — he always seemed like a prince, with his noble walk and aristocratic bearing."

Of course, how Leone uses Fonda's "beautiful way of moving," his prince-like way of walking with one foot in front of another, is distinct to Leone's films. Fonda's physical grace is perhaps most striking during the massacre of the McBains, where he appears from behind the sagebrush and strides up to the small child he intends to murder (in mea-

*Three. Ford and* Once Upon a Time in the West

51

sure to Morricone's lush soundtrack, to which the actors were listening to as they filmed their scenes). As De Fornari ably notes, "Henry Fonda's calm presence and clear-eyed glance which have so often portrayed the Olympic serenity of the just man, here give a priestly gravity to the gestures of the evil character."[17] This is a very precise summary of what Leone does with his iconic references. He patiently creates a ritualistic dance for Fonda that takes advantage of his elegant stride, his "priestly gravity." Leone's characteristic close-ups delivers Fonda's "Olympic serenity" in greater volume than ever before. He taps into the potential of all there is in having Fonda in his film, folding the beauty and drama of Ford's films into his own. A significant part of the beauty and majesty of Leone's films is this great respect for Hollywood, for Ford, for the Western, and most of all for *us*, for the feelings he knows these icons engender in us. He uses those feelings in us to fuel his own drama. He taps the potential for drama that exists simply by having Fonda in his film.

But he does not stop there, because, despite his reverence for Ford, Leone was very clear where his view of America and the Western separate, and there is always in Leone's films a rebelliousness or contrariness to Ford that co-exists with his reverence for Ford. Though at times he is respectful of the beauty of Ford's optimism, other times he strikes at that optimism as part of the machinery of lying myth in American history. Leone bites the master's hand while feeding from it. The introduction to Fonda is characteristically slow, dramatic and mythic. No actor could ask for a more reverential introduction. After the appearance, like a spirit, out of the swirling dust and sagebrush, and the elegant march to the boy, Fonda stops. The camera (which is perched high above Frank and his men, shooting them from behind) takes Fonda's arrest in motion as its cue to start to move. The camera elegantly tracks, in a respectful curve, from behind Fonda to before him, before settling down and letting us gaze in leisure on Fonda's face in a near shot for the first time. Leone's intentions in resting the camera on Fonda here are obvious. He wants us to realize two things: first, that this is Henry Fonda, and secondly, and quickly on the heels of the first realization, that in this movie Fonda will be a murderer. Leone wanted the audience to be struck "in an instant by this profound contrast between the pitiless character Fonda is playing and Fonda's face, a face which for so many years has symbolized justice and goodness."[18]

This is a typical Leone moment, where a reverence for Hollywood, for Ford, for all that Fonda represents in film, is matched by a very Italian, Socialist cynicism. There is a point where even the reverential Leone goes cold on Fonda's legendary goodness. "The vice-presidents of the companies I have had dealings with have all had baby-blue eyes and honest faces and what sons of bitches they turned out to be! Besides, Fonda is no saint himself. He has had five wives. The last one fell out of a window while trying to murder him. He stepped over her body and went to the theater to act his part in *Mister Roberts* as if nothing had happened."[19] Here, we have a pretty good example of how Leone's adoration for American mythology could be matched by a disdain for the realities of American culture. The glee and hyperbole with which he relates this episode from Fonda's life attests to Leone's hostility and strong desire to counter antiseptic American myths of "justice and goodness." Leone's cinema aims to deepen and respect the myth of the American Western, but at the same time challenge and refine it, make it more truthful.

Leone said that he wanted to build on John Ford's idea of casting Fonda as a heavy in *Fort Apache*. In that film, Ford cast Fonda as un unpleasant martinet of a colonel who deals cruelly with both the Indians and his own troops.[20] And it is true that this Ford film, in which Fonda plays a darker character with nebulous morals, would seem the obvious parallel to Fonda's performance in *Once Upon a Time*. But, oddly enough, when I watch *Once*, Fonda's performance brings to mind his performance in those Ford films where he *did* play an icon of middle American goodness: *My Darling Clementine* or *Young Abe Lincoln*, for example.

Henry Fonda on the set of Ford's *Fort Apache*. The brittle martinet of a colonel that Fonda played in this film inspired Leone to cast Fonda, against type, as a bad guy in *Once Upon a Time in the West.*

In many ways, Fonda was out of character in *Fort Apache*. The character was too brittle and petulant to draw out the best of Fonda. Fonda, in *Once*, is what Fonda was always at his best. He strides with the same stately, calm elegance that he did in his best films. He speaks in epigrams, the honesty of which seem to be proven by time. Even when Frank says things as awful as "people scare better when they are dying," Fonda articulates the words with such a calm, quietly humorous,

*Three. Ford and* Once Upon a Time in the West

53

Lincoln-esque intonation that we cannot help but smile at the truth of what he is saying. It is a testimony to Leone's insistence on holding back as far as he can from moral judgment that he taps into the great positive virtues of Fonda's iconography in representing the evil Frank. Fonda is not reduced by his bad guy role in *Once*. He is allowed to air out his greatest acting virtues, but this time in order to lend beauty and gravity to the side of evil.

Of course, Frank is not completely or invincibly evil. In many ways, he is the most vulnerable character in the film, marked from the outset for doom. Morton sees through him and is amused by Frank's naive belief that he, old warrior that he is, might transform himself into a modern businessman. Harmonica is not impressed with Frank either. Even when Harmonica is tied up, he seems to have power over Frank, reducing him to blank fear when he recites the names of all the men Frank has killed. In the end, Frank accepts the two truths he has been running from: that he will never be a businessman, and that he must subject himself to execution by Harmonica. When he finally understands his true role, that of a passing mythic figure, a titan from the past, his character grows fully into the power of Fonda's persona. When Harmonica says to Frank, "So you found out you weren't a businessman after all, huh, Frank?," and Fonda responds, "Just a man," there is no longer a contradiction between the character and the actor. Fonda packs a lot into those three words, articulating them with a measured finality, tinged with humor, that makes them seem to represent the moment at which he was meant to arrive in this film. It is a line worthy of Ford's Fonda, with his "Olympic serenity" and calm honesty. Leone underrates his own cinema when he compares Frank to the colonel in *Fort Apache*. Frank, despite his evil, is more reminiscent of the calm dignity of Wyatt Earp than he is of *Apache*'s petulant colonel. Frank may be the film's worst character but he represents Fonda at his Fordian best.

## Woody Strode

Leone draws a similar power from Woody Strode's cameo in the opening sequence. Strode brings to any film the associations he earned from Ford's films where he was an icon of strength, stoicism and loyalty. His lean, strong physique and his dark, clean shaven head seem to embody these virtues. When he appears at the outset of this film as a gunslinger in Frank's camp, he brings to his character, as Fonda does to Frank, a quiet majesty. And Leone uses Strode's quiet dignity in much the same way he does Fonda's, this icon of goodness and loyalty as a murdering outlaw. And yet Strode's role does not seem to diminish, or to stand in contradiction, to his persona. He has never seemed so gloriously himself. As he positions himself under the porch roof, waiting for Harmonica at the beginning of the film, he assumes a look of impassivity that is in keeping with the general rock-like solidity of his body, for which he was famous. His face and figure here are about as close as the human form can get to absolute immobility. As the first drop of water slaps off his bare scalp (a physical trait that Leone sought to ironically emphasize, as he did Jack Elam's wandering eye in the same sequence), his face barely moves, but his eyes cloud with irritation. As he very slowly and ceremoniously places his hat on his head (his movements can only be described as glacial) and the water bounces off his hat, Strode's eyes just barely perceptibly narrow, and the edges of his mouth just barely curl into the slightest hint of a cruel and confident smile. Leone's close-up here is striking in the way it registers the most fleeting of expressions and in the way it suggests, as quietly as possible, a disturbing sadism about this man. There is something scary about a man who can get angry with a drop of water. That his anger is so quietly registered only makes its seem more powerful in potential.

Leone relished shooting Ford icon Woody Strode. Strode felt he had never been shot so effectively — high praise from a Ford veteran.

This is one of those moments that puts the lie to Leone simply quoting Ford in his films. Here Leone develops what Ford began. He may be capitalizing on the iconic stature Strode gained in Ford's films but Strode had never been filmed like this before. Ford, of course, had never put Strode's singular presence in the service of evil. But Leone does more than dirty Ford's icons. Ford had also never given Strode such glorious close-ups or filmed him with such reverence and majesty. This is something Strode recognized. He effused over the attention Leone lavished on him. "The close-ups," he said, "I couldn't believe. I never got a close-up in Hollywood. Even in *The Professionals*. I had only three close-ups in the entire pic-

**Three. Ford and** Once Upon a Time in the West

55

ture. Sergio Leone framed me on the screen for five minutes."[21] Fonda, too, reported that he had "never had such wonderful close-ups" as he had in *Once Upon a Time*.[22] James Coburn took the job on *Fistful of Dynamite* based on Fonda's recommendation of Leone as "the best director I ever worked with."[23] The praise dished up by Fonda and Strode is so hyperbolic as to almost seem to represent a betrayal of Ford. On the other hand, Ford and Strode probably both realized that if Leone filmed them well, he did so, at least in part, because he saw the drama in their presence that Ford had first discovered. In filming them, Leone was tapping into Ford's power as much as their own. Leone's treatment of Fonda and Strode is typical of his tendency to study concepts and icons from Ford's film and to steep them in his own slow and reverential film process, until he had brought out even deeper and richer qualities in them.

# FOUR

# Harmonica and Cheyenne

Harmonica, Cheyenne and Frank represent three archetypes from the mythic past. Robert Cumbow sees them as representatives of a "a privileged race" who stand to the rest of the Westerners in the film "as Titans to Olympians. They are older, tougher, simpler, less flexible and doomed."[1] Of these three members of the "ancient race" to which Harmonica says he and Frank belong, Harmonica stands out as the most ancient, the most primitive and the furthest removed from the contemporary West of capitalism and train tracks.

Of the three titans, only Harmonica passes through the film without pretending to himself that he could put down roots in the new West. Cheyenne is more of the earth than Harmonica. Cheyenne would have liked to settle down with Jill and watch Sweetwater grow. Morton's bullet puts an end to that fantasy. Frank wants to be a businessman. He thinks he can shake his ancient habits and be like Morton. Like Cheyenne, he is attracted to Jill and even indulges himself momentarily in imagining that he might marry her and settle down. Alone of the three, Harmonica is not susceptible to Jill's charms. The sight of her in the bathtub only provokes him to teasingly hand her a brush for scrubbing her own back. He may think she is a "remarkable woman," but she knows he has "something else on his mind." In the end, when she expresses her hope that he will return to Sweetwater someday, Harmonica looks at her with a distant, bemused smile.

Harmonica is no more tempted by the world of finance than he is the world of romance. He passes through this film without ever participating in its monetary system. Both Frank and Cheyenne find Harmonica in saloons, try to intimidate him, and end up paying for his drink. We never see Harmonica open his purse. He buys back Jill's farm for her (at the cost of $5000) by trading in Cheyenne for the $5000 reward on Cheyenne's head.

When Frank tries to insult Harmonica by offering him $5000 for the land, plus one dollar ("You've got a right to make a profit too," Frank says mockingly), Harmonica ignores the insult and the offer, using Frank's extra dollar to pay for his drink, which just happens to cost a dollar. Harmonica does not buy and he does not sell. He simply exchanges other people's money. He stands above and outside the world of profit and ownership. "I don't invest in land," he explains to Jill in giving her back the land. Harmonica is no capitalist. He is moved by McBain's dream to develop Sweetwater, but he has no use for such ventures himself. By the end of the film, Frank catches on to Harmonica's ways when he abandons his burgeoning capitalist habits and surrenders to Harmonica in a duel. "Nothing matters to us any more," he tells Harmonica. "Not the land, not the money, not the woman."

But even with this realization, Frank does not reach Harmonica's titanic heights. Since Frank and Cheyenne are more earthbound than Harmonica, they are doomed to die mortals' deaths. They pass with the old West. Harmonica simply rides away with Cheyenne's body, suggesting nothing so much as an angel ascending to Heaven, bearing the body of a saint. Harmonica's character is both an avenging angel whose purpose is to find and punish Frank and a guardian angel sent to protect Jill and establish her garden on Earth. Jill may be sarcastic but she is also right when she identifies Harmonica as "the noble defender of poor, defenseless widows." This kind of line is typical of the way Leone traffics in conventional archetypes and iconography and at the same time playfully tweaks those conventions.

## Bronson

Leone was attracted to Charles Bronson for the role of Harmonica because he felt Bronson's face conveyed the toughness of an ancient race. "He is destiny himself," Leone said, referring to Bronson's physiognomy, and particularly his hard, pockmarked face: "a sort of granite block marked by life." Frayling comments that Leone's assessment of Bronson was reminiscent of Jean-Luc Godard's comment about Gary Cooper, that his "face belongs to the mineral kingdom." With his "face made of marble," Bronson was the perfect representation of this character "who knows just how long to wait," who "must always have an impassive look on his face. He doesn't talk much. He expresses his sadness with the harmonica. His music is a lament which comes from deep down. It is visceral — attached to ancestral memory."[2] There is a striking contrast between the emotional sound of Harmonica's harmonica and the impassivity of Bronson's face. Leone wanted Harmonica's sadness over his brother's death long ago to be so deeply rooted that it was nearly invisible to the audience, expressing itself only in Harmonica's music.

These words that critics use to describe Bronson in this film — marble, impassive — would hardly win him rewards in the world of method acting, but are recommendations for an actor in a Leone film. Tonino Valerii, Leone's director of photography noted that Leone learned a great many of the "precious secrets" of the Hollywood directors when they journeyed through the Cinecittà Studios of Italy. One "secret" was how to compensate for wooden acting by shooting around the actor, for example, giving the actor nervous habits or tics that do not require dialogue, or expressing character through costume, or shooting the actor in close-ups that break the actor into concrete details — eyes, hands, boots. " A good editor," said Valerii, "will always be able to make something decent out of all this."[3]

Leone uses these tricks in filming Bronson. He dresses Bronson in his

Leone saw Bronson's face as "a sort of granite block marked by life," perfect for the role of Harmonica, a character who represented "destiny himself."

trademark weathered gear, keeps him very still and moves the camera around him, pulling a performance out of his still subject through a virtuosic assemblage of close-ups and pans. He films *around* Bronson as often as he films him. Many critics have opined that Bronson's performance in this film is the best of his career and it is no coincidence that it is a film in which he speaks very little. Harmonica speaks in brief aphorisms that finish just in time so that we remain, for the most part, unaware of Bronson's nasal voice and New York accent. In the meantime, the camera coaxes from the lines and creases of his face a presence that de Fornari describes as "primordial," as hard-baked and primitive as the stone monuments of Arizona that would serve as his backdrop. Leone's technique of directing actors here is strongly reminiscent of that of other great directors, such as Robert Bresson (with his insistence on referring to his actors as "models") or Hitchcock (famous for battling with Method actors such as Montgomery Clift and Paul Newman), who tried to get their actors to neutralize their acting technique so that they might capture with their camera the unique presence implied by these actors' physiognomy.

## A Man of Destiny

To reinforce his sense of Harmonica as a visitor from an another world, a visiting god or avenging spirit, Leone likes to surprise us with Harmonica's appearance. Harmonica seems to appear out of nowhere, his image often preceded aurally by the wail of his harmonica. The train exits the station in the opening sequence to reveal Harmonica to the three men he will soon kill. The gunmen are introduced to his presence on the scene by the sound of the harmonica, a clarion call to attention. When they turn around, he is there. For all we know, he might have been unloaded like a statue from the train, because Leone avoids, whenever he can, recording Harmonica's pedestrian movements, such as stepping down from a train. Harmonica never rushes into a scene. He is usually revealed as if he had always been there. We discover him, for example, in the back of the desert tavern, only after much action has occurred in that sequence. The final sequence of the film finds him lodged solidly on a fence whittling a piece of wood. Everyone else in the scene comes riding up to him, or gazes at him through their windows. Robert Cumbow makes the excellent observation that Frank's movements are often tied to Morton's train. We see, several times, Frank riding up to, and away from, the train, like a bee coming and going from a hive. Cumbow notes that after Morton has been slaughtered and the train disabled, Frank drifts into Harmonica's sphere and influence. In their duel together, Harmonica stands like a monolith in the middle of the circle inscribed around him by Frank, his satellite.[4]

When Harmonica does enter a scene, he does so mysteriously, often coming out of the shadows. He peers from the shadows of the bar in the flickering light of Cheyenne's lantern in the desert bar. Jill knows Harmonica is outside her house only by the sound of his harmonica and the flash of his match in the dark. He appears in her barn the next morning as a shadow in her loft.

Or Harmonica enters a scene in very distinctive manner, reserved for him and no one else in this film — in close-up profile from the direct left or right of the screen. (In the shooting script of *Once Upon a Time*, Leone indicates Harmonica's arrival by writing, "the man enters in his usual way.") In these shots, we are not given any spatial context, any sense of where he is or where he comes from, until his face has entered the scene. The close-up profile further reinforces Harmonica's granite monumentality, as if Mt. Rushmore were on the move.

Leone's sense that Harmonica is "destiny himself" is reinforced by the scene in which Harmonica whittles as he waits for Frank to arrive for their duel. "What's he waiting for out there?" Jill asks Cheyenne. "He's whittling on a piece of wood," answers Cheyenne. "I've got a feeling when he stops whittling something's gonna happen." Harmonica's whittling emphasizes the vastness of his patience. He is the man who can wait forever, the man who has time on his side. The idea that things will happen when he stops whittling suggests he is the author of all that will come to be, the block of wood suggestive of the various fates that Harmonica has been sculpting throughout the film.

Frank seems to know that it is part of his fate to deal with Harmonica when he describes him as the "man who makes appointments." Harmonica is Frank's ultimate appointment. Harmonica's presence in Frank's life represents the evil of Frank's past catching up to him.

Harmonica alerts Frank to the assassin hidden behind the painted clockface by saying, "Time sure does fly." This little snippet of dialogue operates on several levels. Literally, Harmonica is referring to where the assassin is. Metaphorically, he is reminding Frank that time is catching up to him in the shape of Harmonica and his revenge. There is also a little dig at Frank's recent pretensions to being a businessman. Frank has begun to pick up the businessman Morton's obsession with time, to follow the American business dictum that "time is money." Frank and Harmonica represent a sharp contrast in their approaches to time. Frank is running out of time, both with Morton (who has given up on him and is trying to kill him) and with Harmonica, who is seeking to make him pay for his past.

Harmonica, on the other hand, represents the fullness of time. He is the man who whittles, the man who can wait. He seems to be the master of time, the one who knows when everyone's appointment is. "It's not time to leave," Harmonica tells Jill, the first time she waivers in her resolution to stay on the McBain farm. Later, after the auction when he has handed over the deed of the ranch, he tells her "it's time to go home." Harmonica seems to see through Frank and Jill, to understand them and the schedule of their lives better than they do.

As befitting a sage, or oracle, Harmonica does not say much. When he does speak, he tends to express himself in brief aphorisms and even these are so simple and pure as to achieve a mathematical purity. Harmonica asks the three men who meet him at Cattle Corners train station, at the outset of this film, whether they have brought him a horse, since they have not brought Frank, as directed. The character played by Jack Elam looks at the three horses he and the two other gunmen have brought, just enough for them to ride out on, and laughs, "Looks like we're shy one horse," he says, indicating their intention to kill Harmonica. Harmonica's response is certain. "You brought two too many." In Harmonica's world, things and people often have a way of washing out, accounting-wise. Cheyenne is worth $5000. So is the farm. The extra dollar Frank tries to bully him to take for the McBain property is just enough to pay for his drink.

Cheyenne, who develops the kind of camaraderie with Harmonica that we often see develop in Howard Hawks films, a friendship that is expressed by a mutually understood code language, takes to Harmonica's talking in numbers also. After Cheyenne has given Harmonica two reasons why it could not have been his gang that slaughtered the McBains (along with some jibes about his harmonica playing), Harmonica says, "Well, you know music and you can count ... all the way to two." "All the way to six if I have to," says Cheyenne, holding up his six-shooter, "and maybe faster than you." When Harmonica introduces Cheyenne to the auction crowd, announcing that Cheyenne is worth $5000 in ransom, Cheyenne comments, wryly, "Judas was satisfied with 4970 less." Harmonica and Cheyenne like to turn to mathematics to express their good-natured jibes. It is a kind of stripped-down language, devoid of flowery sentiment. And it expresses things with certainty, a kind of language of fate. Leone conveys to us that Cheyenne will be sprung from his confinement on board the train simply by having two of his men order tickets for the same train. "Two tickets to the next stop, amigo," they say, in classically ominous Mexican bandit tones. The next four syllables they pronounce slowly and musically, as if they contained the entire gist of their message: "One way only."

If Harmonica carries with him the power of time and destiny, it is no surprise that the other characters in the film feel the presence of death when he is near. "People like that have something inside them, something to do with death," Cheyenne says about Harmonica when he explains to Jill why she cannot count on Harmonica settling down with her. Both times Frank asks him who he is, Harmonica responds with a litany of Frank's dead victims. Here he seems like a man who has traveled through Hades and is well-acquainted with death. The death Harmonica has "something to do with" is, of course, the death of his brother, which he is avenging, and which the flashbacks make clear still haunts him, both because of the cruelty of Frank's means of murdering his brother and because of Harmonica's own sense of culpability in not being able to support his brother on his shoulders when his brother had the noose around his neck. The death he has something to do with is also Frank's death, which seems to be his sole, unswerving goal, a punishment he so relishes that he is willing to save Frank's hide, even kill on Frank's behalf, so that he can kill Frank in just the way he wants to, at just the right moment and place, following a planned ceremony. Looked at in terms of plausibility, Frank realizing who Harmonica is at the very moment he draws his last breath is very unlikely. It is the kind of revenge that really can only be dreamed of. It has a pre-ordained quality that lends more basis to Harmonica's presence as a spiritual avenger with special knowledge about the wheels of time and an exact knowledge of when it is right to do things.

The death Harmonica has something to do with has metaphorical implications as well. As critic after critic has noted, *Once Upon a Time in the West* (more literally translated as *Once Upon a Time There Was a West*) is about the death of the old West as it makes way for the new West of industrialization and cultivation. Harmonica's archetype, the heroic loner, the lone gunslinger, is passing away, as are Cheyenne's wild outlaw and Frank's hired gun. The death Cheyenne refers to is the death of Harmonica's type. With the wound in his side as he says these words, Cheyenne too has something to do with death too. He too will pass away.

Even in films that do not take such an allegorical approach to the West, the characters Harmonica resembles often have "something to do with death." These men have no place in the world they help settle. Tom Doniphon, in John Ford's *The Man Who Shot Liberty Valance,* has a nice farm and is even building an addition on it for Vera Miles' character, Hallie, and their projected offspring. But he is still too connected to the violence and anger of the old West to realize this fantasy. He is no competition for Ransom Stoddard who brings, with his courtship, the promise of culture and beauty. Countless gunslingers, like Shane, have helped homesteaders ward off evil and brought Fisher King husbands back to life, only to disappear because they had no real talent for domesticity. These cowboys, too, have "something to do with death," too much to do with death to ever settle down.

# The Duel

*Once Upon a Time*'s final scenes underline the fixity of Harmonica's presence in the film. Harmonica bears a strange resemblance to Leone himself in the way he carefully choreographs the end. The duel, he has decided, will take place on the McBain farm, the site of Frank's last slaughter. Leone had drawn specific parallels between Frank's viciousness to Harmonica as a child and his viciousness to little Timmy McBain, the boy he murders early in the film. In both the killing of Timmy McBain and the flashback with Harmonica, Leone orchestrates one of his patented staredowns between the child and Frank. That Leone wants us to draw parallels between Harmonica's childhood confrontation and Timmy McBain's is emphasized also by the bells that toll in mourning in the final notes of the score that accompanies Timmy's murder. The murder of Harmonica's brother also coincided with the sound of bells, as his noose was tied to a bell hanging from an arch. During the flashback scene, as Harmonica falls to the dust, we hear the bell chiming, thus signaling his brother's death. (Leone further reinforces the linkage of death and bells tolling in the death scenes of Cheyenne and Morton, both of which finish with sounds of bells.) The parallels between Timmy McBain's death and Harmonica's childhood trauma suggest that when Harmonica squares off with Frank at McBain's farm, he is paying back Frank for two crimes, his own victimization as a child and that of Timmy McBain as well.

It is also fitting that the duel takes place on the land that Frank was unable to acquire. The Irishman's crazy dream of saving one piece of land from the voracious grasp of the railroad has been Frank's undoing. He will be buried on the land he thought to steal. He will not be awarded Cheyenne's ascension into cowboy Heaven, or at least cowboy Hades. Like a warring medieval baron, this titan's bones will become part of Sweetwater's foundations.

The duel itself visually accentuates the fixity of Harmonica's purpose. Harmonica stakes a piece of ground and stays on it. Frank circles around him, calmly but scurrilously looking for an advantage, and stopping when he has the sun behind him and in Harmonica's eyes. Harmonica seems to know that he will need no such advantage. Visually, one has the sense of Harmonica and Frank representing a kind of compass, with Harmonica as the fixed point and Frank tracing a circle around him. Harmonica is the planet, the destiny around which Frank circulates. Leone chooses this sequence for the longest, tightest close-up of Harmonica in the film. Harmonica has his prey in his eyes. The prey is moving but he is not. Leone relishes every fold and pore in the blasted granite of Bronson's face. This is the scene for which he chose Bronson, where the rock-hard monument of his face matches the ancient fixity of his purpose.

## Harmonica and McBain

Harmonica is a mythic man of granite with a tender side. He is "destiny himself," a kind of exterminating angel, but Harmonica also stops along his path of vengeance to do a few old-fashioned things, characteristic of the more conventional Western hero, such as defend the virtue of a woman and aid in the realization of a poor sodbuster's dreams to tame and cultivate the West. Critics often over-estimate the coldness and viciousness of Harmonica's character and underestimate the way he fights for the Fordian virtues in the film. If Harmonica's quasi-divine wisdom is evident in how he seems to see right through Jill and Frank, and the way he seems to know everything that is going to happen and when it should, it is also evident in his understanding of the dreamy Irishman McBain's dream to bring "sweet water" to the arid West. Harmonica is the first to figure out the significance of the building materials sent to McBain, the first to understand McBain's dream. And he is the one who brings the dream to realization, already measuring out the buildings as he explains McBain's dream to the befuddled Cheyenne. In this scene also, Harmonica is associated with a kind of mathematical precision as he lays down the lines of the future community. The way he talks here, while measuring out distances and walking in strict lines, echoes the way he enters scenes in sharp profile, directly from the left or right of the screen. Everything about Harmonica is characterized by clarity and fixity of purpose. Through Harmonica's movements, Leone emphasizes, that he is an instrument of some larger design.

Harmonica is surprisingly moved by McBain's "dream of a lifetime." He understands far more swiftly than does Cheyenne that McBain's goal was more than to make money, that he dreamed of developing a community. Harmonica seems to want to make this dream of progress and cultivation, the dream of John Ford's Westerns, come true, even if it is not a world he can ever enjoy. There is a great self-sacrificing quality to Harmonica. He helps bring to fruition a world in which he no longer has a place.

Leone, who rigorously avoided any excessive expression of optimism, must have found the ending of *Once Upon a Time* a little too stirring, because in his interviews he often emphasized that the film's ending was not a happy one, depicting as it did a newer, more pedestrian West, governed by women and characterized by labor rather than style. Nevertheless, there is nothing cynical in the way Leone shoots Harmonica taking one last satisfied look out Jill's door at the swarming community coming into existence before him. "It's gonna be a beautiful town someday, Sweetwater," he says, finishing with a quietly triumphant pronouncement of the name that symbolizes McBain's dream. This moment indicates how important it was to Harmonica to realize McBain's dream. In fact, it is almost comical how much more Harmonica's thoughts are with McBain at this moment than they are with Jill who, a few feet away, waits breathlessly to see if Harmonica has enough love for her to stay with her. Harmonica, however, as we know, is not the type to settle down. His thoughts are with the past (his brother) and the future (McBain's Sweetwater). True to his ephemeral nature, he shows little interest in the present world. But he is not just an assassin, and the movie does not just follow the rhythms of revenge. Harmonica's purpose was not just to kill Frank but also to bring McBain's dream to life.

# Cheyenne

Harmonica and Cheyenne's relationships is one of the most carefully articulated and successful in the film. It represents a reprise of the kind of gruff male camaraderie we see between Monko and Mortimer in *For A Few Dollars More* and between Angel Eyes and Tuco in *The Good, the Bad and the Ugly*. Cheyenne's character was conceived as a kind of parallel to Tuco's— another crazy Mexican bandit to counterbalance the preternatural calm of the film's hero. But not much of the Mexican nature of the character survives the casting of the WASPy Jason Robards as Cheyenne. (Some viewers are not even aware that Cheyenne is meant to be a Mexican brigand.) And Robards' performance is miles from the broad comic work of Eli Wallach in *The Good, the Bad and the Ugly*. Hence, the relationship of Harmonica and Cheyenne ends up being more reminiscent of Monko's and Mortimer's friendship than it is of Angel Eyes' and Tuco's. Harmonica and Cheyenne, like Monko and Mortimer, are men of quiet dignity, despite Cheyenne's reputation for violence (which we see infrequently). And Robards approaches his role with a profound leisure that moves his performance into a more elevated category than the caricature of Wallach's Tuco.

I would argue, however, that Harmonica and Cheyenne's relationship is even more carefully rendered than that of Monko and Mortimer. Part of that is due to Donati's careful script, so good at avoiding clichés and reducing all communication to pleasing riddles. Harmonica and Cheyenne manage to express great amounts of affection for each other without recourse to the weepy barroom treacle that has become the standard of the male buddy film (and that we even get touches of in *Fistful of Dynamite* and *Once Upon a Time in America*). But a large part of the success of this relationship is due also to Robards, who has a congeniality on the screen that the stiff Van Cleef cannot match.

Donati did not like the choice of Robards for the role. He felt that Robards was a theater actor, an actor who "doesn't get past the screen. He hasn't got the eyes, I think that's where the problem lies."[5] Robards certainly has the most patrician, or least Leone-like, face in the film. But of all the American actors on board in this project, he also seems to have the most Italian soul. He caught on, as well as anyone in the film, to Leone's Visconti-like, tired, elegant rhythms and to the Chaplinesque pathos that Leone was looking for in his spirited brigands, his so-called "ugly" characters, whose feeling hearts match their violent temperaments. In Robards' hands, the tired Cheyenne — with his endless sacrifices for Harmonica, Jill and McBain, his quiet bouts of philosophy, his puppy dog eyes for Jill — represents something like the heart of the film.

Cheyenne is often justifiably lumped together with the other "ugly" members of Leone's cowboy trios: Tuco in *The Good, the Bad and the Ugly* and Juan Miranda in *Fistful of Dynamite*. In each of these films, Leone feels most deeply for this character. What he says of Tuco applies equally to Cheyenne: "My most profound sympathy always goes towards the Tuco side … he can be touching with all that tenderness and all that wounded humanity. But Tuco is also a creature of instinct, a bastard, a tramp."[6]

Stuart Kaminsky does a nice job of summarizing the essential ingredients of the "ugly" character in these three films, capturing that same mixture of amorality and sentiment in them that Leone prizes (and which was central in Chaplin's Tramp character). The "ugly" character is "physically coarse, bearded, a bit dirty, but vibrant, alive, and, in contrast to the morality of the 'good' and the immorality of the 'bad,' he is amoral. The 'ugly' character is hyper-human, can show great affection, great hatred and violence. He has no cunning, is open, direct and shows an earthy simplicity and sense of humor." Kaminsky notes that we react with "amusement and affection to Wallach, Robards and Steiger, although they are shown to be murderers. The murders they commit are all matters of survival or angry emotions without calculation; and this is seen by Leone as being sympathetic. In all three films in which this character appears, the 'good' guy's emotional distance is penetrated by the honest earthiness of the 'ugly.'"[7]

All this is generally true, but it is important to distinguish Cheyenne from the other members of the "ugly" grouping. Cheyenne is not quite as coarse and amoral as Juan and Tuco and is probably a bit more cunning. Leone did not want Wallach to play Leone because he did not want Cheyenne to be tainted by the coarse humor Wallach would bring to the role. Leone saw Cheyenne's character as similar to Eli Wallach's in *The Good, the Bad and the Ugly* "but there is more warmth in him, a humanity which, with a mixture of drollery and sadness, gives him a particular philosophy of life."[8] Leone saw Cheyenne as a gentler, more philosophical entry into the ugly tradition. When, according to Leone, he was trying to convey Cheyenne's character to Morricone, he described Cheyenne as "a bandit and a lout, a son of a bitch, but he has the capacity for friendship. So there shouldn't just be violence in Cheyenne, but also a great tenderness, because he's a sweet, romantic character, proud and full of love."[9] The words Leone uses to describe Cheyenne — warm, humanity, friendship, tenderness, sweet, romantic, love — are not words one associates with Leone's film and they go along way to explaining why Cheyenne is such an important character, and one that is crucial in seeing the difference between this film and Leone's other Westerns. Cheyenne brings a warmth, charm, a world-weariness, a mixture of "drollery and sadness" that is a big part of why this film stands out among Leone's as having a vaster emotional as well as pictorial scale. Nichols is right when the says that "the Romanticism of Cheyenne's character is unique in Leone's work."[10] Cheyenne is a Romantic in every sense of the word. He is Romantic because he is the man in this film with the deepest appreciation of women. But he is also Romantic in the larger sense of the word, because he is someone with a nostalgia for what has passed, for lost opportunities, for what might have been. Cheyenne *is* a philosopher. He understands destiny (Harmonica) and he understands love (Jill) and he has a paradoxical understanding of life as both sad and sweet, a beautiful garden that we are not allowed to enjoy.

## Harmonica and Cheyenne

De Fornari refers to Cheyenne as the "sage brigand." Cheyenne, he says "is always ready for a chat and never misses an opportunity to pontificate."[11] De Fornari contrasts Cheyenne's verbosity with Harmonica's silence. I am not sure that if you actually counted the number of lines accorded to Cheyenne and Harmonica, respectively, you would find that Cheyenne says a great deal more than Harmonica. Everyone in this film speaks in maxims and aphorisms. But I know what De Fornari means

Harmonica (Bronson, center). "Instead of talking, he plays. And when he should play, he talks."

because Cheyenne does serve as a translator of sorts for Harmonica. Leone described the structure of *Once Upon a Time* as being like "a jigsaw puzzle, like a mosaic where if you move one piece it ruins everything. Because none of the characters talks about himself, it is always someone else who judges him, reads him."[12] There is a great feel of dignity to this film's script. It avoid the clichés and embarrassments of self-analysis, the self-absorption of the psychoanalytic age, which is, in many ways, out of step with the ethos of the Western.

It is Cheyenne's role to talk about Harmonica, to explain him to us, and to save Harmonica from undignified self-exposition. It is interesting to watch Cheyenne's relationship with Harmonica develop as the film moves along. Initially, Cheyenne is utterly confused by Harmonica. When Cheyenne and Harmonica first meet at the roadside tavern, Cheyenne does not understand what Harmonica's harmonica-playing means. As he tells Jill later, "Instead of talking he plays, and when he should play he talks." The comment is remarkably similar to the comment Tuco addresses to the dead man who took a little too long in trying to kill Tuco in the bathtub in *The Good, the Bad,* "If you're going to shoot, shoot, don't talk." The bandit or "ugly" character in Leone's films—Tuco, Cheyenne, Juan Miranda in *Fistful of Dynamite*—is not the most intellectual of Leone's heroes (though he may be the most philosophical). He tends to be confused or annoyed by too much chatter. Harmonica effortlessly wins his first battle of wits with Cheyenne at the desert tavern. Cheyenne does not understand the meaning of Harmonica's music or his words.

By the end of the film, though, after their camaraderie and their partnership in helping Jill have developed, Cheyenne is the only one who *does* understand Harmonica. Frank remains mystified by Harmonica up to the bitter end and Jill too harbors false illusions about a life together with Harmonica, based on a deep misunderstanding of his character. Only Cheyenne gets Harmonica. By the end of the film he knows Harmonica so well that he can tell Jill exactly what Harmonica will do: that when Harmonica is done whittling, there will be gunfire; and that when the gunfire is over, he will walk in the door, pick up his gear and say adios. He has come to understand Harmonica, to become his translator, the spokesman on earth for this otherworldly creature.

If I were to search for a feature that serves to oppose Cheyenne and Harmonica, it would not be how much they talk but the nature of their Western persona. Harmonica, "destiny himself," is characterized by fixity and immobility. He knows what is going to happen and what he is going to do. Cheyenne is characterized by chaos and improvisation. Our introduction to Cheyenne (in a typically allusive Leone manner) is off-screen through a riot of sounds—gunshots and horse whinnies—as he single-handedly slaughters the police guard that was leading him to prison. Later, while Harmonica, like Odysseus passing the Sirens, remains tied to a post in Morton's train carriage, Cheyenne ranges all over Morton's train car, inside and outside of it, employing extraordinary resources of trickery and improvisation to wipe out, one by one, Morton's men. This scene parallels the duel between Harmonica and Frank in which Frank draws a circle around the fixed point that is Harmonica. It is the other men in this film, not Harmonica, that are forced to scramble for their existence. Harmonica carries with him the leisure of eternity.

Cheyenne's final gunfight is again registered off-screen. Frank returns to Morton's rail carriage to find the vestiges of an unholy massacre, with dead scattered all about. Wherever Cheyenne goes there is the gleeful display of violence, though it should be noted that the only men he kills are those who try to confine him or Harmonica. Cheyenne is the true representative of the wild West in the film, the dime-store novel cowboy who blasts his way through the West.

That said, Leone seems to have enjoyed suggesting rather than showing just how crazy Cheyenne can be. We tend to hear about the "fired-up" Cheyenne. We tend to see the tired Cheyenne who just wants a cup of coffee. In fact, when he comes into the roadside tavern after having singlehandedly killed some number of men, he seems less the wild outlaw and more the tired business manager. His men were supposed to have met him at a time designated for his breakout. They were not there on time and he was forced to escape himself. In another subtly comic use of sound, the frantic sound of their speeding horses hooves trampling up to the tavern precedes the equally comic image of the men bursting though the tavern door with great bravado, too late to be of any use to the tired Cheyenne, who is already having his drink at the bar.

By the time we (the viewers) have caught up with Cheyenne, he is no longer the wild man of the West. Leone gives us one glimpse of the manic energy that earned him his reputation in the scenes where he busts Harmonica free on the train. Otherwise, we meet mostly the man who is tired of fighting, tired of riding with buffoons. The Cheyenne of this film is the one who wants simply to rest, to drink a good strong cup of coffee, to look at a beautiful woman, to slap her on her behind from time to time, to sit on the front porch, like a retired soldier and watch a town being built. The Cheyenne of this film is a man of simple pleasures, a tired, earthbound man whose fantastic struggles and exploits have taught him how pleasant life is when there is a moment of calm.

Jason Robards in costume for playing the part of Cheyenne in *Once Upon a Time in the West.*

The poignancy of Cheyenne's character is that his acute sense of the beauty of the world comes hand in hand with his sense of having lost that world. The archetypal arrangement of the film will not let him survive. He is from a different era. He would like to settle down and love Jill, but she is more interested in Harmonica. By the time she realizes that Harmonica will not stay for her and that Cheyenne is "sort of a handsome man," Cheyenne has a bullet in his gut. Besides, one wonders even if he and Jill *had* been able to get together whether Cheyenne might have concluded like Frank, who also contemplates marrying Jill, "It's me who wouldn't have been any good as a husband." It is easy to see the tired Cheyenne stop for a cup of coffee. It is more difficult to see him having the volition or the energy to build Sweetwater.

Cheyenne has a particularly sad role to play in this film. He is the only one of the three titans, the ancient archetypes, who has a feel for this new West. Harmonica is only passing through. He is so hardened in his sadness, in his preoccupation with death, that he never lets himself believe that he has a place in this new world that is coming to life. Frank is only interested in exploiting it, only interested in the money it generates. Cheyenne likes this new West. He likes the woman, he likes the town. Through Cheyenne's character, Leone expresses an affection and warmth for this new matriarchal West that he so often disparaged in his interviews. Cheyenne likes Jill because she reminds him of his mother. His interest in her, like Harmonica's, is a great deal less sexual than it seems at first glance.

The Harmonica-Cheyenne partnership is so close by the end of the film that it is not difficult to see them as two halves of the same entity, Harmonica representing the celestial half, Cheyenne the terrestrial. Harmonica wants to build Sweetwater out of respect for McBain's "dream of a lifetime." Cheyenne's motivations are more earthbound. He is doing it for Jill. He wants it to be the "first thing she sees when she gets back" from her confinement with Frank. Harmonica is "destiny himself," Cheyenne is a man–warm, loving, chaotic and tired. When Harmonica carries away Cheyenne's body at the end of the film, ascending into the hills outside Sweetwater, it is difficult not to see Harmonica as a god carrying away his son. Frank, the Luciferian character in this drama, deserves to be left in the dust of Sweetwater. But Cheyenne is one of us—a tired, suffering man. We are glad he is being taken care of. Like Harry in *The Snows of Kilimanjaro*, who in his last moments of consciousness ascends to Kilimanjaro in the small airplane, Cheyenne is returned to the mountains. He gets the death he deserves.

# Playing

The trajectory of Cheyenne and Harmonica's relationship is recorded with great allusiveness. One of Leone's principal criticisms of the conventional Western was how talky it had become. He was dedicated to a script in which his cowboys spoke in maxims and aphorisms that were as hard and chiseled as their faces. In a sense, he was drawn more to film noir language than Western language. He stressed the parallels between his first Western, *Fistful of Dollars*, and Dashiell Hammet's *Red Harvest*. The most cursory glance at Raoul Walsh's gangster films reveals how carefully Leone scrutinized their technique and their ideas. In all of his films, Leone's cowboy villains move with the elegant and casual evil of Walsh's gangsters. Leone's dialogue is just one of the ways his films represent an interesting fusion of the Western and film noir genre.

Harmonica and Cheyenne's dialogue often brings to mind Howard Hawks' dialogue and the way his heroes would form a partnership or camaraderie based on a mysterious and poetic code language that only they understood. Their first conversation, for example, is allusive and thick with word play. The recurrent theme in this first conversation is a parallel between playing a harmonica and shooting a gun. Cheyenne's first cognizance of Harmonica, like most characters in this film, is through his harmonica-playing. Cheyenne rightly interprets this playing as a challenge or announcement, the call to judgment that it represents throughout the film. But Cheyenne insists that Harmonica back up that kind of statement with gun skills. "Do you only know how to play or do you know how to shoot?" he asks Harmonica, sliding a gun towards him. "Can you play music from that?" Cheyenne's use of the word "play" here has a lively ambiguity. He seems to be asking Cheyenne, like a Hawks hero would, whether Harmonica is "one of them," a gunslinger. Can he play the game of the West? But by comparing the gun to a musical instrument, he also seems to be suggesting that he, Cheyenne, is virtuosic with a gun, an artist of sorts and he wonders—at this point, doubts—if Harmonica is.

A man seated nearby suddenly makes a motion for his gun, which Cheyenne easily anticipates. He outdraws the man, shakes his head at him and says slowly with a wise look on his face, "You can't play." This moment is typical of the way a hero in a Hawks films can, in a moment, size up the moral stature of another man. He knows instantly that this man does not represent the challenge that Harmonica does. Nevertheless, he insists that this man play his instrument a little also, forcing the man to shoot away the chain of his handcuffs. "Bravo," he responds to the man's shot, insisting again on critiquing gunplay with the vocabulary of a music critic and

Howard Hawks (center) and Montgomery Clift (right) on the set of Hawks's great Western, *Red River*. Cheyenne and Harmonica, in their silent, reluctant (but unswerving) morality are highly evocative of Hawks's heroes.

acting as though he has given this bystander his first lesson in what it takes to be a Westerner.

Cheyenne returns to the metaphor of shooting as playing just before he leaves the desert tavern. Harmonica, having nothing more to say at this point, has returned to playing his harmonica. "Go ahead and play," Cheyenne says as he leaves the bar. "Play so you can't bullshit. Only watch out for those false notes." At this point, Cheyenne thinks Harmonica is all talk. He has noted the bullet hole in his shoulder (left from his gunfight with the three men at the train station). He does not believe yet that Harmonica has the skills to back up his eerie call to destiny. As he leaves, though, Harmonica intentionally hits a false note. Leone times the sound to match a squished close-up of Robards arriving before the planted camera. The sound seems to match the image, as if Harmonica were expressing Cheyenne's confusion. Cheyenne had suggested that he would be there to take advantage of, possibly destroy, Harmonica, the first time he hits a false note, at the first lapse in his playing. By immediately then hitting a false note, Harmonica challenges Cheyenne, lets him know that he is not afraid. Cheyenne's consternation suggests he is beginning to suspect there is more to this stranger than meets the eye. Cheyenne may even, for a split second, glimpse the sour note in his own destiny, that this stranger may have something to do with his own demise.

Harmonica will prove that he is a virtuoso with a gun, that he can play too, when he kills the assassins Frank has sent to murder Jill. Cheyenne watches from a distance as Harmonica cleanly dispatches Frank's gunmen, commenting wryly, "He not only plays, he can shoot too." "Playing" takes on a broader meaning here. Cheyenne had been standing by to help Jill if she needed it. He seems surprised not only that Harmonica shoots as well as he does, but also that Harmonica too has decided to team up with, or defend, Jill. Playing may now mean not only shooting well but shooting for the right reasons. It may take on a moral quality as well as one of virtuosity. "Playing well" to Cheyenne is not just a question of shooting well. It also involves questions of style and dignity. Harmonica shoots with a purpose in mind.

Cheyenne will show Harmonica that he can play too, the day he saves the bound Harmonica from Morton's men, with a carnival-like display of sharpshooting. As he presents himself to the still-trussed Harmonica after killing all of Frank's men, he is puffed with pride and awaits Harmonica's expressions of praise and gratitude. But, in the world of Hawks and the American Western, praise does not come too easily. "Do you only know how to shoot?" Harmonica asks. "Or you can cut too?" The line is a reprise of Cheyenne's first line to Harmonica ("Do you only know how to play, or can you shoot too?"). This line is Harmonica's way of announcing that they have both, now, proven to be virtuosos with the gun and have both proven to be on the same side. The line seals their friendship. Cheyenne responds with a smile and they both head off to save Jill, who is, at that moment, being pursued by Frank. Harmonica displays a paternal attitude toward Cheyenne here that will be reinforced later in the film when he carries his body away. He only grudgingly allows that Cheyenne can "play" and, by teasing him for just standing there, reminds him they have work to do.

Ironically, Cheyenne is killed by a man who cannot "play." The nervous businessman at the bar does not get him, but Morton does. "Hey, Harmonica," Cheyenne says, suffering grievously from his stomach wound at the end of the film, "when they do you in, pray it's someone who knows how to shoot." Frank at least had the luxury to be killed by someone who knew what he was doing. Cheyenne has been shot by a bumbling member of the new West, someone who does not know how to shoot, someone who is not part of his and Harmonica's world, someone who does not know how to "play."

Or perhaps it would be more precise to say someone who does not know how to play the old game, because the word "play" has come to be associated with Morton as well. When Morton very ingeniously bribes Frank's men by dealing $100 bills rather than cards during their poker game, one of Frank's gang says, "How do you play this game, Mr. Morton?" "It's very simple as long as you don't lose your head," Morton responds. In the game of money Morton is an expert.

Earlier in the film, Leone had made explicit parallels between guns and money as two different ways to power in the West. The gun, Leone emphasizes, was the old way. Money is the new. And money, Morton argues (and his opinion is borne out in the film), is a much more effective weapon than the gun in the long run. So, in a sense, Morton knows how to play, just not by Cheyenne's rules. Cheyenne's lingering death makes clear that the quick, decisive laws of the past are gone. He does not know how to play the new game.

# FIVE

# Jill

## Leone's First Woman Character

It would be an understatement to say that Leone is not a woman's director. Trained in one masculine genre (the Cinecittà *pepla*) and master of another (the Western) until *Once Upon a Time*, he had pretty much avoided developing any substantial women characters. He felt that the vast majority of Westerns he had seen would have been improved if the woman's role had been cut out. Frayling writes that, confronted with charges of misogyny, Leone would reply that his films were mythic or Homeric, having to do with "a simple world of adventure and of uncomplicated men — a masculine world."[1] Bertolucci, whose memory seems more trustworthy than most of the collaborators on *Once Upon a Time*, claims, and takes pride in, the development of Jill's character, recalling that he had to bend Leone's arm to make her a more substantial character in the film. That Leone retained some negative feeling for the female element in the film is evident in his constant description of the film as being about the emasculation of the West. The final image of Jill carrying water out to the railroad workers, as her theme music swells majestically, was for Leone both stirring and depressing. Stirring because it showed that "a great nation had been born." But, from Leone's point of view, depressing as well, for it showed that the West had given way "to the great American matriarchy, the worship of 'Mom.'" Leone was fond of characterizing the survival of Jill at the end of the film as coinciding with the "beginning of a world without balls."[2]

It is curious how central a character Jill is to *Once Upon a Time,* and how strong a character, given how little precedent there is in Leone's work for significant female characters and how hostile he had been to the notion of a principal female character in a Western at all. All three of the principal male characters — Harmonica, Cheyenne and Frank — are defined to a great extent by their relationship to Jill. Jill's survival will provide Harmonica with his second mission (after killing Frank) and, perhaps, his more morally significant one. Cheyenne's character softens and deepens through his relationship with Jill. Helping Jill provides the basis of Harmonica's and Cheyenne's camaraderie. And underestimating Jill proves to be a large part of Frank's undoing.

Even Leone's most sympathetic critics have often been dismissive of Jill's character. Robert Cumbow sees Jill as "an independent woman of the world molded gradually into a coffee-making, house-cleaning, water-carrying, semi-respectable, dependent 'lady.'"[3] Noel Simsolo sees her only as an archetypal convention, "the repentant prostitute, nothing new here."[4] Frayling describes her in his earlier writings (he seems to change his tone in his later, lengthier study of the film) as "a rather passive, reactive figure. At no stage in the story, until the very end, does she take initiative."[5]

These criticisms all have some truth to them but generally miss the larger picture of Jill's character. Cumbrow is right that Jill is characterized by an increased domesticity. Cheyenne heralds her for her coffee, which he compares to his mom's, and encourages her to be patient with coarse men's advances. The final scene of the film reveals that she has spruced up McBain's house and brought a feminine touch to the place. But, at the same time, Cumbow may too breezily equate being a prostitute with being "an independent woman." In fact, Jill, stepping off the train in Flagstone in all her finery at the beginning of the film, is much more of a "dependant lady" than she is at the end as she carries out water for the men, shoulders bared to the sun *a la* Sophia Loren. Cumbow ignores how the film parodies the dreams of marriage and domesticity with which Jill steps off that train, consigning her instead to a life of reduced happiness, solitude and labor.

I would also argue with Frayling's notion that Jill is a purely "reactive" character. I agree that she has the most reaction shots, but that is as indicative of a character who is meant to be reflective as it is of one who is passive. And though she is brutally handled and traded back and forth by all the male leads, Jill also confronts, and competes with, these men. She easily backs down Cheyenne, transforming him from a "fired-up Cheyenne" to a little boy with mournful eyes who wants her to be his mom. She manipulates Frank's emotions long enough to escape his clutches. And, contrary to what Frayling says, Jill takes initiative from the very beginning of the film, when she lets the townspeople of Flagstone know that she is not the fragile little lady they think her to be and that she will be staking her claim to the McBain homestead.

For example, at the funeral for Jill's slaughtered family, an old, well-meaning woman expresses sympathy for Jill, saying with great feeling, "On the day, the very day of your wedding. Poor little Miss." But Jill seems to only find the old lady's sympathy demeaning. "Mrs.," she responds tersely. "Mrs. McBain," signifying both that she is not a helpless little girl and that she intends to stay and make this property hers. She reiterates her determination to stay to Sam, the coach driver who assumes he will be driving her back to Flagstone and that she will soon be going "home." "*This* is my home," Jill says. Both the old lady and the coach driver assume Jill is delicate enough to have been undone by this tragedy and will beat a hasty retreat. But Jill chooses to stay and fight.

Just because Jill is strong does not mean she is noble, however. Leone quickly cuts from the line "This is my home" to a shot of Jill rifling through the house looking for whatever hidden treasure has brought violence on the McBains. Leone means to contrast, in this segue, the Fordian, noble sentiment she utters with the baseness of her real intentions. We are not meant to excessively ennoble Jill. She is the female version of Leone's typical Western gang—conniving and self-interested as well as powerful and impressive.

Leone's frustration with women characters in Westerns was not just that they existed but that they were so passive and undeveloped in character. "Even in the greatest Westerns," he said, "the woman is imposed on the action, as a star, and is generally destined to be 'had' by the male lead. But she does not exist as a woman."[6] It was very important to Leone to avoid this way of handling a woman in his Western. The male lead does not "have" Jill in *Once Upon a Time*. There is no conventional love or sex scene. All three men in this film circle around her but none gets her in the end. Leone's wife Carla felt that women were such an important part of Leone's life (he had two daughters) that he was incapable of just using them "as props" in his films.[7]

Leone and Bertolucci were inspired, in their characterization of Jill, by an earlier strong woman character from a Western, Joan Crawford's Vienna in *Johnny Guitar*. Like Vienna, Jill is a woman with a questionable past who is taking control of her fate, moving, in a sense, from employee to management. Like Vienna, she will be in charge of transforming a dream that is simply a collection of architectural models. Like Vienna, she has to battle forces that want to remove her from her land while she waits for the train and its riches to reach her land. Some of the strength of Jill's character is attributable to the film's source material, as well as to Bertolucci's contributions. Leone picked up some of Ray's desire to subvert Western traditions by handing power over to the woman. As Frayling notes, "Since Leone was so set on bucking Western conventions, it was appropriate on this occasion to centre the film on a resourceful and powerful woman," a

somewhat different estima-
tion of Jill, on Frayling's part,
from that of his earlier writings where he saw her as
"purely reactive character,"
and evidence that, upon
closer analysis, Jill emerges
as something more than a
passive figure in this film.

## Jill and Cheyenne

It is nevertheless easy to
see how one could still be
uncomfortable with Leone's
handling of Jill's character.
There are two scenes in which
the two "good guys" in the
film, Harmonica and Chey-
enne, seem to threaten her
with rape, and another in
which she is forced to sleep
with the "bad guy," Frank.
The sex scene with Frank is
particularly troubling because
Frank suggests that she cannot help enjoying sex with

Cardinale was to get the only substantial feminine role in Leone's Western oeuvre. She
would introduce a Fordian theme of the feminization of the West, but she would be an
earthier, more robust feminine lead than was
ever seen in Ford's films.

him, even though he is forcing it on her (though it is very important to
note that this is *Frank's* interpretation of her feelings). One need only look
at the rape sequence in *Fistful of Dynamite* in which the stern old maid
seems partially excited by the threat of being raped at the hands of Rod
Steiger's bandit to know that Leone was susceptible to some ugly approaches
to sex. Add to this Cheyenne's admonition to Jill at the end *Once Upon a
Time* to be patient with the railroad workers when they pat her on the
behind and you have a variety of scenes in which Jill is asked to be disturbingly patient with male sexual aggression.

That said, a close look at the scenes in question suggest that Harmonica and Cheyenne are not nearly as sexually aggressive as they seem
to be. In fact, the joke in these scenes may be that they only seem to be
about sex. And Frank may be guilty of a classic male over-confidence in

assuming that Jill is enjoying sex with him. Moreover, it is through his over-confidence in the bedroom that Frank makes the mistake of letting Jill go without killing her and in turn loses the property he sought to gain from her. He was more right than he realized when he taunted Jill that she was willing to do "anything" to save her neck. Jill is even willing to sleep with him if it allows her to stay alive long enough to escape his grasp and see him dead in the end — which it does. It is laughable to make a case for Leone as a feminist in this film, but it is equally wrong to write him off as a misogynist, based on Jill's character, which reveals itself, even in the film's strange sex scenes, as strong, defiant, clever and ultimately triumphant.

The scene in which Cheyenne first confronts Jill is a case in point. Cheyenne is angry about having the McBains' murder pinned on his gang and demands that Jill tell him what she knows about the murder. When Jill does not comply, he threatens her, saying that a "fired-up Cheyenne ain't a nice thing to see" though every indication, including his gently comic theme music, suggests that he is not particularly fired up and that the only people who really have anything to fear from him are any law enforcers who try to lock him up. "I don't think you understand what I'm saying here, ma'am," he says threateningly to Jill. Jill responds with a short speech that is emblematic of her character, perhaps her definitive character statement. "Sure I do. I'm here alone in the hands of a bandit who smells money. If you want to, you can lay me over the table and amuse yourself — and even call in your men. Well, no woman ever died from that. When you're finished, all I'll need will be a tub of boiling water and I'll be exactly where I was before — with just another filthy memory." She delivers this last line with gusto as she slams Cheyenne's coffee down on the table with a deafening thud. A hot tub of water is a significant symbol for Jill. It is the first thing she seeks out after she has escaped Frank. A hot tub of water represents Jill's essential pure or inviolate nature. Jill makes it clear to all men in this film that there is a part of her they cannot reach, no matter what they do.

Cheyenne, whose intentions were probably not as violent as they seem, quickly backs down after Jill's speech and, from that point on, seems more than satisfied with the simple cup of coffee before him. Indeed, we get the feeling that at this time in his life and outlaw career, Cheyenne is tired enough to want coffee more than sex. For the rest of the film, in fact, coffee will be the motif that links Cheyenne and Jill in mutual respect. Not just because Jill, like a good housewife, makes a great cup of coffee, but also because she dishes out some pretty strong attitude with that coffee. After this scene, Cheyenne, takes on a passive, almost childish attitude towards Jill. Jill reminds Cheyenne of his mother, who was also a prostitute and also an impressive woman ("the biggest whore in Alameda and the finest woman that ever lived") and who also made a great cup of coffee. Cheyenne's greatest desire seems to be that Jill step into his mother's shoes and take care of him for a short while. Cheyenne's relationship with Jill is more elegiac than sexual. Just as people on their deathbed often return to childhood memories, Cheyenne, who seems to sense the end of his career is near, finds in his feelings for Jill a way to express nostalgia for his past. Far from depicting masculine sexual aggression, this scene communicates, comically, the "momma's boy" quality in men, even the most grizzled and violent of them.

In this film, a woman's sexual history is not held against her. Cheyenne and Harmonica respect Jill for her survival skills and for how she has suffered in the past. The Western female archetypes that Leone avails himself of here are double-edged. No one needs reminding that in the Western, we get definitively demeaning images of women. And Jill fits that stereotype perfectly. She is the hooker with a heart of gold and the prostitute gone straight. The role of women in the West plays definitively into perceptions of women as either whore or saints.

On the other hand, there is often an acceptance of women's sexuality in the Western that cannot be rivaled by other movie genres. Johnny Guitar does not care how many men Vienna slept with to build her dream casino. And in Ford's *Stagecoach*, Ringo insists on treating the prostitute with care and chivalry, while the supposedly good and upstanding citizens, including our classic leading lady, take turns abusing her. The final image in that film is of the hero and the ex-prostitute riding off into the sunset towards a future of marriage and domesticity. Often women's sexuality in Westerns is allowed to breathe. Women do not even necessarily have to be killed off for that sexuality, as is so often the case in film noir. Leone is respectful of the toughness of the saloon girl. She is not scrappy in a pure way, like Jean Arthur in *Shane*. She has had to endure extraordinary degradation, like a survivor of a war. Harmonica and Cheyenne respect Jill for how she has stood up to men and survived them.

The scene in which Cheyenne shifts quickly from sexual threats to a fatigued desire for a good cup of coffee brings to mind a story Bertolucci told about Leone's tendency to neutralize sexuality in his film. Bertolucci had a scene in mind for *Once Upon a Time* in which Harmonica, after being shot and wounded in the opening sequence, is carried to an inn. A young woman, in ministering to him, lays him on a bed and begins to massage his feet. The scene, Bertolucci said, was to be the beginning of an erotic encounter. "But Leone interrupted me: 'Yeah. Yeah. She massages his feet slowly, very slowly ... and he falls asleep.' He had a tendency to neutralize the possibility of a sexual relationship."[8] For Leone, the attraction of this scene would not be to provide "an erotic encounter" but to hoodwink the audience, to pretend that he was going to give them a sex scene, surprise them with an anticlimax, and then get back to the real business of the Western.

Leone's tendency to neutralize sexuality is evident in Cheyenne's scene with Jill, where he plays the role of the sexually threatening criminal (in a tired kind of way), but actually just wants to sit at a kitchen table and be served a cup of good, strong coffee. Leone had great respect for the exhausting nature of the Western archetype's life. The Western outlaw, condemned by mythology, like Sysyphus, to bust out of prison day after day, is a tired man looking for just a few creature comforts.

It seems likely that Bertolucci and Leone, in writing the scene between Cheyenne and Jill, had in mind a speech from *Johnny Guitar*. Like Cheyenne, Johnny is tired from years of gunslinging. He has put away his gun, changed his famous name and come back to Vienna with the hopes of settling down. And he has developed a taste for coffee. "There's nothing like a good smoke and a cup of coffee," he says in the scene where he plays peacemaker between Emma's and the Dancing Kid's respective gangs. "You know, some men got the craving for gold and silver. Others need lots of land with herds of cattle. And there's those that got the weakness of whisky and women. When you boil it down, what does a man really need? Just a smoke and a cup of coffee." Like Johnny, the tired Cheyenne's craving for women seems to have given way to a craving for a good cup of coffee.

## Jill and Harmonica

Leone neutralizes Harmonica's sexuality even more than Cheyenne's. We get the sense that Cheyenne entertains fantasies of settling down with Jill. If he did not have a bullet in his gut in the end and if Jill cared for him as much as she does for Harmonica, and if he were not, by design in this film, a vanishing Hollywood archetype (the outlaw who roamed free before trains and women arrived out West), it is clear that Cheyenne would have liked to stay in Sweetwater with Jill. "It would be nice to see this town grow," he tells Jill near the end of the film and asks Jill to shave him while he looks out the window at the workers building Sweetwater.

There are no such suggestions that Harmonica would like to settle down. Harmonica is hardly a physical man. Rather, as I discuss in Chapter Four, he seems fate personified, a visitor from the past, here to settle an old score. Harmonica knows that archetypes from the past like him have no place in the new, more feminine West. He agrees with Frank that in the end "none of that matters," not even "the woman." Harmonica never, for one moment, evinces a sexual feeling for Jill.

Leone fools us, as he did in the scene with Cheyenne, into thinking that Harmonica is a criminal and sexual predator in the scene in Jill's barn in which Harmonica rips off the white lace beneath the bodice of Jill's dress. As Frayling notes, this act, that seems to betoken sexual aggression and to anticipate rape, is actually one of protection. Harmonica represents no more of a sexual threat than Cheyenne does. What Harmonica realizes, and Jill does not, is that Frank's sharpshooters wait for her in the hills above her house and that the white of her dress makes her an easy target. He might have explained this situation more carefully to her, of course, but Leone's characters seem to almost thrive on, or to court, ill opinion. Moreover, when Harmonica's shots ring out at the well and Jill realizes he is actually intent on protecting rather than brutalizing her, the effect is all the more dramatic for his having given her no hint of his intentions. Leone's heroes do not like to wear their morality on their sleeves.

Later, during the sequence in which Harmonica saves Frank from the treachery of his own men (so that he can have the pleasure of killing Frank himself, later on), Harmonica charges into Jill's room and discovers her soaking in a bath. This archetypal image, drawn from numerous Westerns, is meant to titillate the audience but it has no such effect on Harmonica. Jill looks at him and her expression suggests a couple of things. Partially, she seems to be looking at him with defiant anger, as though she were wondering whether he was going to finally reveal his true coarseness and confirm her generally cynical view of men. But she has also, by this time, come to care for Harmonica and her expression seems also to suggest a hope that Harmonica might take a break from his gunplay and spend some attention on her. Certainly John Wayne was beginning to be seduced by Angie Dickenson by this point in *Rio Bravo*.

But Harmonica does not respond to her fears or her hopes. Jill flinches as Harmonica bends down towards the tub, but, as so often in Leone, sexuality gives way to comedy as Harmonica picks up her fallen scrub brush and hands it to her with a mock chivalry. (Psycho-analytic critics can go to town with both the phallic nature of the item in question and the fact that it allows Jill to take care of herself.) Harmonica's gently mocking expression here suggests that he knows what she is thinking and that has no intention of taking advantage of her. He is neither a cad nor a suitor.

Even before this scene, Jill seems to have caught on to the fact that Harmonica is interested in helping her, but not in falling in love with her. When Harmonica tells her she is "a remarkable woman," Jill responds in a faintly irritated voice, "And you're a remarkable man, but you have something else on your mind." And she is right. Killing Frank and realizing McBain's dream of building Sweetwater are of much more interest to Harmonica than courting Jill.

Cheyenne is acutely conscious of Jill's feelings for Harmonica and also of how they are not reciprocated by Harmonica. In the final scenes of the film, he tries to communicate to Jill that it is futile to think of sharing her life with a man such as Harmonica. In their final scene together, after Cheyenne has shaved and tidied up some, Jill says to him, "Hey, you're sort of a handsome man." But Cheyenne does not for a moment allow himself to think he has any future with her. "But I'm not the right man," he tells her. He has only moments to live and he knows she cares more for Harmonica anyway. Seeing Harmonica in her thoughts, he adds, "And neither is he." Cheyenne tries to explain to Jill why she can expect nothing from Harmonica. "People like that have something inside them, something to do with death. If that fellow lives, he'll come in through that door, pick up his gear and say adios." This is less a theory than an exact premonition. When Harmonica returns from his gunfight with Frank, he acts out Cheyenne's words as if they were stage directions.

The final scenes between Jill and Harmonica are touching, as Leone quietly registers Jill's gradual realization that Harmonica will not be staying. When Harmonica appears at the doorway after his gunfight with Frank, Leone films Jill's reaction in close-up. Her face is fearful and apprehensive as she hears his steps approach the door. She is not sure whether she will be seeing him or Frank. When he appears, she is grateful he is alive and greets him with a smile. Leone cuts to Bronson's stony expression in response and then back to Cardinale. Her smile fades as she realizes that Cheyenne is right, that Harmonica is not the type to hang around after he has settled his business. Harmonica prepares to leave, as Cheyenne said he would. But before he goes, Harmonica allows himself to bestow an approving comment on Jill's enterprise. "Gonna be a beautiful town someday," he says, and then pronounces the town's name with great satisfaction, "Sweetwater." Jill responds to this overture hopefully. "I hope you'll come back someday." Harmonica's look in response to what Jill says is still stony but a slight smile strays across his face. He look at her curiously, as if she had just said something mildly amusing. Her hopeful look again freezes and fades and is again replaced by a sad, chastened expression. Harmonica leaves and Cheyenne relieves the pressure of the scene by providing a final comic epilogue. "Yeah, I gotta go too," Cheyenne says archly, commenting ironically on how little any one is noticing him at this moment and how little his departure means to Jill next to Harmonica's. She does not even seem to take in Cheyenne's words, as she continues to stare at the door through which Harmonica has just departed.

This is the extent of Jill's romantic relationships with Cheyenne and Harmonica and, seen in the full context of her relationship with the two men, it becomes apparent that those initial scenes that seemed to imply rape were just frightening decoys, the purpose of which was to save Leone's heroes from appearing too obviously or conventionally good. Leone was as horrified by the prospect of his men, as well as his women, being too pure. Both Cheyenne and Harmonica are archetypes too removed from contemporary times to actually respond to Jill in a physical way. Both of those initial scenes are the bluffs of men trying to impress women, and a bluff on Leone's part, a joke on the audience and their anticipation of sexual clichés. In these scenes, Leone neutralizes the sexuality, as he would have in the foot-massage scene Bertolucci tried to get into the script.

## Jill and Frank

Jill's sexual relationship with Frank is more confusing than her relationships with Harmonica and Cheyenne, but here too Leone makes things look different than they are actually. The sex scene between Jill and Frank is troubling in that it is a rape scene handled like a love scene. We know Jill is being forced to have sex and yet the music is Jill's luxurious theme, rendered in the gentlest of tones. Frank adds to our queasiness by suggesting that Jill is enjoying making love to him, that she "likes the feel of a man's hands all over your body, even if they're the hands of the man who killed your husband."

As usual with Leone, there is more here than meets the eye. The music is intentionally misleading. Leone often uses music that works against the visuals rather than reinforces them. The music here may sound like a love theme but it stands in stark contrast to Frank's vicious monologue, in which he reminds Jill, as he caresses her, that he still intends to kill her and taunts her with his newly gained knowledge ("great invention, the telegraph") that she was a prostitute in New Orleans.

Even Frank cannot convince himself that Jill is sincere in her attention to him, despite his theories about her sexual hunger. He expresses explicitly that Jill is trying to manipulate him. "What a little tramp. Is there anything you wouldn't do to save your skin?" "Nothing, Frank," Jill responds, making it clear that she *is* willing to do whatever she has to, that she is ready to make deals. Cardinale's line here is interesting. Post-synchronized, like all the dialogue in the film, it does not even quite match the image. Jill continues to play the role of amorous kitten. But her voice sounds hard and angry as she says this single word. It seems to spell out Frank's demise.

This is not a love scene as much as a quiet, vicious duel played out in soft gestures and to soft music, a kind of amorous equivalent to the other scenes in Leone films where he finds slower, more drawn-out ways to approach the violence of the West. If we had not picked up how much making love to Frank is a practical operation to Jill from the way she says "nothing," we certainly do in her conversation with Harmonica after the auction. "You don't look anything like the noble defender of poor, defenseless widows," she says to Harmonica, "but then again I don't look much like a defenseless widow." There is self-recrimination in the last part of this comment, emphasized by a quiet expression of self-hatred that crosses Jill's face as she says this. Harmonica sees in her expression both what she has done to survive and how she hates herself for what she has done. "Cheyenne was right," he says, "you're a remarkable woman." The reference to Cheyenne here is exact. Harmonica has picked up on Cheyenne's respect for Jill's toughness. And like Cheyenne, Harmonica does not judge Jill for her sexual compromises but rather respects her for her survival skills.

Harmonica seems to almost have mind-reading skills when it comes to Jill, which is consistent with his other-worldly nature. Nothing gets by him. Watching her belt down drinks in this scene, he tells her "You have something on your mind." The drinks, it becomes clear, are to steady herself after the horror of her experience with Frank. What she has on her mind, she tells Harmonica, is "hot water. A bathtub full of hot water." This is an obvious reference back to what she had told Cheyenne, that if he followed through on his threat of rape all she would need is a bucket of hot water and she would be exactly the same woman she was before, "with just another filthy memory." That Frank is the new filthy memory is even more explicitly pointed out as he walks in at that moment and Jill says, "Time I filled that bathtub."

It is hard to see Jill here as Frayling's passive woman, only reacting to the men around her, because she has used Frank here. By making love to him, she has saved her life. Like Harmonica, she has sniffed out Frank's weaknesses. Throughout the film, Leone has made it clear that Frank does not understand himself, that he has been trying to transform himself from gunslinger to businessman, that he foolishly thinks there is a place in the new West for a dusty old archetype like himself. By the time Jill is through with him, Frank has even gotten to the point of fantasizing about settling down on the McBain ranch and marrying Jill. "Hey that's an idea. I could marry you," he says to her. "And maybe you'd make a perfect wife." Jill confuses Frank. Once again, he delays in finishing the McBain business. He forgets his gunslinging ways, with his fantasies of business and marriage. And Jill buys enough time to save her life and her home.

## Jill and Water

The motif of water is central to both Jill's character and the film as a whole. Water is used to represent several things in the film. As we have seen, water is important to Jill as a means of washing away filthy memories, a means of self-purification. It is a symbol for the unassailability of her self-respect, her essential strength.

Jill is also associated with the bringing of water to the West. It is often noted that *Once Upon a Time* finishes with Jill following Cheyenne's final instructions to bring water out to all the railroad workers. Earlier too, Harmonica orders her to the well to "get me some water. I like my water fresh." Moreover, she finishes by bringing to realization McBain's dream of building a place called "Sweetwater" in the middle of the desert, picking up on Ford's metaphor in *Liberty Valance* of irrigation as a symbol for the fruition civilization would bring to the West, replacing Tom Doniphon's cactus rose with Ransom Stoddard's garden rose, the genuine article.

The metaphor of water makes an odd alliance between Jill and Morton, who is often associated with water as well. Morton started his railroad at the Atlantic Ocean and aims to see it reach the Pacific. Seeing the water of the Pacific is the holy grail of his life, as evidenced by his fetishistic devotion to the oceanscape hanging in his train carriage. Sounds of crashing waves accompany the music Leone and Morricone chose to evoke this dream and, of course, he dies crawling through a mud puddle, Leone's mocking replacement for the ocean Mortimer would never see.

By allying Jill and Morton, Leone is only reinforcing a point Ford made in many of his films but perhaps most notably in *The Man Who Shot Liberty Valance*: the industrialization of the West and the feminization of the West occur hand in hand. For Ford, this emasculation of the West was a good thing. It meant the death of power by force, the advent of farming, church, education, beauty. Hence, there are scenes in Ford's films you would never find in Leone's: inaugural dances on the floors of half-constructed churches, the first touchingly inept school classes, etc. For Leone, as we have seen, this feminization of the West was more troubling. Water is an ambiguous symbol for Leone. The shot of Jill carrying the pails of water to the men is inspirational in its composition and because of the soaring music that accompanies it. But Leone's ultimate attitude towards water may be expressed by Lionel Stander's bartender in response to Jill's request for a glass of water. Stander seems genuinely offended when he responds— angrily, as though someone had insulted his mother —"Water! That word is poison around here."

This has been the most recurrent interpretation of Jill in criticism of the film — as a water bearer, an earth mother of sorts bringing a nation to birth, and sustenance to the men who struggle to build the nation. Frayling notes that Leone was perfectly aware of Cardinale's performance in Fellini's *8½* five years earlier in which she played the young girl at the springs who offers spa water to the depressed film director (Marcello Mastroianni), helping to restore him to life.[9] And Cardinale in this final image of the film fits into a particularly Italian reverential attitude for robust womanhood that we also see in the films of Sophia Loren and Anna Magnani.

## Jill as Loner

This is a legitimate interpretation of Jill and, as Leone's interviews make clear, certainly one he intended in his conception of the character. But sometimes there is such a great emphasis on Leone as the master of adult fairy tales that the subtlety of his characterizations goes unnoticed. Allegorical interpretations of Jill as the great earth mother have had two negative consequences. One is to distract us from appreciating what is a unique and carefully wrought characterization of a strong individual woman she is, and the other is to play into the hands of those critics who would view Leone as demeaning to women because he can only see them as ancient stereotypes. Marcia Landy, for example, writes that when women are present in Leone's films, "they are either like Jill in *Once Upon a Time in the West*, carriers of economic value, as kept women, prostitutes, or heirs to property, or they are figures of nostalgia, as in *Duck, You Sucker*."[10] To reduce Jill to a "carrier of economic value" is to ignore the interesting ways in which her character develops and to ignore the toughness Leone accords her character. I think Nicholls understands her character better when he writes that Jill is "at the center of the film because she is the only character capable of change."[11] Jill evolves in this film, from a New Orleans lady of the evening, with delicate domestic fantasies and lacy finery, into a rugged woman who accepts her essential aloneness and turns her shoulder towards helping build the new West. We feel great sympathy for Jill at the beginning of the film. There is a touching contrast between the hopeful expectation she wears on her face, as she disembarks from the train, and the cruel reality that we know awaits her at the McBain ranch. But Leone respects her more at the end, when — worn, tired, resigned — she has ditched conventional female fantasies of being take care of and taken on her key role in building Sweetwater. He likes her more as the manager of a town than as a hopeful bride.

I would argue that Jill is as an existential hero of sorts, not unrelated to certain masculine heroes of Hollywood, for example in film noir, who dream of a better life that they know they will never see and in the end persevere in the world given them. At the outset of the film, Jill believes a conventional life of domestic peace and harmony is within her grasp. She has been infected by McBain's dream and believes she might be happy. Her speech to Cheyenne testifies to how susceptible she was to McBain's dream of conjugal bliss, how much she wanted to believe she could leave unhappiness behind her in the brothels of New Orleans. She recalls that McBain "looked like a good man." He had "clear eyes, strong hands. And he wants to marry you, which doesn't happen often, and he says he's rich, which doesn't hurt. So you think, 'Damn you, New Orleans. Now I'll say yes and go live in the country. I wouldn't mind giving him half a dozen kids after all. Take care of a house. Do something. What the hell.'"

Jill quickly discovers that dreams of domestic harmony have little place in the Leone Western world when she arrives at her new home only to find her entire family stretched out and ready for burial. Cheyenne makes some tentative steps to replace McBain in her life. "You deserve better," he tells her, but her response suggests she is no longer willing to believe her life will change: "The last man who told me that is buried out there." As Cumbow has noted, Jill's words are prophetic. Cheyenne, the second man who makes some noise about taking care of her, dies in the end as well. By now Jill is catching on that she may not be meant to be either married or happy.

Jill, as we have seen, does set her stakes on Harmonica, but that is also not meant to be. Not for a moment does he seem to entertain the idea of taking care of her, in terms of settling down with her. The loving (but also gently mocking) smile with which he responds to her hopes that he will come back someday tells her that she was meant for a life of solitude and service.

And that is how Jill finishes, alone. In a sense, nothing has changed for her. She might as well still be in New Orleans. She still has to take care of herself. All of the men who seemed potential partners are gone. She is still surrounded by, and expected to serve, men. The dreams of the woman who stepped off the train and which were exemplified by the lacy white dress she wore, are gone. She's Sophia Loren now, a woman of the earth again.

Still, much has changed. She can believe in what she is doing now. This is not prostitution. This is building a town, and one that lies outside the rapacious grasp of the railroad barons. With Cheyenne and Harmonica's assistance, she has picked up McBain's dream. She will finish what McBain started and perhaps could not have finished himself. His fiery temper, coupled with the dialogue with his daughter that suggested he was not even sure he could finish his project, make us wonder whether McBain would have seen his plans through. She has become the bearer of the Fordian optimism, even in the midst of so much Leone pessimism.

Moreover, Jill can carry herself with the swagger of Vienna in *Johnny Guitar*. Early in *Johnny Guitar*, Johnny taunts Vienna by suggesting she has not changed much in the five years they have been apart. He left her in a saloon and he found her in one, he points out. Vienna is quick with her response: "The difference is, I own the place now."

The same is true of Jill. She may still be surrounded by men for whom she will have to care. Her life may still be one of solitude and perseverance, but she owns the place now. She is not, as Landy writes, a "carrier of economic value" shunted back and forth between the film's men. She is the manager, the establisher of economic value. And the men who she might have depended on, the men who traded her back and forth, are all gone. She has become Vienna, a leader of men. Leone may lament the matriarchy that he sees taking over America with the arrival of the train, but it is not bad news for Jill.

Jill comes into this film alone and leaves it alone. Her introduction makes an interesting contrast with our final view of her. When Jill arrives, she is confused that there is no one there to greet her, a situation that is emblematic of her role for the rest of the film. Leone punctuates the famous, gorgeous tracking shots in this sequence with point-of-view shots from Jill's disoriented perspective. We look at a busy Western town from the point of view of the outsider. There is an extraordinary amount of bustle and activity (in contrast to the sleepiness of the Western towns in most Westerns) and none of it seems to have anything to do with Jill. No one pays her attention. Only the two luggage bearers seem to register consciousness of her arrival. The West looks strange and distant from Jill's vantage. Leone gives us the West from a perspective of alienation. It reminds one of the strange beauty of the farmlands from the point of view of disenfranchised workers in Terence Malick's *Days of Heaven*.

The final image of Jill is an objective shot of her with men crowding around her as she passes out water. Once alienated by this environment, she now owns it. In fact, she is the center of this world, the wellspring, its source of life. All that suffering she experienced in New Orleans seems to have paid off in the West after all. It provided her with the toughness she needed to survive out West. In what has to be his final word on the marriage of capitalism and femininity, Leone once said (returning again to, apparently, a favorite metaphor) that America was founded by "women with iron balls." He often advanced the notion that "Rockefeller's grandmother came from a whorehouse in New Orleans."[12] Not the words of a feminist to be sure, but Leone's attitude to women in Westerns should not be written off simplistically, as sexist or misogynist. Jill is not simply "had by the male lead" and she does "exist as a woman," something that, as Leone complained, cannot be said of Rhonda Fleming in *Gunfight at the O.K. Corral*. It is a testimony to Leone's desire to challenge Western traditions in this film, as well as pay homage to them, that at the front and center of this film is a story of a woman with "iron balls."

SIX

# Morton and the Politics of
# *Once Upon a Time in the West*

## A Disillusioned Socialist

An essential element of *Once Upon a Time in the West* is its critique of American capitalism. And though Leone's critics often accused him of playing the '60s sage in his interviews, in believing a little too much in the philosophical and political wisdom his interviewers accorded him, Leone's political commentary in this film is generally accorded respect. Here, as De Fornari points out, Leone had "the good taste to not take himself too seriously."[1]

Leone was adamant that political commentary be expressed through, and subordinate to, the traditional structures of myth and genre. "I don't like political films, the film as a political rally," he told De Fornari.[2] The fad for political films in the late '60s and early '70s was, he felt, "getting to be a fiasco."[3] "Militant cinema should only be shown to members of a party," he complained.[4] He lauded "indirect political movies" like Billy Wilder's *The Front Page* "which, he felt, hit the audience harder than party slogans could do." His mentor in using film for social commentary, he said, was Chaplin, whose comedies, he felt, did more for Socialism than any political leader ever did.[5] In fact, the scene in *Fistful of Dynamite* in which Rod Steiger accidentally finds himself at the head of a group of liberated prisoners represents an homage to Chaplin's *Modern Times*, where the Tramp happens onto political leadership quite accidentally, by turning a corner and walking in front of a Communist parade. If Wilder and Chaplin are your political models, the politics of your films are not going to be explicit, and that is the way Leone wanted it. "Through fables and spectacle, I try to say things that are of political importance."[6]

A great part of Leone's success in refreshing the Western genre was in saving it from verbosity, from the self-analysis and preachiness that had crept into Hollywood after the war. Westerns increasingly tended to take themselves too seriously, as if their directors had lost faith in their ability to explore serious ideas through the indirect language of myth and genre. "I use myth like an instrument of linguistic communication," Leone wrote in *Cahiers du Cinéma,* "to interpret a contemporary sensibility, all the while conscious of its distance from that sensibility and open to the poetry of irony."[7] Leone's films explore myths and their relationship to the reality they mythicize. His films, as has often been noted, are neo-realist fairy tales, a unique fusion of the Hollywood tradition he learned at Cinecittà Studios and his Neo-realism heritage as an apprentice to the likes of Vittorio De Sica. But he is always careful to make sure his neo-realist observations do not overwhelm the fairy tale elements of his film, which he believed in with a child's ardor. Leone never labored under the illusion that he could hide his Italian nature. He did not try to deny his European sensibility any more than he tried to hide the obvious Italian qualities of the majority of faces he photographed in his films. He knew, moreover, that the Western provided a forum through which he could communicate his very strong opinions about America and the American West. But he understood that political statements lose power in inverse proportion to their explicitness. Conversely, political statements always take on greater resonance when yoked to a powerful myth or fable rooted in a tradition and a shared history.

Leone's ardent critic Lucino Vincenzoni laughed at the very notion that Leone had a political point of view. Serge Donati described Leone derisively as a "qualunquista," that is, someone who is non-committal politically and tends to mock both sides of the issue. Leone himself recognized that his commercial success as a filmmaker did not square well with Socialism. He often said that one could not be a Communist and own a villa.[8] Moreover, he had soured on Italian Socialism because of its tendency towards internal squabbling and because of the unrewarded sacrifices he felt his father, an ardent Socialist, had made for his politics.

This "qualunquista" aspect of Leone's politics gets its fullest expression in Juan's speech in *Fistful of Dynamite,* "I know all about the revolutions and how they start. The people that read the books, they go to the people that don't read the books— the poor people — and say, 'Ho-ho, the time has come to have a change' ... And the people that read the books, they all sit around the polished table, and they talk and talk, and eat and eat. And what happens to the poor people? They're dead!" Leone exorcised a great deal of his frustration with revolutionary politics through this film.

He often spoke with pride of a father who approached him in a restaurant. The man's two sons had been political revolutionaries until they had seen *Fistful of Dynamite*. The film had convinced them to abandon their political extremism and the father expressed profound gratitude to Leone for having brought his sons back into the family fold. Whether or not this story is true, Leone's pride in it reveals how much more important he felt the personal, the family, was to the political. *Fistful* was a very contrary film to be made by a man who swam in an intellectual leftist milieu at a moment, historically, of ardent political activism.

Still, we should not overemphasize Leone's indifference to politics, or buy too easily into his Northern Italian intellectual friends' assumption that he was not capable of a political point of view. Leone jokingly referred to himself as "a moderate anarchist who doesn't go around throwing bombs," but was probably more truthful in describing himself as a "disillusioned Socialist." Despite his cynicism about political filmmaking, his movies suggest that he remained a Socialist at heart if not in practice and the substance of his work backs him up when he makes claims for its anti–Fascistic qualities. "I always tend to defy the official version of events—no doubt because I grew up under fascism. I had seen first hand how history can be manipulated. So I always question what is propagated. It has become a reflex with me."[9] Seeing first-hand the repression inherent in a Fascist regime left Leone with a kind of punk contrariness that is a hallmark of his films and a large part of what gives them their edge. Even towards the American Western, which represented a kind of religion to Leone, he evinced such questioning cynicism that some are unable to see any reverence for the genre that survives.

The presence of World War II is also stamped in Leone's films—foremost in his films' obvious adoration for American myths and culture. American films were banned in Italy during World War II and, as such, a forbidden pleasure. In his childhood, said Leone, "America was like a religion," and by "America" he meant the America he saw in films, the America that was not allowed in Italy. He responded to the freedom represented in the spatial representations of the country in film ("the wide open spaces, the great expanses of desert," "the long straight roads which began nowhere and end nowhere") and freedom suggested by its "extraordinary 'melting pot,' the first nation made up of people from all over the world."

Later, of course, Leone would meet actual Americans, his first being the GIs who came to Italy in the wake of the war, "men who were materialist, possessive," and his reverence for America would be hugely qualified. But American movies were always defined for Leone in the context of World War II as essentially anti–Fascist in their sensibility.[10]

There is also a noirish or Existential emphasis on dignity in suffering in Leone's Westerns that often is more suggestive of a World War II atmosphere than that of the traditional Western. And there are specific visual references to the horrors of World War II and Fascist regimes. Leone was inspired in *The Good, Bad and the Ugly* by photographs of the horrible condition of Civil War prison camps such as Andersonville but also had in mind Nazi concentration camps in the scene where the cries of tortured prisoners are drowned out by the orchestra. The scenes of the prison camps have a double impact, both questioning America's official line on the Civil War (it is striking how few Westerns emphasize Civil War prison camps) and commenting on the eternal recurrence of wartime atrocities by bringing twentieth century political touchstones into a nineteenth century story.

As Frayling has ably documented, *Fistful of Dynamite* is full of "historical cross-referencing" between the Mexican Revolution and World War II. The brutal Col. Gunter Reza is presented like a Nazi tank commander, the cattle wagon belonging to the Ferrocarril de México is clearly meant to be analogous to World War II death camp trains. The local revolutionary units are paralleled to Resistance fighters and Frayling feels that the behavior of the agents of Huerta's regime as they cling to their power parallels the decadence and cruelty of the last days of fascism in World War II.[11] Donati may be right when he criticizes this film for being heavy-handed and "rhetorical" in its politics. But the film does not support his comments that Leone was a "qualconquisto" or indifferent to politics. There is simply too much effort spent on analyzing the technique of fascism to support that line on Leone.

## Leone and America

Leone's attitude towards America was complex and lively. First and foremost, he was an aficionado of American myths and dreams. This love of American mythology was obviously born from watching these American films that, as Frayling notes, "by being banned, became more magical."[12] Leone's fascination with American film was fostered by growing up in Cinecittà Studios, the Hollywood of Italy, and later by his apprenticeship under American directors like Mervyn LeRoy, Robert Wise, Raoul Walsh, William Wyler, Fred Zinnemann and Robert Aldrich, from whom he learned many tricks of the trade. Leone manifested a childlike glee in Westerns. According to Clint Eastwood, Leone would even dress up like a cowboy on the set, replete with hat and gun, looking, with his plump figure, like no one so much as Yosemite Sam from the old Warner Brothers cartoons.

Some critics may make the mistake of underestimating Leone's pure affection for Hollywood and the West. *Once Upon a Time* is renowned as a kind of final statement on the Western, a representation of the Western's death. And Leone was careful to avoid optimistic clichés and to draw a sharp distinction between his violent West and Ford's idealistic one. And yet a love of the West is etched in the film, not so much in its dialogue or script, but in its very being, the mythic structure that Leone presents with so much awe and reverence, the physical world he transcribes with such love and exactitude.

That said, Leone's frustration with American should also not be underestimated. The negative opinion he conceived of Americans through the soldiers he met in World War II was only confirmed by his experience working with certain great American directors, who felt they were slumming when they worked at Cinecittà. He cherished the craft they brought to them but found that many of his heroes, Robert Aldrich for example, were less impressive in person. And he continued to feel more deeply as he grew older the materialism of American culture.

Leone's ambiguous relationship with America is typical of Europeans and European filmmakers, who often cherish the idealism and simplicity they find in American film, but despise the economic cruelty they perceive in its political and economic system. Think only of the recent success of Lars Van Trier's, *Dancer in the Dark,* at once an ode to the American musical and condemnation of the American judicial and penal system, a film that criticizes America for not living up to the beauty of its myths.

But Leone seems to have had a rather extreme case of this "double attitude." Few wax as enthusiastically about the American dream as Leone, but few were simultaneously as suspicious as Leone was that Americans did not understand and could not live up to their dreams. He often spoke and wrote about American myths as something he cherished more and understood better than Americans themselves. "America is really the property of the world, and not only of the Americans, who among other things, have the habit of diluting the wine of their mythical ideas with the water of the American life."[13] Leone's reference to the watering-down of America reminds one of how he used water (through associations with Jill and the weakly Morton) as a symbol of the new feminization or matriarchy of the West in *Once Upon a Time.* We have to chuckle also at the typically European slam on American wine.

Americans, Leone warns, have only "rented" the American dream "temporarily. If they don't behave well, if the mythical level is lowered, if their movies don't work any more and history takes on an ordinary day-to-day quality, then we can always evict them. Or discover another America.

The contract can always be withheld."[14] Leone felt that the America represented in Hollywood was world property. His words here testify to Leone's emergence as a filmmaker at a time when Europeans were discovering virtues in Hollywood's cinema to which Americans themselves were blind. And, really, Leone did in his Westerns just what he threatens here. The "mythical level" of the Western *had* "lowered." Westerns were not "working" any longer and the history they depicted had lost a Fordian, epic grandeur. Westerns were subject increasingly to a bland realism. Leone evicted Americans from their own genre and discovered on his own, a new American Western, set in the Spanish plains, peopled with Italian faces, and expressive of a European sensibility.

Leone's frustration with America is more evident in the film's Italian title, *C'era una volta il West,* which translates literally as *Once Upon a Time, There Was a West* than in its conventional translation, *Once Upon at Time in the West. Once Upon a Time in the West* has a nostalgic feel. It suggests that the film you are going to see will tell a story from the distant past. It emphasizes only the mythic, fairy tale aspect of Leone's film. *Once Upon a Time, There Was a West* is a title with more bite to it. It expresses Leone's frustration both with America and with American film, as if saying once upon a time you had a West, a world of mythic grandeur, but you no longer do. Or, once upon a time there were Westerns but there no longer are. It expresses Leone's sense that Americans have not been true to, and do not understand, the power of their own mythology.

When Leone was inveighing against the decline in American film, he often turned to Doris Day's films as a touch-point for what he most detested in contemporary American film. He felt the vision of America in those films was "totalitarian and quasi–Soviet! A world without conflict, Abel without Cain." Whereas Leone had found in American films as a child and during World War II a refuge from fascism, he now found in its contemporary blandness, its Doris Day films, a Fascist, Soviet-style propaganda. He detested "all those grinning white teeth. Hygiene and optimism are the woodworms that destroy American wood."[15] Not surprisingly, Leone, the collector of antiques, saw himself as a restorer of the antique wood of the Western. His goal was to bring out, and back, the grainy texture of the West as no one since Ford had. But what is really curious about these comments is the way in which the typically apolitical Leone describes himself as staging a political battle between two Americas in his film. He is fighting the modern Fascist American film on behalf of the anti–Fascist film of his childhood. Leone saw himself as varnishing away the smooth plastic surface of Doris Day and rediscovering the fine grain of Raoul Walsh and John Ford.

Apparently, it was a political struggle that Leone's '60s audience could appreciate. Amazingly, Leone was able to take that most conservative of genres, the Western, replete as it was with America's most fundamental home beliefs, and make it palatable to a generation that was hostile to almost everything for which that genre stood. And he did it without throwing the baby out with the bath water, because every moment of this movie, despite its strong pessimism, evinces a reverence for the Western. As Nichols notes, "Leone's Westerns were Americanized European movies for an Americanized but anti–American audience, and found immense popularity with the children of Marx and Coca-Cola, including those of us who loved John Wayne but detested his politics."[16] Youthful audiences in the '60s saw a reflection of their own horror at 1950s hygiene in the gritty textures of Leone's film (the dusters the gunslingers wear *Once Upon a Time* would be the subject of a brief fashion craze), as they would in the spate of realist Westerns that would follow Leone's. Ironically, Leone won this modern audience, not by catering to them, that is, by modernizing the West, dressing it up in hippie garb — but by restoring it to its proper antique texture.

In the end, it is no easy feat to summarize Leone's politics. Born into an intensely Socialist and political family, he tended to feign political indifference and to aggravate his intellectual friends and to oppose the times by making films that were overtly apolitical and, in the case of *Fistful of Dynamite,* hostile to the highly charged politics of the time. At the same time, he made Westerns that found strong allegiance in the youthful radical crowd of his day, the "children of Marx and Coca-Cola," as Godard referred to these young people who were a mixture of radical politics and consumer privilege, who found in the feel of his Westerns something parallel to the politics of the time. And, indeed, this was in keeping with Leone's goals to express his politics "through fable and spectacle." Leone's films, with the possible exception of *Fistful of Dynamite,* are careful to avoid explicit political rhetoric, but one nevertheless senses in them the presence of the "disillusioned Socialist." Throughout Leone's films, there is a strong and consistent hostility to fascism that expresses itself in a resistance to all forms of propaganda, political and filmic, and in a youthful tendency to shock his audience and challenge their myths and clichés.

# Mr. Choo-choo

The majority of Leone's political commentary in *Once Upon a Time in the West* is expressed through his conception of the role the transcontinental railway played in transforming the West. The transcontinental railway of course is as much of an archetypal player in stories of the old West as are the archetypal characters in this film — the lone gunslinger, the hooker with a heart of gold. The arrival of the railway out West is a standard theme in Hollywood Westerns, from John Ford's *The Iron Horse* to the Henry Fonda subplot of *How the West Was Won*. Frank Gruber categorizes the *Iron Horse* story as one of the seven basic plots in the genre.[17]

In many ways, Leone satisfies the requirements of the *Iron Horse* genre in his film. To be sure, he is not nearly the idealist Ford is. While Ford could express nostalgia for the death of the old West that the coming of the train represented, he could also see the train as a harbinger of culture and civilization, something that would bring economic order and law to the West, help the West blossom and prosper. Leone could never summon the kind of optimism for the train that Ford could, but this film does at times, particularly in the final scene, celebrate the majesty of the train and of the culture that appears in its wake. Like the other *Iron Horse* films, it explores the ambiguity of meaning inherent in the train's arrival, which signals both the death and the birth of the West.

But at certain times in this film, particularly in the scenes involving Morton and his influence on Frank, one senses a cynicism about the transcontinental railroad and a cynicism about business in America in general that is not in keeping with previous *Iron Horse* films. In these scenes it becomes apparent that at the helm of this film is not a good idealist, like Ford, or an American capitalist, but an Italian Socialist (albeit a frustrated one).

As Nichols has noted, Morton is "a familiar type from Italian political cinema, his physical debility symbolizing the corruption of a system which gets its way though the power of hard cash."[18] Morton is more than just a man. He is a limping, wheezing personification of the disease that the railroad represents. Like a train, Morton is stuck on two tracks, the crutches he uses to walk. As Cheyenne says to Morton, "You leave a slime behind you like a snail, two beautiful shiny rails." Cheyenne is referring to Morton's train tracks, of course, but also to the tracks he leaves with his crutches. We cannot help but remember Cheyenne's words when we see the two lines leading to Morton's dying body in his death scene. Morton moves on tracks above him as well as below since he uses the tracking device that drops down from the ceiling to pull himself along when he is not using his crutches. Morton's neck-brace locks him into a mechanical structure and gives him the stiff, metallic look of a train. As Morton lurches across his rail car while the train is idle, Leone times his movements to the wheezing breaths of the train as it expels steam. The effect is that the train's

The film's implacable force, representing death to Cheyenne, Harmonica and
Frank: the railroad.

breath seems to be Morton's or that he is encased in a kind of huge iron
lung.

It is Morton's bodily weakness encased within the iron shell of the train
that makes Cheyenne compare him to a snail. Frank picks up on the same
idea. "You look like a turtle out of your shell outside that train," he says
when Morton comes to visit Frank's hideout. Both Frank and Cheyenne see

Morton as a weak, slimy creature, encased by a hardened shell. There is a doll-within-a-doll quality to Morton and his train. Within the hard shell of the train resides a man; within the train-like frame of this man's support devices resides a man; within the brittle shell of that man resides a disease. Frank in particular likes to remark on the rot that is eating Morton from the inside, commenting derisively about Morton's "tuberculosis of the bones" and reminding Morton that "I could crush you like a wormy apple." A corruption hides within the seemingly powerful metallic body of the train. This train carries a virus that will eat away at the fabric of Western man. "Who knows how far you could have gone on two good legs," Frank taunts Morton, but he might just as well be addressing his comment to the modern Westerner.

The business practices that Morton brings with him, the cash that issues from the train, like a virus, will spell the end of the Western warrior. From now on, power will go to the weak and diseased, those who thrive in diseased environments like the plush interior cabin of Morton's train, a room so dolled up in red velvet it looks like a bordello. This is a different environment than the hard-baked monuments that provide the furnishings for the archetypal cowboy. Cheyenne, Frank and Harmonica, who thrive in the hot sun of the day, will not survive this dank and diseased atmosphere.

Typically, though, Leone refuses to draw Morton as a purely evil character. Leone, as we have seen, is as unwilling to make his bad guys purely bad as he is his good guys purely good. Harmonica does not look "anything like the noble defender of poor defenseless widows," Jill does not act like "a poor defenseless widow" and Morton does not act like an evil capitalist. In fact, he is one of the gentler, dreamier characters in the film. And despite his speeches to Frank about the power of money, he sometimes seems less interested in money than in what it can get him, which is the fulfillment of his dream to reach the Pacific Ocean and thus complete the first transcontinental railroad (a feat accomplished by no single man in reality).

Oddly enough, Morricone and Leone save some of their softest, most impressionistic music for Morton as he stares into the Romantic seascape painting in his train carriage. This scene is shot in first person and as we look through Morton's eyes at the painting, it dissolves into a blur, as though Leone were encouraging us to fall into Morton's own internal reveries. Water is all this man cares about now. His business dream has become a kind of mystical obsession. He seems to have transposed his own sense of his coming death (his disease is spreading quickly) into a heavenly dream of baptism, the ocean representing the final stage of his diseased body's dissolution and purification.

Morton might be a study in megalomania, a study of a man so caught up in his private vision of glory he does not see or care what devastation his technology will wreak upon the country. Frayling sees Morton as representing "an essential, but self-destroying 'stage' in capitalist economic development. He is the entrepreneur who will be made redundant by the technological imperatives he plays a key role in unleashing."[19] Frayling refers here also to the self-devouring quality of Morton, the way he caves from the inside. Looked at from this point of view, Morton is a kind of Frankenstein, devoured by his own creation, his dream run amok, a victim of a vision that is both beautiful and terrible. Leone liked the conjunction of beauty and terror. One need only look at the lushly rendered massacre at the McBain ranch to see that. The way he films the train pays tribute to its beauty and majesty, but he also describes it as a frighteningly unstoppable force. *Sui generis*, it has destroyed its creator and exists on its own accord, like a force of nature. Like Harmonica, it seems to be "destiny himself." Hence, the repeated first-person shots of the train from below as if it were barreling over and making victim of us, the audience, as well.

Morton's death is both pitiable and pitiful. Wounded by Cheyenne, watched by a glowering Frank, he drags himself in the mud toward a muddy puddle, a mocking substitution for the ocean he will never reach. His ocean theme and the sounds of waves provide the background sound to his death. The ocean sounds are artificially introduced, since there is no water nearby, signaling that we have entered into Morton's "death consciousness." Morton dies immersed in his fantasy of water, leaving the train to power through the parched land on its own. As he dies, we hear the distant clanging of an ocean buoy's bells, evoking both the sea and the funereal sound of a church bell.

As in the scene in which Timmy McBain is murdered, which also finishes with the tolling of bells, the sound of the bells in Morton's death scene segues to the screech of a train arriving, this time at the quickly developing Sweetwater depot. Morton had thought to rob Jill of Sweetwater, but this editing makes clear who was killed to make way for the train. And this editing reinforces the notion of Morton as a Frankenstein destroyed by his own creation. The train seems to have run him over here. It has unleashed itself from its owner and is on its own power now.

As I discussed in my chapter on Jill, Morton and Jill are linked by the water symbolism that surrounds both. Jill is associated with water in the many references she makes to using water to purify and strengthen herself after the victimization she suffers from men and in the references to her as the girl of the well, who first brings fresh water to Harmonica and later is encouraged by Cheyenne to bring water, like an earth mother of sorts, to all the laborers on the railway. Water is used to suggest something strong and noble in Jill. With Morton, it represents something more mystical, a holy grail of sorts. But it is the same water Ford talks about in *The Man Who Shot Liberty Valance*, the water of civilization that would come with the train and with the presence of women out West and which would irrigate this parched land, creating gardens of culture and civilization.

Not that Leone uses water in exactly the same way Ford does. Leone is on record more times than can be counted describing the ending of this film as marking a new matriarchal age in the West, and both Morton and Jill contribute to this softening of the West, this "watering down" of Western strength. Ford's films also describe this feminizing of the West. But for Ford, feminizing the West was much more of a good thing than it was for Leone, whose first goal in making Westerns was to rid them of women. For Ford, a culture in which women could prosper meant the building of schools and churches, dances, gardens, once dangerous cowboys transformed into touching and stuttering pupils, peaceful ritual and celebration, dances against vast, pure, blue skies. For Leone, it meant "the momism" that he felt seeped into American culture from this point in time, a kind of emasculation that would reach its pinnacle in the Doris Day films that he often cited with disgust as evidence of America's bland and materialist culture. And this "watering down" of the West meant a more stagnant environment that was much more suitable to diseased capitalists, like Morton, who would find, more and more, the plush interiors where the disease of capitalism could thrive.

## Morton's Protégé: Frank

Leone takes his shots at capitalism and its insidious effect on the mythic beauty of the West, not only through Morton's character but through the relationship between Morton and Frank, who is a hostile (but nevertheless willing) pupil of Morton's. At the outset of the film, it is clear that Frank aspires to replace Morton. Like Cheyenne, he seems to be able to sense the end of the West. He too seems to be tired of fighting and violence. Morton picks this up. "You used to take care of things personally," he taunts Frank, after Frank's men are unable to dispatch Jill. "Now, you're staying in the background. You'll end up taking orders." This last line amounts to one of the film's many premonitions, because in the end, the tired Frank will submit himself to Harmonica's meticulously choreographed death process. He ends up taking orders from Harmonica.

Frank senses the end of the old West and his old powers and he antic-ipates the power of the train and of Morton's money. Early on, he tries to recast himself as a businessman. "Didn't expect that," he says of Jill's sur-prise arrival that throws a kink in his and Morton's plans. "Happens in business." When he sits down at Morton's desk, Henry Fonda exhibits a tight restraint that does not entirely mask the childlike glee Frank experi-ences in playing the role of the businessman. When Morton asks him how it feels, Frank tells him that "it's almost like holding a gun ... only much more powerful," as he caresses the wood of the desk and the leather of his chair. This scene represents one of many times in which Leone draws a parallel between the power of money and the power of the gun. By doing so, he clarifies the means to power in the old West (violence) and in the new (money) but he also lends a sinister tone to the character of capital-ism. This money is not meant to seed the Edenic growth of Ford's West. It is simply a newer, more hidden and insidious weaponry. As Morton tells a gun-wielding Frank while waving a wad of bills at Frank's gun, "There are many kinds of weapons, and the only one that can stop that is this."

From Frank's point of view, there is not much to Morton as a man. The inner physical corruption, so symbolic of the inner moral corruption, has rendered Morton a pretty pitiful physical specimen from the point of view of the hard-baked Westerner. But Morton finds the spectacle of the violent Frank trying to slide into the clever and oily world of finance com-ical in its own right. It is interesting to note that Frank, sitting behind Mor-ton's desk, seems to feel its power, and uses it as a base from which to mock Morton. But as soon as Morton takes his place behind the desk, he seems to regain his ascendancy over Frank. "I'm sorry for you, Frank," Morton says as he settles in his chair. "You're doing your best. But you'll never suc-ceed in being like me." When Frank asks why, Morton says "Because there are things you'll never understand," and as he says this opens a drawer to his desk. Frank, hearing the drawer open, spins on his heels and draws his gun, assuming Morton has pulled a gun out of the drawer. Instead Mor-ton only pulls out the money. Frank is too violent, too instinctual a crea-ture to make it in the cool and clever world of finance. "Easy, Frank," Harmonica says when Frank is anxious to conclude the deal for Jill's prop-erty (a deal that Harmonica has no intention of making); "taking it easy is the first thing a businessman should do." Harmonica has sensed the same weakness in Frank that Morton has. Frank does not have the patience for business. His trigger finger is too itchy.

Harmonica catches on to Morton's superiority in business before Frank does, as he watches Frank's men assemble in various hiding places in town with the intent to ambush and kill Frank, at the behest of Morton.

Harmonica calculates Frank's situation as easily as he does Jill's, with that supernatural skill he has of reading signs that others miss. Frank had left Morton guarded by guns. But money, in the form of bribes, had easily dispatched the guns. "I got an idea Mr. Morton could teach you a lot more," Harmonica taunts Frank.

Harmonica disturbs Frank for two reasons. One is that Frank does not understand who Harmonica is or why he is hounding Frank. To his queries on this subject, Harmonica only responds with the litany of Frank's murder victims. Frank queasily intuits that Harmonica represents some form of retribution or judgment for his crimes. But Harmonica bothers Frank for a second reason also. Harmonica can see through Frank and he confronts Frank with the foolishness of his business aspirations. When Harmonica tells him "you sound like a real businessman, Frank," or "Yes, Mr. Morton has shown you a lot of new ways," Frank knows exactly what Harmonica means. Frank knows what he himself thinks of Morton, who he compares to a "wormy apple," and he knows that Harmonica is calling him soft too. And he knows that Harmonica is right. Because, as a gunslinger, Frank is slipping. He sends other men to kill Jill and they fail. He fails to kill her himself when he gets her.

There is a touch of comic pathos to Frank's character. He is indisputably nasty and violent, a real bad guy. But he is also hopelessly confused, the character who least understands the role has to be play in the Greek tragedy unfolding. Too interested in being a businessman to be a good gunslinger, too violent to be a good businessman, hounded by the shadow of Harmonica's exterminating angel, Frank keeps making a muddle of things. He rides through this film like a hunted animal, something which Henry Fonda seems to have well understood, judging by the frightened eyes that peer out from his otherwise immobile face in so many of Frank's scenes.

One of the comic ironies of *Once Upon a Time* is that it attacks the contemporary notion that financial success, or clout in the world of business, adds up to masculine success. In Leone's world, business softens and emasculates the Westerner. How absurd, Harmonica seems to be saying to Frank, it is for a Western gunslinger to dream about sitting behind a desk, like some gross parody or reversal of the conventional fantasy, the fantasy of the average man to be a part of the freedom and mythos of the old West. Harmonica kills Frank, but not before he has salvaged Frank's dignity. "When gangsters start sitting behind desks, I start losing interest in them," Leone said, in explaining why he turned down the offer to direct *The Godfather*.[20] The idea that a man can who can emerge from the sagebrush or ride a horse the way Frank does (which is to say, of course, the way Henry Fonda does) aspiring to worm his way into Morton's satiny and diseased den is laughable. Harmonica kills Frank, but not before he has helped Frank regain some dignity and reminded him that he is not a businessman, "just a man."

# Time

If Frank has picked up Morton's softness, he has also caught Morton's obsession with time. Morton is anxious to reach the Pacific Ocean before he dies. Time is running out for him. One of the points this film makes is that the cost of business is to become the slave of time. "We're running out of time," Morton yells at Frank when he realizes Frank has not successfully acquired the McBain ranch. It is ironic that Morton is compared to slow creatures such as a turtle and a snail. There is a sense in this film that time is most constrictive for those who are most concerned with it, that the more you panic about time, the more you slow down.

Frank becomes infected with Morton's sense of hurry. In bed with Jill, and maybe a little bit moved by the crazy Irishman's dreams both for Sweetwater and Jill, Frank flirts with the idea of marrying Jill and developing the land himself. "Hey, that's an idea. Maybe I could marry you. Then the land would be mine. And maybe you would be the perfect wife." This may be Frank searching for escape yet again from his fate as the doomed gunslinger, this time in a domestic fantasy rather than a business one. He quickly concludes this venture would require too much patience. "We'll have to think of another solution. Simpler. Quicker."

Carrying as he does a sense of eternity, Harmonica of course finds the impatience of Morton and Frank's laughable. When Harmonica cleverly alerts Frank to the assassin hidden behind a painted clock face by saying, "Time sure flies, don't it, Frank?" he is not only pointing out the assassin, but mocking Frank's doomed race with time. Critics have often seen this line as a reference to the fact that, through Harmonica, time (Frank's past) has caught up with him. But the reference also fits into a general framework in which Leone teases Morton and Frank for being so obsessed with conquering time. Harmonica, "destiny himself," is the master of time in this film, not the anxious capitalists, and the spectacle of them running around like chickens without their heads is laughable to him.

There is a contrast in this film between the anxious nature of contemporary business time and time as it is experienced by the archetypal figures from Westerns past. When the three outlaws waiting to kill Harmonica take over the railway station at the outset of the film, they ostensibly stop time. They pay no attention to the old clerk's fee schedule and rip out the telegraph line for the simple reason that it makes enough noise to irritate Jack Elam's character. They steal the station and render it timeless. By the time they have settled down, we are in a world in which time is dilated, a world so quiet and still that the sounds of a buzzing fly, a creaky windmill and water dropping on a hat echo loudly. The mythic characters of this film occupy a time of immensity and leisure. They recognize the train, with its speed and slavish devotion to the clock represents the destruction of their world, as does Jill's stagecoach driver (another denizen of the ancient West) who laments that the train has "caught up with us again," as if it were tracking his kind down. Of course, when Leone stops time in the opening sequence or in the gunfight between Frank and Harmonica where seconds seem stretched out to minutes, he is not only asserting the beauty of antique notions of time but the power of cinema to confront the cramped modern notions of time. If his script takes on the businessman's great friend, money, his camera asserts the power of the businessman's great enemy, time.

As I emphasized in the introduction, there is a Romanticism at the heart of *Once Upon a Time* and it is most apparent in Leone's attitude towards, and rendering of, time. Like a Romantic, Leone reveres and mythizes, the past. Cumbrow sees in Leone's Westerns a respect for the "permanence of mythic time." Nichols describes Leone's West as "a sun-drenched desert outside of time and place."[21] Correspondingly, and also like a Romantic, Leone has a great deal less respect for sunny visions of progress and the future, which he sees as the more pedestrian dreams of the materialist and industrialist, those who can only find man's purpose in his material accomplishments and have no savor for paradises lost, no sense of spirituality or the significance of memory.

Like a Romantic, Leone respects the persistence of memories, the way in which the past does not die or refuses to let us go. Nichols notes that "as Leone's budgets got bigger, several things happened: characters motivated by something other than money appeared; an obsessive concern with time and memory grew to great importance."[22] *Once Upon a Time in the West, For a Few Dollars More* and *A Fistful of Dynamite* all build themselves around narratives that emphasize the inescapability of the past, the way in which the past represents a greater, more powerful reality than the present. Mortimer's pocket watch and Harmonica's harmonica are clarion calls of the primacy of the past. *Once Upon a Time in America* is positively drenched in Leone's sense of the melancholy beauty of the past.

Like a Romantic, Leone urges the relativity of time in his cinema, speeding and slowing it much more aggressively than other directors. Despite

Leone's reputation for violence and broad gestures, *Once Upon a Time in the West* is a richly contemplative film in which the characters are constantly drifting into reverie — Jill about what her life might have been with McBain, Cheyenne about what his life might have been with Jill, Morton about the mystical ocean, Harmonica about his haunting past — before they are suddenly snapped back into reality by a sharp sound, a rude moment that signals the return of regular, pedestrian time, so much quicker, and less interesting in its movement. It is to these rich contrasts in the representation of time that Nicholls refers when Leone has sublimated his Romanticism into the style of his films. Leone builds into the pace of his film a Romantic respect for the immensity and leisure of inward time and the crudeness and pointlessness of relentlessly forward moving, exterior time.

In the end, Frank realizes that he belongs to mythic time and that he has no business trying to follow the schedule of a train. Finally, he abandons his business aspirations. "Morton once told me I could never be like him," he says to Harmonica, after riding up to him and presenting himself for the duel. "And now I know why. It wouldn't have bothered him to know you were alive." Here, Leone starts to reclaim Frank as one of the three powerful and moving men in this film. Frank seems to recognize here that he is motivated by something other than money. And he seems to realize that a quest for financial gain was for him, as it is for many, just a way to avoid confronting his destiny.

Leone brought Hollywood cowboy regular Jack Elam into his film. Leone's tight close-ups allowed him to take full advantage of Elam's famous wandering eye.

"So you're not a businessman after all," says Harmonica, in the tone of a mentor or spiritual guide. In one of the film's most effective lines, Frank answers simply, in words that take on gravitas through Fonda's elegant drawl, "Just a man." This line provokes one of Harmonica's strongest responses in the entire film. He looks up sharply at Frank, as if Frank has said something of great significance. Harmonica's eyes glaze over slightly before he responds with an addendum: "An ancient race." This is one of the film's most suggestive moments. Harmonica, who, like all of Leone's heroes rarely expresses a respect for, or faith in, anything, here expresses a profound respect for humanity in the raw, stripped of pretensions and worldly pursuits. With this comment, Harmonica almost seems to welcome Frank back from the world of high finance and technology, and into the fold of the old West. By recognizing that he is "just a man," Frank is stepping off the train and confronting Harmonica on his own.

All of Leone's heroes, in the end, confront their aloneness and self-dependence. Jill has to give up her fantasy of domestic bliss. Cheyenne is not able to get his mother back through a relationships with Jill. Frank will not be able to shelter himself with money. Despite the distance of their epoch from our own, the fantasies that the characters in this film have to abandon in confronting their essential aloneness in the world are disturbingly similar to our own.

From this point on, Frank and Harmonica are in complete synchronization, more friends than enemies. In a line that is so expository as to almost be out of step with this determinedly enigmatic and elliptical script, Harmonica says, "Other Mortons will be along. Then they'll kill us off." Harmonica and Frank share a joint enemy now, Morton and the powers of civilization and wealth that will make the old West obsolete. Frank's final response clears the battlefield of all the detritus that has distracted both of them from their mutual destiny. "That doesn't matter to us. Nothing matters now. Not the land, not the money, not the woman." There is something almost Sartrean in Leone's insistence, throughout this film, that dreams of romance, ownership and wealth are just distractions from dealing with death, the one thing we all have to confront by ourselves.

## The Other Businessman

There is one more capitalist in this film, besides Morton and his "pupil in business" Frank, and that is the rancher McBain. At first glance, McBain seems to be a symbol of the simple pioneer trying to better his life and being thwarted from doing so by evil forces of capitalism. His fiery nature, Irish heritage and dreamy nature are all homages to the optimism of Ford's films that moved but did not necessarily persuade Leone. On the other hand, he does not seem, like Ford's pioneers, to be rooted in community. There are no church readings, no schemes of education associated with McBain. Like a typical Leone Westerner, he seems to be in it for the money, promising his daughter that one day she will be cutting fatter slices of bread than she ever dreamed. Like Morton, he is an entrepreneur with a dream.

The thing that distinguishes McBain's dream from Morton's is that Morton's dream is of his own glory, or, at the very best, the attainment of a kind of mystical height that is significant only to him. McBain's dream grows out of love for others. He communicates his dream of financial reward to us through his assurance to his daughter that he will provide a better life for her. The way he floats off into a dreamy state when he reads Jill's letter to his son suggests that the dream of Sweetwater is tied into his love for Jill and his dream of providing her with a new life of family and domesticity and saving her from a life of prostitution. And it seems to be McBain's plans of taking care of and providing for Jill that moves Harmonica and Cheyenne to help her. Here again we must remind ourselves to not fall too hard for Leone when he constantly dwells on the pessimistic and elegiac nature of this film, referring to the death of the West and sneering at the new matriarchy left in its wake. McBain may be a businessman, an entrepreneur, and he may not have the social spirit of a Ford settler, but the dream of Sweetwater is founded on the principle of love. It may be a doomed love, for all the men who love Jill — McBain, Cheyenne, Harmonica, even Frank — are doomed, but it is still love.

The final image of Sweetwater, with workers flocking around Jill who carries them water, almost suggests that Sweetwater exists independently of an owner. We know Jill owns the place, but having lost Harmonica, with whom she dreamed of settling down, and having been counseled by Cheyenne on service management, her goal seems less to make money than it is to carry on McBain's principles of decency and to take care of her workers. There is a positive feel to this final image, despite Leone's tendency to emphasize the pessimism of the film's ending. We have seen how Leone's Westerns, while determinedly apolitical, often contain visual references (particularly in scenes of massive scale, like this one) to more contemporary historical and political situations, such as the references to Nazi death camps in *The Good, the Bad and the Ugly* and in *Fistful of Dynamite*. Here the disillusioned Socialist seems to transpose the dream of twentieth century socialism on to the terrain of the old West. The final image of the film depicts a world in which the destructive machinery of capitalism has given way to a respect for workers and their comforts.

# SEVEN

# A Neo-Realist Fairy Tale: Leone's Set Design

## Feel of Things

Leone was meticulous in his set design. Even colleagues like Vincenzoni, who tend to emphasize Leone's intellectual and literary poverty, cannot help but extol his appreciation for the grain and texture of the past. Vincenzoni (whose comments on Leone before they feuded during the making of *Fistful of Dynamite* are much more charitable than afterwards) tended to be most effusive about Leone's sense of set detail. Vincenzoni was, for example, struck by the care Leone took in choosing and filming guns in his film, "how lovingly" he handled them, as though they were precious jewels. He was, Vincenzoni says, a man who loved objects, citing Leone's knowledge in art, furniture and eighteenth century Roman silver. "He has a great knowledge of visual things. He is one of those rare directors for whom you may write a scene with a potential of ten and you get it back from him with a potential of a hundred."[1] It is interesting how Vincenzoni connects Leone's love of antiques and beautiful objects to his ability to enrich, or amplify, a script. Vincenzoni refers here to a key aspect of Leone's art — his ability to transcribe a narrative into visuals and concrete detail. "Expression through compression," is how Robert Bresson described this aspect of the director's job. "To put into an image what a writer would spin out over ten pages."[2]

Serge Donati also noted Leone's love of the feel of things. He recalls Leone polishing his antique jewels on weekends and saying, "If I were a woman, I would absolutely love these things."[3] Leone's wife Carla similarly notes Leone's passion for well-made things: "He loved the feel of the materials themselves — the marble, finely carved wood, precious metal and inlay

... the workmanship of antique silver—cutlery, plates, birds and animals. The way the material was worked by skilled hands of the past."[4] This director, so famous for his operatic bombast, had a cult for the fine, delicate and miniature. Leone's cinema is often as memorable for its fine detail as it is for its broad and sweeping gestures.

Ted Kurdyla, "production liaison" for Leone's *Once Upon Time in America* shoot in New York, described Leone as "a combination director and art director," and numerous accounts bear out that description.[5] Leone was a kind of amateur archivist of the West and so brought the collector's knowledge and fascination to his set designs. It is interesting to hear Leone describe his frustration, early in his career, with working at Cinecittà as assistant director to some of America's greatest directors such as Raoul Walsh and William Wyler. He laments the projects these greats had been reduced to and also how much he could have helped them make real films had they the resources. "I was more in love with the idea of the America than anyone you could imagine; I had read everything I could on the conquest of the West, already building up a huge archive of the subject, and I was obliged to spend my time in tatty versions of antiquity, directing Roman circuses in pasteboard Coliseums."[6]

Leone had begun storing visual ideas on the West years before he started making Westerns. Many of the images in his Westerns are straight out of his archives. Mickey Knox was incredulous about the verisimilitude of attaching a cannon to the end of a train in *The Good, the Bad and the Ugly* until Leone showed him the image he had copied from an American history book.[7] Ernesto Gastaldi, screenwriter for Leone's production *My Name Is Nobody*, said that before he worked with Leone, research had always meant consulting other American Westerns and simply copying the atmosphere from them. Only with Leone did he begin to read history books about the West and consult original photographs from the Civil War.[8] Gastaldi's comments reinforce the idea that Leone's great contribution to Westerns was not to recreate them but to strip away meaningless artifice that had accumulated on the Western legends, to restore the Western to its original luster, as if it were one of the antiques he so treasured.

Leone also brought a well-trained painterly eye to the Western. He had a great taste for Surrealist art, particularly the *trompe d'oeil* of Magritte (like Buster Keaton and Jacques Tati, Leone had a sharp sense of the film screen's potential for visual puns) and De Chirico's looming angles. His fascination with Goya is evident in his use of backlighting and in the studies of rustic faces that many of his close-ups represent. Degas' off-balance compositions influenced his arrangement of space.

Leone found a sympathetic eye in cinematographer Tonino Delli Colli,

Seven. A Neo-Realist Fairy Tale: Leone's Set Design

113

who began working with him on *The Good, the Bad and the Ugly*. Both agreed that excessive color had made a good many Westerns look tacky. Leone had a particular horror of blue, which he practically banishes from his films. He and Delli Colli shared the fundamental belief that Westerns should not be too colorful.[9] Leone says he showed Delli Colli a "series of Rembrandt prints. I was after that monochrome color."[10] The Delli Colli– Leone palette was one of subdued shades: blacks, browns and off-whites that worked with the wooden buildings of the West and freed the vivid colors of the landscape to express themselves. They chose colors that grew organically out of, and did not overwhelm, the environment, a "sandy color" in *Once Upon a Time*.[11] Leone's color scheme was highly influential on Westerns that followed his. The most cursory look at Westerns from the late '60s and the '70s reveals that the majority of that period's gritty Westerns adopted Leone's earthy but colorful palette.

Leone applied the same discriminating idea to costume. Leone loved to tell the story of how he bypassed the "newest things" offered to him at Hollywood's famous Western outfitters, Western Costume, preferring to find his costumes in their "warehouse left-overs," which he found a great deal more authentic in their worn dirtiness. He was right in claiming that after his films, costumes in films like *Butch Cassidy and the Sundance Kid* reflected a new attention to Western grit and grime. When people praised his costumes and asked how he had arrived at their invention, he boasted that he had not invented anything, simply gone back to the original. American filmmakers, he felt, depended too much on other screenwriters and did not consult vigorously enough their own history.[12]

One is struck by the originality and authenticity of detail in set design as well in *Once Upon a Time*. The tavern in the middle of the desert represents the kind of interior one had rarely seen in Westerns before and at the same time the kind of structure that much more likely would have existed at the time. The tavern is a mixed-use environment, serving as a stable and feed center for the horses as well as a watering hole for humans. Customers are also shown bathing and sleeping. Cavernous, darkly lit, seemingly devoid of windows, it much more closely approximates the necessities of desert architecture in the nineteenth century. As Mickey Knox notes, most "Westerns showed bars just like the bars today in the sense of lighting. But, that wasn't true at all. Leone's use of lighting was very authentic."[13] Leone's camera occasionally pauses very lovingly over the rough-hewn textures of the old West: the curved and cracked roof tiles of Flagstaff's train station that pass under our noses as the camera pans over the station during Jill's arrival, the heavy, roughly shaped coffins of the McBain family, the straw casing for the oversized bottles at the tavern.

Carlo Simi's comments about the Cattle Corners train station platform in the scenes at the beginning of the film apply to many of the sets in the film: "We wanted a non-construction, which had grown out of bits and pieces over time." Leone's sets have an organic quality. They match the landscape so well that they seem to have grown out *of* landscape. Interestingly, Simi was aided in his mission to convey the weight and feel of the West by a consignment of huge wooden logs, which had been used in Orson Welles's *Falstaff*.[14] There is something fitting in this inheritance of one meticulous set director from another. Leone and Welles had in common a desire to use only quality materials in their films.

## Documentary Myths

One should be careful not to make undue claims for Leone as a historian. No one has made a systematic study of his films for anachronisms and it is not to be expected that a director who films so much out of the visual memory of other Westerns would be perfectly realistic. Certain people recoiled at the way Leone could take such a proprietary attitude toward the Western. Many comment on Leone's attitude towards the Western as being more childlike than academic. Donati and Bertolucci recall him playing with Western accouterments like a child might. As I mentioned earlier, Eastwood found it comical the way Leone would dress like a cowboy on the set. Eastwood never bought Leone's image as Western archivist. Leone, Eastwood argued, "doesn't really know anything about the West. He's just a good director." Eastwood, in fact, emphasizes that it is Leone's naïveté about the West, "his very open, adolescent-type approach to film," that gives his Westerns their originality; his bravado, not his authenticity.[15]

Frayling poses Eastwood's comments as oppositional to Leone's claims for authenticity, but they really are not. Leone's taste for verisimilitude and his childish glee in approaching the West are probably responsible in equal measure for his films' success. Leone always emphasized that, though he had the taste of an archivist, his films were not archives. He repeatedly described his films as a mixture of fairy tale and realism. He spoke of applying a "documentary obsession to myth," of his tendency to "nourish my fairy-story with a documentary reality," of "mixing games with a documentary feel." The significance of his historical details is not that they are perfectly realistic, but that they are realistic enough. "I love the authentic when it is filtered through imagination, myth, mystery and poetry. But it is essential that, at base, all the details seem right. Never invented." The

**Seven. A Neo-Realist Fairy Tale: Leone's Set Design**

115

key word here is "seems." Leone stresses that his realistic details are never just for the sake of historical accuracy, but to "make the fable more believable."[16] Leone criticized one '70s Western, *The Culpepper Cattle Company*, which he recognized was rigorous in its historical reconstruction but which however did not capture "the mythical quality that comes from the legend and, above all, from the Hollywood films." The film failed, Leone noted. "Why? Because they did not find in it what they were looking for: the fable."[17] Leone's comments here suggest successful stage design is a recipe made of three ingredients: authenticity, a good sense of myth and fable and, most importantly, a good sense of the mythical history of Hollywood films—in other words, a literacy in the genre of the Hollywood Western and an understanding of its grammar. The details, no matter how stunning, will not register unless they express the myth powerfully. They will not express the myth powerfully except in the hands of a student of the myth.

Leone justifiably cites his neo-realist roots in talking about his realism. Like De Sica's best neo-realist efforts, Leone's films are gritty, take advantage of natural locales and use unprofessional actors who communicate something real that professional actors never could. At the same time, like De Sica's films, Leone's have a conventional melodramatic structure, with close ties to Hollywood, although with Leone, the touch point is Ford and with De Sica, it is more Chaplin. *Bicycle Thief* too could be described as fairytale inscribed in documentary form.

On the other hand, there is greater artifice to Leone's films than De Sica's. Leone is more wed to Cinecittà and a commercial sort of cinema than De Sica was in his greatest neo-realist films. One is tempted, oddly enough, to compare Leone's approach to his set to that of the consummate studio set director Ernst Lubitsch, whose facsimiles of European settings were patently artificial, but who, through an obsessive attention to telling concrete detail, conveyed the atmosphere of his settings better (that is to say more ideally) than the real thing.

Leone's biography is rich with accounts of meticulousness and ambition in set design. Vincenzoni recalled that if a producer told Leone he could only have two days for a scene and Leone knew he needed six days, he would ask the producer for eight. Leone would shoot beyond the schedule by 20 weeks, racking up huge bills. He would shoot half a million meters of film and only use 4,000 of those meters. [18] It is this kind of over-reaching, Vincenzoni points out, that results in memorable constructions like the Cattle Corners railway platform that serves as the backdrop for the film's first gunfight, where Leone had thousands of railroad ties brought over to construct the platform where Bronson confronts the three killers.

"Another director would have said: 'We already have the grass, the boulders … isn't it the same thing?'"[19] Vincenzoni emphasizes here Leone's verisimilitude, his insistence that his backdrop have the grit and texture of the real West. But equally typical of Leone is the scale of the effort — thousands of railways sleepers when a hundred would do. Leone wanted his sets to be realistic but surprising and expressive as well.

Vincenzoni notes also that Leone, when constructing the "huge drugstore" in the middle of the desert, "wasn't worried that this should be credible" (thought it certainly is); what was important to him, says Vincenzoni, was the fact that it should give a depth to the scene. "For Leone always had to make an effect. Every time."[20] For Leone, Vincenzoni again emphasizes, the primacy of dramatic effect over historical authenticity. The "drugstore in the middle of the desert" has probably been praised as much as any set in *Once* for its authenticity. But authentic as this set is, what viewers most remember about this scene is the dramatic effect Leone arrives at with this authenticity. For example, the scene where Harmonica is introduced so strikingly by the lantern swinging back and forth, making his face appear and disappear in the darkness of the cave-like tavern.

## Set as Protagonist

What was most important to Leone was not that a set created a good backdrop for his film but that it vied for power itself in the film, that it expressed itself. Carlo Simi recalls that Leone requested a Western village in *For a Few Dollars More* that would be like a protagonist in the story.[21] The bank in this town "must be like a character itself." Leone emphasized that his set should not only communicate to the audience but to the actors as well. He felt that a meticulous approach to the particular was "a great help and support to the actor … Visconti has been criticized for being too fussy. You can't be."[22] One thinks of Erich von Stroheim as well as Visconti. These are directors of meticulous set direction, who believed the authenticity of set detail was reflected in the actor's performance. Creating a meticulous set for his actors is the visual equivalent of Leone's habit of playing the theme music on the set for them. Both practices explain why actors liked working with Leone. You did not act in a vacuum on Leone's set. He provided his actors a great deal of dramatic context.

The scenes in *Once Upon a Time* which most reflect Leone's sense of the set as a protagonist are those where Jill moves through McBain's house, first in a frenzied search for clues to his murder and wealth, and then in a fatigued communication with a house that was meant to be hers as a wife

**Seven. A Neo-Realist Fairy Tale: Leone's Set Design**

117

and mother but never will be. McBain's presence is thick in this house. When Jill hurriedly searches through one drawer, she is frozen by the discovery of what would have been her wedding corsage. The corsage is in a drawer next to prayer beads, presumably those of McBain's dead wife — kept, one guesses, more for their romantic nostalgia than for their religious significance. Presumably, this is the drawer where McBain kept his most sacred objects. Jill is like a child left alone in a house, languorously exploring her parents' effects. What she finds either reflects the dead McBain's presence or her dashed marital dreams, both melancholy thoughts, and so these scenes are characterized by a sad and reflective tone.

It is the objects of the set that do the most speaking in these scenes. Jill pulls a model out of a trunk that expresses McBain's dream of building Sweetwater in miniature. It is a carefully wrought piece with a tiny little station sign in front that swings when touched. The toy train station represents the kind of delicate, small scale object (like a harmonica or a musical watch) in which Leone had a penchant for investing the largest meanings of his films.

McBain's picture sits between Jill and Cheyenne in their initial scene together. Both commune with the picture, Jill verbally, Cheyenne silently. Jill says a mock prayer over the picture; Cheyenne studies it carefully after talking to Jill and hearing of her dreams, as if trying to get a feel for who this Irishman was, why Jill would love him and whether he (Cheyenne) might be capable of similar dreams and of similarly settling down with Jill.

Leone is famous for the silent film quality, the Eisensteinian montage, of his gunfights, but there is a different kind of silent filmmaking in Jill's scenes at McBain's house, something more along the lines of a Garbo film, with Jill moving languorously through the house, communing with McBain's spirit, or more precisely, with the spirit of the life she just missed having, as it is expressed in the objects of the house — the objects in the drawers and trunks, the lace of her bed's canopy, through which she peers when she lies down, the mirrors in the house that repeatedly cause her to lose herself in reflection. In these scenes, thought is expressed through a silent communion between an actress and the objects that surround her and with which she involves herself. Here, more than any other scenes in the film, Leone puts "into image what a writer would spin out in ten pages."

Leone conveys changes in Jill's character through the interior of this house. McBain's house has had a makeover by the time we leave it. Jill has tidied the kitchen up so nicely that we have to assume she has resigned herself to her new role out West — not the role of mother and wife, but the lonelier role of water maid to the new West. Jill's kitchen is so much more orderly by the end of the film and so much more light issues into the room than it did the first time we saw it, that, on first viewing of this film viewers may not realize this is the same dingy room in which Cheyenne and Jill had their first conversation. The changes in this interior represent the changes that have occurred in the West in the course of this film. The old West, of bachelor cowboys holed up in dingy places designed to keep out enemies and heat, has given way to a domesticated West. Flowers decorate the room and light pours in. Civilization and security are starting to make themselves felt. In the earlier scenes with Cheyenne, the kitchen was a typical Leone interior, dark and grungy, a challenge to our antiseptic view of the West. In the final scene, it is a Ford interior, more beautifully lit, more open to the outdoors, representative of a unanimity between man and environment.

It was a dictum of Hitchcock's that a set should never be just merely background but should become an integral part of a film. If you make a film set in Mount Rushmore, Hitchcock would say famously, make sure Cary Grant is hanging from Lincoln's nose. Hitchcock's dictum just represents for film an extension of the unities that dramatists had always practiced. If you show a gun in act one, Chekhov would say, make sure it goes off by act three. Leone followed this rule of making use of your set for symbolic or expressive purposes. And the more the object was typical of the Western (a gun, a whiskey bottle, a deck of cards), the more he was tempted to play with that object, make it integral to a scene, or charge it with meaning. And so, when Morton aims to convince Frank's men to betray Frank, he does not use words but rather communicates his idea through the rituals of poker, asking to play a hand, and then dealing hundred dollar bills as if he were dealing cards. (The scene recalls the one in *For a Few Dollars More* when Eastwood prefers to tell his bounty victim that he will be dying by dealing cards rather than speaking.) Frank's men go along with the game, fanning the five bills in their hands and looking at them as if they were a hand of cards before asking Morton how they are to go about playing this game.

## Significant Objects

Leone is often at his most eloquent when he expresses himself through objects rather than words. Jill and Cheyenne's relationship, as we have seen, is delineated through the cups of coffee she makes for him. McBain and his daughter's conversation about their financial future is externalized in the loaf of bread that the girl cuts and that McBain says will be even

Seven. A Neo-Realist Fairy Tale: Leone's Set Design

119

more plentiful in the future. Frank and Harmonica's duel over the deed to Jill's property, after the auction, is physically inscribed in the coin dollar Frank insultingly offers Harmonica as a profit on the deal. Harmonica rejects Frank's offer, not in words, but by promptly using the dollar to pay for his one-dollar drink. He tosses the coin in a glass and the ringing of the coin in the glass represents his answer (and his return insult) to Frank. Harmonica teasingly lets Jill, who is naked in a tub, know her physical attractiveness is not of tantamount importance to him by silently handing her a scrub brush. Harmonica's infinite patience in waiting out Frank and in accomplishing his revenge is expressed through the piece of wood he whittles as he waits for Frank, a classic Hollywood symbol of resigned and wise leisure.

And here, as in *For a Few Dollars More*, the central mystery of the film is contained in a small object, Harmonica's harmonica. Mortimer's watch in *For a Few Dollars More* and Harmonica's harmonica have many things in common. Both are so delicately miniature as to have an almost child-ish appeal. When Leone wanted to get his most deeply felt ideas across, he would turn to finely wrought objects or objects that are inherently intriguing, the kind of things that would catch a child's or a collector's eye. Both the watch and the harmonica are also musical and the music of both becomes part of the action of the film so that they represent a kind of Brechtian portal through which the soundtrack can be smoothly introduced into the action of the film. Both typify Leone's tendency to enclose his film's largest meaning in small and delicate symbols.

*Once Upon a Time* actually has two of these symbols. The harmonica, like Mortimer's watch, signifies the vengeance plot and also conveys touchingly, as Mortimer's watch did, the love of one family member for another. But the tiny train station, also miniature and finely wrought, and attractive to a childlike sensibility, carries a good part of the film's emotional charge as well, conveying McBain's Fordian dream of family and an honest development of culture in the West, not to mention suggesting to Jill the melancholy of all that she just missed having in her new life. Both the harmonica and the toy train sign point to the primacy of the family in Leone's emotions and to the fact that, in his films, the family is most often a dream that cannot find a reality out West.

Of course, the objects Leone invests with the most emotion are the various components of the cowboy's uniform, particularly those all impor-tant three components that sit at the top, middle and bottom of the cow-boy respectively: the hat, the gun, the boots. Mickey Knox remembers Leone spending hours looking through a hundred hats before he could find the right one for Henry Fonda. As we will see in the chapter on Leone's pictorial compositions, Leone used hats both as framing devices and as means of dramatically introducing his cowboys in shots where their hat appears first, before their faces. Leone loved building gags around the cowboy various accoutrements, for example, the hat-shooting duel in *For a Few Dollars More* or the scene with Woody Strode collecting water in his hat in *Once Upon a Time*. Leone conveys Jack Elam's sinister nature by filming him in close-up trying to bottle a fly in the barrel of his gun. The first confrontation between Harmonica and Cheyenne is told, in great part, visually, through close-ups of Harmonica's gun which the two hand back and forth like a hot potato as they make allusive references to the parallels between playing a harmonica and shooting a pistol.

Each of the three cowboys' costumes say boatloads about them. Harmonica's earth-toned get-up ties him into the colors of the southwest and emphasizes, both in color and style, his ties to Mexican culture (as will the set detail of his flashback). In its tan and gray hues, his outfit reinforces (as do Bronson's rock-like features) our sense that Harmonica springs from the rocky desert terrain of the West and that he represents some ancient, timeless force, as solid as granite. That Leone carefully planned the symbolic import of his colors is evidenced by the countless reports of the care he took in establishing his color spectrum. He chose the Sierra de Baza and the Sierra de Los Filabres in Spain as settings for *Once Upon a Time in the West* because "the area had a similar coloring to the red earth of Utah and Arizona." (Only portions of his exteriors were shot in Monument Valley.) When he shot interiors at Cinecittà, he had at his disposal a container "of that particular dust of that particular color all the way from Monument Valley" to make sure there was consistency in his colors. "For the record," he made sure one interviewer knew, "I'm the one who stains the clothes of the actors."[23]

Frank's outfit is blacker than those of Harmonica and Cheyenne, perhaps a nod to his role as the villain, and has a fastidiousness to it that recalls Mortimer's outfit in *For a Few Dollars More*. Frank, the burgeoning businessman, is more the patron of the tonsorial parlor. The spectacle of his pants tucked neatly into his high, elegant boots creates opportunities for using the boots as foregrounding in photographic compositions, just as Leone used the natty Mortimer's boots in the same way in *For a Few Dollars More*. Frank's elegant black boots represent a marked contrast to Cheyenne's weathered, tan, suede ones (often featured in close-up). In fact, the men's boots are shot in close-up enough to represent a reprise of the battle of boots (Mortimer's elegant black boots, Monko's weathered tan) shot in close-up in *For a Few Dollars More*, when Monko grinds his toe over Mortimer's to announce his claim over the bounty they are both

*Seven. A Neo-Realist Fairy Tale: Leone's Set Design*

121

chasing. Leone works a gag out of the cowboy boot also in the scene where Cheyenne's boot, hiding a gun, turns his boot into a lethal weapon.

Of course, the dusters Frank and Cheyenne's men wear express a style in evil that is so memorable that the duster has become, of all the interesting objects in *Once*, the one that is closest to a trademark of the film, even, Frayling tells us, inciting a brief fashion craze in Paris after the film came out.[24] That Leone could set a fashion trend, via a Western, reminds us that his set design and costumes were about authenticity, but even more about style, an expressive parading of that authenticity. For Leone, authenticity was important, but particularly in the way it dramatized his myths.

# EIGHT

# Composition

## Shot Composition: Framing

Leone framed his shots so carefully that he was sometimes criticized for over-composing his shots. He shared, for example, Ford's passion for doorway backlighting, what Robert Cumbow refers to as the "underlaying visual motif of John Ford's *The Searchers*." The menace of the three gunslingers in the film's opening sequence is conveyed by all three appearing as shadowy figures at doorways, behind them the brightly lit vastness of the West. This is one of Leone's favorite ways of introducing characters dramatically. Jill's entrance at the wayside saloon where she stops on her way to Sweetwater is shot in the same way, as is Frank's saloon entrance after the auction when he has come to pay Harmonica the $5,000 for Jill's land. Doorway backlighting is dramatic for a number of reasons. It is a technique that highlights contrast. The brightness of the treeless West contrasts dramatically with the dark interiors of the West, the vastness of the landscape with the cramped interior. And it is a good technique for accentuating drama. The figure at the door arrives as a shadow, thus underlining his power and mystery. The framing of the figure in the doorway further adds a mythic power to that figure.

Of course, Leone's use of backlit doorways is only part of his general tendency to look at the West through doors and windows, to look at the Western landscape from cramped interiors so as to underscore its vastness and through windows so as to frame it majestically. When Timmy McBain hears the shots that have felled his family, Leone chooses to use a point-of-view tracking shot that simulates the child's frenzied dash to the doorway. In this sequence, the wide openness of the exterior landscape comes rushing upon us with great drama as the boy races to the door. When Leone shoots people arriving in doorways, the emphasis is on that person's mythic power, their stature as they arrive. When he takes us out a window or doorway to look at something in the exterior world, the emphasis is on the Western landscape, the vastness that expands so dramatically through our limited portal.

Leone's penchant for composition through doors and windows is, as it was for Ford, part of a larger tendency to frame all of his scenes very carefully. Along with his cinematographer Tonino Delli Colli, Leone was very sensitive to the play of horizontal and vertical lines and could arrive at some dramatic shots with the assistance of only a few deteriorating fences and leaning boards crossing here and there. Here, the reference point to Ford has to be the final shoot-out in *My Darling Clementine*, a dream-like collision of swirling dust bisected by the maze-like lines of the O.K. Corral's fences and entryways.

Leone was defensive when he was accused of complicating his pictures just to make them attractive. "They call me a perfectionist and a formalist because I watch my framing. But I'm not doing it to make it pretty; I'm seeking, first and foremost, the relevant emotion. You have to frame with the emotion and the rhythm of the film in mind. It takes on a dramatic function."[1] Leone's framing is not arbitrary. It fits the emotions of the scene. The more elaborate framing devices tend to happen during the most dramatic scenes.

The opening sequence in *Once Upon a Time* is the one that most recalls Ford's strong use of vertical and horizontal lines for framing devices. Leone avails himself of every line available — doorways, windows, the pillars of the roofed walkways outside the station and the line of the roof itself, the receding line of the railway, the endless lines of the vast train platform, shaped of thousands of crudely jammed-together planks of wood, the legs of the water and windmill towers. His three villains pace majestically through and around these lines, looking for the perfect spot to situate — that is, to frame themselves. They seem to have an instinctive sense for the spot that best heightens their grandeur, particularly Strode, who is shot in both near shots that emphasize his place within the lines of the porch and far shots that place him dramatically between the vastness of the train and the vastness of the water tower. The more inspired Leone is by his subject, as he was certainly in shooting Strode, the more dramatic become his framing devices.

Similarly, in the Frank–Harmonica duel, Leone films Frank in close-up as he circles around the fixed Harmonica, looking for the best spot to stop for the duel. Frank's glances to the sky tell us he is looking for a spot that is to his advantage, with the sun behind him. Just before he finds the spot, Leone shifts to a far shot of Frank settling on a spot. As Frank comes to a decisive halt, we note that the vertical line of his body matches four other vertical lines, in the background: two wispy trees filmed from such a distance that we really only see the vertical lines of their trunk and two vertical fence posts. Frank's body lodges so naturally into this field of vertical lines that we get the sense of him having arrived at the only spot he could have, a kind of pre-destined spot that he has not so much chosen as fallen into. This shot is an example of framing that is photographically attractive but also reinforces the drama of the situation, the feeling that we have finally arrived at *the* moment of confrontation.

Trying to choose the best framing compositions in a Leone film is a pretty frustrating exercise, given the abundance of choices, but certainly one nominee has to be the shot of Harmonica waiting for Frank to ride into the newly built-up Sweetwater at the end of the film. The shot is from Jill's point of view as she looks out her window. Leone has already posed Bronson amidst a tangle of lines. Harmonica rests on a fence, his back to a post. A variety of fence lines, posts and leaning boards add linear complexity to the shot. Layered on top of these are the lines of Jill's window frame. The end result of all these lines is that from Jill's perspective, though the window, Harmonica, who is so tiny in this shot as to be barely perceptible, takes on the quality of a bird nestled in its nest or a spider in a web waiting for its prey. He has made a home in this tangle of lines. And he will not move until Frank arrives.

This shot is followed a few minutes later by another of Leone's most carefully framed compositions, the shot where Cheyenne looks through the window of Jill's kitchen at Harmonica and Frank readying for their confrontation. This time we see, through the window again, Frank and Harmonica squaring off for their duel. We see Cheyenne's profile in close-up on the left (a match to the earlier shot with Jill's profile on the right — Leone *was* a perfectionist) and Frank and Harmonica cleanly divided by the vertical line of a post, and horizontal post lines above them, into two boxy areas. These frames are, of course, framed, themselves, by the window. The framing here serves to enhance the mythic quality of Harmonica and Frank as they finally face each other. But the framing in this shot and in the earlier one too, where Jill looks out at Harmonica through the window, fits the narrative strategy of the scene as well. It is in these scenes that Jill will ask Cheyenne what Harmonica is doing, what he is waiting for, and in these scenes that Cheyenne, the closest thing to a chorus in this tragedy, tries to explain Harmonica's character to Jill. It is only fitting that Harmonica would be framed in the distance. He is the subject of analysis, in much the same way Charlie Kane was in the famous scene in *Citizen Kane* when his parents contractually wrangle over his future while he, framed by a window deep in the background, plays innocently in the snow. One has the sense here of watching a kind of pageant, with Cheyenne narrating to the side of the stage, and Frank and Harmonica acting out his narration in miniature in the background, like puppets or a film within a film.

## Composition in Depth

Leone also shares Ford's taste for composition in depth, though Leone carries that proclivity to greater extremes. Leone works some of his richest compositions around the image of railroad tracks receding straight to the back of the screen. Though at times Leone's train track compositions suggest encroaching civilization, more often the way they recede into nothingness suggests that Leone has situated his drama in a no-man's-land of sort, a world that is evocative of the empty Surrealist landscapes Leone was fond of in his art collection.

With the frightened Indian woman, who, minutes into the film, runs from the three outlaws directly into the back of the image, and the nothingness of the desert landscape, Leone seems to be signaling to us that this is a film that will operate on a backward and forward axis, not one that moves left to right. (This shot may also be a comic reference to Natalie Wood's run for her life in Ford's *The Searchers*.) When the wounded Cheyenne arrives in Sweetwater at the end of the film, we watch him (from the waiting Harmonica's point of view) appear from the back of the film's busy image of men working on the railway, riding slowly right up to the waiting camera. When Leone shoots scenes on Morton's train, he abandons the customary habit of treating the carriage like a room on wheels with a left-right or horizontal axis. Instead, he composes most of his shots along the central walkway of the train so that we are always conscious of the narrowness of the carriage, the walls on each side and the ceiling above. Whereas other directors might be constrained by shooting on a train carriage, it coincides perfectly with Leone's visual tendency, which is to film on a axis that runs from backward to forward, not left to right.

It is interesting to see how Leone avoids horizontal composition, even in his shots of dialogue. Leone tends to avoid match-cutting dialogue. He keeps both conversing figures within the same frame. He puts one person a little closer to the camera, the other a little further back, so that their dialogue begins a recessional composition that is usually continued throughout the frame by other visual elements. Leone then adjusts this recessional approach to dialogue according to the mood of the scene. The more dramatic the scene, the closer to the camera one person is, the further away from the camera the other. In these shots, the person who recedes into the frame tends to become more the subject of the shot, the person close to the camera tends to become the vehicle of the shot, the point of view.

This tendency to film human interaction on two planes leads to what has to be one of the most emblematic of Leone shots, that in which one character, squeezed off to the side, in massive close-up, partially cropped at the film's edge, looks back into the frame. Deep in the back of the frame is the subject of his regard. Of course, this is another framing device. The cropped close-up of the face creates a vertical line that frames the right or left of the frame. If the person in the foreground is wearing a cowboy hat, and they often are, the hat creates a horizontal line along the top of the frame. Leone often uses this shot that so strongly contrasts background and foreground when he wants to show a character surveying a scene of some significance. So we survey the carnage at Morton's train, after Cheyenne's escape, from the point of view of Frank, whose profile in close-up lines the right of the image as the brim of his hat lines the top. Or we view Cheyenne's body, just after he has taken his last breath, with Harmonica, Harmonica's profile and hat framing the left side and top of the image.

These compositions also point to Leone's fondness for Edgar Degas' paintings and their disorienting angles, so far from the Renaissance compositional guidelines that Ford follows. Leone, Frayling tells us, respected Degas for the way Degas would use his figures to create perspective, for example, placing his ballet dancers in the distance and another in the foreground in extreme close-up, the depth of the plane suggested only by the relative size of the two figures.[2] Degas' ballet stage and the Western landscape have this in common — they are both blank and wide open, and can lend themselves to compositions with no intervening objects to create lines of perspective, so that the end result is compositions characterized by surprising conjunctions of the near and the far.

There is an abundance of striking examples of these shots, in which the image is framed by a profile in the foreground. The shot in which Harmonica kicks down the door to find Jill, deeply recessed in the room and in a bathtub, is one striking example. The dominance of Harmonica's profile here emphasizes his power (which he will not abuse) and Jill's vulnerability. The shot is not simply one of a woman in a bathtub, but a man watching a woman in the bathtub, as though Leone wanted to emphasize the inherent voyeurism in this bit of archetypal Western erotica. Harmonica's profile looms powerfully in the foreground. Jill seems caught like a trapped bird in the line of his vision.

The shot in which Cheyenne's man watches from the foreground of the screen as the sheriff brings the bound Cheyenne to the train for transport to prison is another good example of this kind of shot. Here, the foreground presence of Cheyenne's man emphasizes his menace, and gives us confidence that Cheyenne's men will spring him from his confinement on the train with ease. These shots point towards Ford in their relishing of composition in depth. But whereas the shots of train tracks receding into the background or of the vastness of the West spreading out from windows and doorways seem to be lifted right out of Ford, the suffocating nature of the close-ups in these compositions, the abrupt contrast of close-up and far shot, the oblique angles, particularly in the relationship of the foreground to the backgrounds, marks these shots as more Expressionistic and peculiar to Leone.

## Choreography of Men

Leone also inherited Ford's tendency to carefully compose groups of men. In *My Darling Clementine*, for example, Walter Brennan's gang fairly spills through doorways but always in carefully arranged, almost Renaissance-like compositions. Or Ford films men deliberately arranged along the receding line of exterior, roofed walkways or lengthy bars. Leone too puts great care into the arrangement of his men's bodies and loves to position them along a line that recedes into the image's depth.

At the heart of both Ford's and Leone's way of arranging men is a respect for the tendency, in classic Hollywood composition, to group figures in threes. The opening sequence of *Once Upon a Time* is striking for the various arrangement of the three men on the vast train platform. The tracking shots of Jill searching for her family in Flagstone are dramatized that much more by her being flanked by two porters, both slightly behind her, like pages, and each carrying her luggage. When Frank emerges from the sagebrush after the massacre of Brent McBain's family, he does so only after one of his men has taken his position to the left and another has taken a position to the right. Frank marches through these two posts like royalty being presented to his subjects. Leone likes to work in threes and to flank his principal characters with courtiers like this, to give his villains the stature of aristocracy.

Leone also shared Ford's fondness for arrangement of men in which one side is over-stacked against the other. In *Stagecoach*, Ringo's lonely march into a duel with three gunslingers who, splayed out and draped by shadows, seem to so overwhelm him, finds an echo in Leone's one-on-three

**Three against one. Evocative of the final shoot-out from Ford's *Stagecoach* and illustrative of Leone's great gift for dramatic composition as well as his excellent sense of texture, both in set and costume design.**

arrangements in his shooting of the duel between Harmonica and Frank's three men who wait for him at the train station at the film's beginning. In *Stagecoach* also, five men, among them a drunk, a gambler and an outlaw, gather in a hulking line over a newborn baby. Ford had a fondness for this kind of scene which brings the brutishness of the West into collision with symbols of innocence and delicacy — a cactus rose or a baby, for example. Leone seems to nod to this scene when he shoots, from behind, five outlaws in their elegant dusters, looming over small Timmy McBain in the scene of the McBains' slaughter. The difference in these scenes is obvious. Ford's barbarians are kneeling before innocent beauty, Leone's are going to snuff that beauty out. As I discussed in my chapter on Leone's relationship to Ford, Leone often delighted in sending up Ford in this way, taking a Ford shot, the purpose of which was to exalt innocence, and using it for much darker purposes.

Leone, like Ford, also takes particular pleasure in choreographing the movements of the various bands of thugs in the film, giving them an elegance that balances nicely their natural brutishness. When Cheyenne's men arrive at the wayside tavern, too late to help Cheyenne with his escape, four men pour through the door, *a la My Darling Clementine*, with two more following in their wake. As the four move forward into the room, the two take their post on each side of the door. The effect of these scenes is regal and ceremonious. One of the great aspects of Leone's cinema is that it is characterized by a neo-realist sort of naturalism, emphasizing strongly the dusty, oiled leather of the West, and yet that it moves with the ceremony of a church processional or the courtliness of medieval ritual. It is this treatment of his heroes like aristocracy that probably most closely connects Leone to that other great operatic director, Luchino Visconti. As Frayling has noted, Leone sees his figures from the old West as aristocrats from the past, threatened and doomed by a new bland, plebeian and materialist culture, much like Visconti's aristocrats were threatened by the encroaching materialism inherent in democracy.

The three scenes where Leone's choreography of groups of men is most elaborate are the opening sequence of the film, the scene where Harmonica and Cheyenne unpack McBain's lumber, and the scene where Cheyenne is arrested and led to the train. All three of these scenes represent a dance of sorts, with men moving around, sometimes in silence (as in the opening sequence) sometimes while talking, exchanging places with one another, creating shifting backdrops for each other. For example, when Keenan Wynn's character, the sheriff, brags to Cheyenne that he will be going to a penitentiary from which he will never escape, Wynn's character is framed by a man on his left and Cheyenne on his right (from our point of view)— a typical Leone composition of three. While the sheriff is talking, he moves to the other side of Cheyenne, leaving a gap between the two of them. Into that gap steps a cowboy with his back to the camera, creating a new grouping of three. As that cowboy turns to the screen, another cowboy lines up behind him, gracefully introducing a recessional depth into the image.

Then Cheyenne and the man in the middle, behind him, begin their march to the train. As they do, the sheriff catches up to them and assumes the position to Cheyenne's left so that Leone can film yet another formation of three men, this time as they walk through the town. As these three pass one of Cheyenne's men, who is leaning against a building, Cheyenne makes eye contact with this man and we get a tag team effect of sorts. The camera stays with Cheyenne's man, with whom new arrangements are created.

Whereas Leone is prone from time to time to static images, particularly in moments of epic grandeur, like Frank and Harmonica's duel, at other times his compositions keep toppling onto and tumbling out of each other in a neverending movement, as they do in this scene. The good-natured dance here captures the wry humor of the scene. This is a humorous moment in the film, both because Harmonica has hoodwinked Cheyenne, by trading him in for bounty money, and because we know that the fatigued Cheyenne is having to gear up for yet another daunting escape. The jovial nature of the scene is reinforced by the jaunty dance across town.

## Camera Movement

The quiet partner in these highly choreographed scenes is the camera, the central point around which all movements are arranged. Leone's camera, like all other aspects of his cinema, can be obtrusive sometimes, and quietly elegant or classical another. Whenever analyzing Leone's camerawork, it is worth keeping in mind cinematographer Tonino Delli Colli's comment that Leone "had very precise feelings" and that "a little movement that someone else might find insignificant says something to him. And when the film is shown you notice this. The audience is not aware of it on a technical level, but feels its psychologically."[3] This comment says a great deal about Leone's art. First, that despite its highly formalized, ritualized feel, it is a highly intuitive art, with Leone making decisions about camera movement instinctually, according to how it feels. Secondly, that it is an art that tries to speak to its audience in non-verbal language, through movements and rhythms. And finally that Leone can be characterized by a classical restraint, expressing himself through the slightest of movements. The great scenes of operatic choreography–the slaughter of the McBains, Harmonica and Frank's duels— are the masterpieces of the film. But there is a great pleasure in watching this film in trying to detect the quieter movements of Leone's camera.

One of Leone's defining gestures in camera movement is to arc away from his subject while the subject, in its turn, arcs away from the camera. Leone seems to have had an instinctual feel for the sweeping feeling that accompanies this dance between subject and camera. One of the most striking scenes in the film and most typical of how Leone can achieve a quiet elegance in his camera movement is when Frank and his men saddle up outside Morton's train and ride off to capture Jill. The shot is characterized by three movements. The men are before the train and both they and the train begin moving to the left at the same time. But the train veers off to the upper left corner of the screen, the men to the lower left. The camera films this movement in a tracking shot that follows the men to the left but then veers off itself to the lower portion of the screen even before the men do. The scene has the effect of a fountain, with three lines of movement spraying out to the left. It is similar to the way Ford's line of soldiers would split at crossroads, only here the camera tracking away from the other two lines of movement give them a more dramatic and balletic effect.

Sometimes Leone's camera movements are more slight and quizzical. In the barn scene where Harmonica confronts Jill for the first time, the camera tracks him in close-up as he moves towards her but then swings away from him and back, resting in the carriage which sits in the foreground and onto which Jill aims to climb. As the camera arrives in the carriage, Harmonica arrives at Jill's side and holds her back from stepping up to the carriage. The effect of the shot is comically cruel as we view the scene from the place Jill would like to reach. It has an almost taunting effect. We feel like children who get to go for a ride when others cannot.

When Frank arrives at the scene of carnage left by Cheyenne outside Morton's train, the camera stops with him to survey the scene. Then Frank walks up to and enters the train. We expect the camera to follow him on to the train, but it hangs back as if it wants to decide its own course. Just then a horse in the foreground starts to move to the right and the camera decides to accompany the horse, rather than Frank, in a tracking shot to its right. The horse acts as a kind of guide to a gruesome underworld of sorts, as in its trail we see the long string of bodies left in the wake of Cheyenne's explosive escape from the train. The lazy indifference of the horse and the relaxed pace it sets for our camera contrasts nicely with the horror of the scene.

Leone's camera registers Cheyenne's death in a couple of lovely, quiet movements. We see and hear Cheyenne take his last breath in close-up but we do not actually see him die. Just as Cheyenne takes his last breath, Leone cuts to Harmonica, who is posed in one of Leone's trademark ways, his head down, the top of his cowboy hat filling the screen. From off-screen, we hear Cheyenne's body slump to the ground — the actual moment of death transpiring off screen, as so many of Leone's deaths do. As Harmonica lifts his head, the camera pans gently to the left (it had been sitting slightly to his right). This is typical of the way Leone liked to have his camera and his subject move in divergent paths. Bronson's face moves up while the camera pans left. We experience that small charge that comes when Leone moves us in two contrasting directions at one time. For a moment, Harmonica and the camera pause to stare at one another. Bronson's face is as impassive as ever, but somehow Leone's camera, in tight close-up, catches a glimmer of sadness in Harmonica's eye for his fallen comrade. Then the movement picks up again. Harmonica turns his head to the left and looks behind him, opening up the right side of the screen. As he does, the camera continues to move to the left a little, until it is behind Harmonica's head, and then tilts a little to the right, opening up even more the right side of the screen, which soon reveals Cheyenne's crumpled body. We have the sense of having stared into Harmonica's eyes at the moment of Cheyenne's death and then turned with him to look at the body. The effect is that we feel we have shared Cheyenne's death with Harmonica, watched it with a friend.

Leone cuts back to a close-up of a grim-faced Harmonica, shot a little from below, staring at Cheyenne's body. Just then the train coming into Sweetwater whistles shrilly and Harmonica inexplicably looks up to the sky. The camera, in another of Leone's small curious camera movements, follows his gaze, then leaves him, rising up to the sky just as the train appears in the lower portion of the screen in the far background. One has a sense at this moment of a connection between the train's arrival and Cheyenne's departure, as though the two entities, one from the old West, one from the new, could never share the same terrain or as if the train were somehow responsible for Cheyenne's death (Morton has shot him). Cheyenne's spirit seems to ascend into the sky with the train's smoke. This idea of Cheyenne's death as an ascension is reinforced by the distant image of Harmonica carrying Cheyenne's body up into the mountains in the final shot of the film.

These are the kinds of little camera movements to which Delli Colli refers when he says that "a little movement that someone else might not find significant says something to" Leone. The quiet little musical moments in his film are often ignored in studies that concentrate on his famously large and operatic set pieces.

## Camera as Destiny

Leone likes also to set up his camera at a halfway point between his character and that character's destination. For example, in the sequence where Frank discovers the carnage at the train in the wake of Cheyenne's escape, Leone starts by shooting Frank in a Ford-like far shot as he rides from a great distance away towards the camera, all to the rhythm of Morricone's majestic score. As he arrives at the hill on which the camera sits, he pauses for a short while, allowing the camera to register his face at it surveys the damage near the train. The camera has stepped back discreetly, though, as he rides up. As Frank picks up his gallop to the train again, it now films Frank from behind, as he recedes into the depth of the frame, having just risen from it.

This is classic Hollywood stuff, very reminiscent, for example, of the scene in William Wellman's *Public Enemy* (a film where one senses a kindred spirit of Leone's) in which Jimmy Cagney marches across a street to the building where he intends to kill all those responsible for his friend's death. Cagney walks right up to a waiting camera, positioned somewhere in the middle of the street, to the point of a tight close-up shot that registers his determination, then is filmed for the rest of his march from behind as he disappears into the building. These shots create the sense of characters both approaching, and descending into, their fates. Here the camera is not so much another partner in choreography, but an observer from a fixed position, conveying a much more fatalistic point of view. Jean Cocteau said of Orson Welles' films, "Not a shot is left to chance. The camera is always placed just where destiny itself would observe its victims."[4] The same seems true of Leone's cinema. Often the camera just waits in the spot reserved for the characters' destiny. The camera is already there on the ground at the spot where Frank will fall to his death, poised to register in close-up the blank expression of death. And it is there at the bottom of McBain's grave starting up, in a point-of-view shot at the mourners scattering dirt on it.

Cheyenne seems to have a privileged relationship with Leone's fatalistic camera, probably because there is something so philosophical and fatalistic about his character. The camera often seeks out Cheyenne so that he can deliver a scene's final line. After Harmonica has surprised Jill and Cheyenne by defending Jill so ably at the well, the camera pans up to Cheyenne who has been watching the scene from high up in the hills, and approaches him in close-up so that he can finish off the scene with the line, "He not only plays, he can shoot." More often, however, the camera stakes out its own spot in a scene and waits for Cheyenne to step before it as he utters his scene-concluding epigrams. When Harmonica turns Cheyenne in for the bounty money, Cheyenne compares him to Judas, who he says was satisfied with $4,970 less than Harmonica (the bounty was $5,000). "They didn't have no dollars back then," Harmonica responds irrelevantly. As Harmonica says this, the camera, which has been on the move, stakes its spot, waiting for Cheyenne to step before it and terminate the scene with his final line, "But sons-a-bitches, yeah."

Similarly, as Jill and Cheyenne await the outcome of Frank and Harmonica's duel, Cheyenne counsels Jill not to expect Harmonica to return to her or settle down. "People like that have something inside them," he says before stepping before the camera, which shoots him from below but still in close-up. "Something to do with death." The drama of the word "death" here seems to match the drama of the camera angle from below.

A shot like this is characterized by finality. It finishes the scene and the dialogue it records is about death and the end of Jill's hopes in love. And the way in which Cheyenne steps before the camera and is locked into place before he utters his eulogy gives the shot its greatest sense of finality.

Leone's camera often records a scene from the point of view of destiny, rather than from the point of view of one particular character. One of the more striking scenes in the opening sequence is of the gunmen squaring off for their duel from the distant point of view of the windmill that has been relentlessly squeaking throughout the sequence, giving the scene its strange, lonely rhythm. The torturously slow and monotonous rhythm of the rusty windmill noise has seemed throughout the scene to capture the slow relentlessness and indifference of time, unfurling in all its ancient leisure. The shot from the point of view of the windmill, with parts of its fans in close-up, the gunslingers small as ants below, reinforces the sense that a distant God watches Leone's cowboys and that their most violent actions kick up, in the long run, a negligible amount of dust.

## Leone and Keaton

We should not make the mistake of too closely associating Leone with Ford's cinematic language, or that of classic Hollywood, despite how much he respected, and drew from, that language. As I have already emphasized, Leone often takes Ford techniques and puts them to extreme uses. Ford loved low angles, but (for example) probably would have avoided the morbidity of shooting from the point of view of a dead man in his grave, as Leone did in McBain's funeral scene. That is a case in which he would have found the camera too obtrusive. And Ford liked a gradual recessional depth but would have avoided the stark contrast in those shots of Leone's where massive close-ups co-exist with extreme far shots. Leone could be as disruptive in his composition as he was in his editing. Just as he would gleefully and abruptly shift his tempos, so he would move abruptly from far shots to close-ups without the graded intermediaries that the classic Hollywood hand would have employed.

For certain Leone far-shots, the point of reference seems less John Ford than Buster Keaton. The scene in which Cheyenne scampers all over Morton's moving train, on his mission to kill all of Harmonica's captors, suggests Keaton in the way it plots on such a huge scale and the way it sees the train as a kind of huge toy with which to create visual gags on a large scale. Leone does not limit himself to the typical run along the top of the train, as in conventional scenes of this sort in Westerns. Cheyenne ranges all over this train like a centipede. He clings underneath, runs along its top, hangs before its windows.

Certain shots in the sequence where Harmonica helps Frank survive the ambush of his own men suggest Keaton too. In one shot, for example, Leone shoots from enough distance to record one entire building and parts of another. Frank, minuscule in the lower left of the screen, is completely unaware that one of his stalkers climbs a slanted roof behind the building on the far right of the screen. Leone shared Keaton's affection for these large-scale shots that give you the entirety of the action, without cuts, and which record several fields of action at one time. In this kind of filmmaking, the large-scale substance of the world, buildings and trains, for example, are treated like elaborate playgrounds, in which humans scamper about, appearing and disappearing in a dance characterized by a mathematical clarity.

The correspondences between Leone and Keaton are many. Both are singular among filmmakers in their technical knowledge of the craft. Leone and Keaton both understood and were fascinated by the machinery of filmmaking. Both even had a history of inventing machinery to aid them in arriving at a desired effect. This solid sense of the machinery of filmmaking is evident in the ways both set themselves up huge visual challenges, that require shots and movements on a large scale and pinpoint timing. Both saw the screen as a chance for game-playing. They both liked *trompes l'oeil* and surprising visual effects. The scene in which Cheyenne's boot becomes a gun is a more macabre version of the kind of stunt for which Keaton was famous; for example, the scene in *Sherlock Jr.* where he effects an escape by leaping through a window, in which his servant has arranged a parcel, and emerging in women's clothing. Leone and Keaton had the same taste for large-scale gags and visual puns—and sometimes both at the same time.

## Leone and the Surrealists

Keaton, with his dreamlike play of space and time, was the darling of Surrealists, and Leone's art is deeply tinctured by surrealism as well. An art collector, Leone's favorite artists were the Surrealists. Of the Surrealists, he granted the most importance to De Chirico and it is indeed De Chirico who seems the key reference in certain scenes in *Once Upon a Time*, particularly the opening sequence and the sequence in which Frank duels with his own men, sent by Morton to kill him.

The opening sequence has qualities that more specifically align it with De Chirico's surrealism. The emptiness of the scene, the sense of timelessness that is introduced when the manic clatter of the telegraph is replaced by the antique wheeze of the windmill, the sense of being in a timeless dream world that paradoxically seems to be governed by a noon-time sun, the vision of small humans next to towering but solitary structures (here the windmill and the water tower), the central role of a circular design or rotating wheel (again the windmill) in a picture governed otherwise by cold lines and angles, lines that seem to recede into nowhere and strange, oblique angles, such as that from which we look down on Woody Strode's character from a high angle, sandwiched between the water tower and windmill — all these elements mark the influence of De Chirico on Leone.

We get the same De Chirico–like sense of bizarre stillness in an abandoned town square, registered through oblique angles, in the shoot-out between Frank and his men. Here again, a small solitary figure traipses through a deserted area that shows evidence of civilization (all the advertisements on the wall only emphasize Frank's solitude) but no people. The shot of Frank from Harmonica's perspective on his balcony seems particularly out of a De Chirico painting. Shot from a sharp angle above, a minute Frank is crowded into the lower left corner of the frame. A faded picture of a clock with no hands towers over his left shoulder. A large building on the right floods the right side of the screen with shadows angled to contrast uncomfortably with the angle of our point of view.

The image of the handless clock resides over the scene, as if to suggest that we are in one of these trademark Leone scenes where time has been dilated, or stopped altogether. One cannot help notice, not only that Leone is fascinated with clocks of all varieties, but how they often take on a visual significance when time stops in his films. In *For a Few Dollars More*, the clock, like the harmonica in this film, represents the inability of Mortimer's enemy to outrun his past, time catching up with him. Close-ups of the watch and scenes in which it is emphasized also provide occasion for time-stopping, for the reverie and the flashback that is the key to the movie.

Similarly, in *Once*, when Jill arrives, the first time she really seems to become conscious that something is wrong is when she looks at the station clock, presumably realizing, clearly now, that her ride is late. Troubled by the time on the station clock, she pulls out her pocket watch, more elaborately tooled than the station clock (and typical of the kind of delicately ornate object the antique-loving Leone liked to feature). At this moment Leone introduces for the first time the plaintive pianola theme that will always accompany Jill in her moments of troubled introspection (of which

Jill has more than any character in the film) and which suggests the memory-inducing sound of a music box (though implicitly here, as opposed to *For a Few Dollars More*, where the watch was also a music box).

Leone, like the Surrealists, was fascinated by the aesthetics of the clock face, both as a collector of antiques and as a practitioner of films that emphasize so strongly the relativity of time and the persistence of memories. The handless clock face suggests Dali's "Persistence of Memory," and Leone often reminds us of that picture in his depiction of a sun-baked world of stillness and timelessness, a dreamscape that aims for vividness of detail rather than hazy effect, a world that suggests that when time stops and memories sharpen, life is apprehended in its greatest clarity.

# NINE

# Leone's Close-ups

Leone also strays far from the filmic vocabulary of classic Hollywood in his extreme and abundant use of close-ups. Frayling notes that Leone in *Once Upon a Time* wanted even more Techniscope close-ups than before.[1] Leone's recurrent use of close-ups in this film reminds us that his homage to the classic Western only goes so far. This was to be his reflection on past Westerns but also his most intense expression of *his* kind of Western. The close-ups also remind us that Leone's films are as characterized by a powerful sense of magnified detail as they are by sweeping *mise-en-scène*.

Leone's use of close-ups may be the most under-appreciated aspect of his work. Those who admire the Fordian expanse and deliberation of his compositions and the sweeping musical effect of his *mise-en-scène* are, at times, liable to sneer at his close-ups, which strike many as too eccentric or extreme — reflective, in a kitschy way, of the frenetic camerawork of the '60s and '70s. And yet Leone achieves some of his most miraculous effects through these close-ups, and these effects are the most distinct to his particular style.

Tonino Delli Colli credits Leone's cinematographer on *Fistful of Dollars* and *For a Few Dollars More*, Massimo Dallamano, for helping Leone find a method for recording close-ups in breathtaking clarity. He was the first one, according to Delli Colli, to realize that the new P2 (two perforations) Technicolor format required a different kind of close-up, one that does not record the entire face, but rather a square from the lower forehead to just below the mouth.[2] Leone's goal was to get the eyes and mouth, the two parts of the face that most betray thought. The combination of this closeness, with the clarity of the new color film stock, resulted in shots that capture the slightest movement of the eye and mouth, that are so sensitive to the play of the eye and the mouth that they manage to record human thought.

*Once Upon a Time* is sprinkled with little moments of close-up alchemy, where the principal purpose of the shot is to capture what Robert Bresson referred to as the "ejaculatory force of the eyes."[3] For example, the scene where Frank and his men confront the little boy Timmy McBain before they shoot him has two striking close-ups, one of Timmy and one of Frank. In the first, we see Timmy surveying the scene of his family's slaughter and then the shape of his doom in the line of gun-toting men staring at him. What is most striking about this close-up is that the child expresses no emotion. He just stares. The most conventional approach here would be to use this opportunity to pluck the audience's heart strings. It would not take much, given the horror of the situation. The slightest whimpering would be wrenching. One can only imagine what Steven Spielberg would do. Leone, however, sticks with something close to absolute neutrality.

Leone used close-ups at times (and certainly Leone often discussed this) to express thought and emotion. Eyes, Leone felt, revealed "everything you need to know about the character ... courage, fear, uncertainty, death."[4] But, as Frayling has noted, Leone also uses close-up to express "complete impassivity." Leone was drawn to actors like Charles Bronson and Clint Eastwood, actors whose chiseled features are more impassive than revelatory. Leone chooses impassivity in his recording of Timmy McBain's face as well. The shot is effective in its avoidance of cheap maudlin effects. The boy's gaze, by its very neutrality, seems to cast a severe judgment on Frank's men, one of whom appears to squirm uncomfortably under the boy's confused and curious gaze.

Frank, however, is impassive himself. In the other great close-up of the scene, Frank stares back at the boy with a repressed smile, a smile that resides almost wholly in the eyes. We search in vain for some sign of guilt. Frank's expression does change, though only very slightly, when the more nervous of his men asks, "What are we going to do about this one, Frank?" Fonda's face remains impassive and even his eyes do not so much move as glint in anger, at having been addressed by name in front of a witness who could now identify him. This is the kind of almost transparent change in temper that only Leone's camera catches, almost the way a camera catches different plays of light as clouds pass over the sun. It is in a shot like this that we appreciate Leone's ability to imply, as quietly as possible, his cowboy's dark thoughts, his "cunning in action."[5]

Another effective use of close-ups is in the scene between Brent McBain and his daughter, just before both are killed. McBain, nervous before the arrival of his wife, scolds his daughter for slicing the bread too thin. He wants an impressive feast for his new bride. His daughter, confused, tells him she is slicing the bread the way she always has, to which McBain responds with an outpouring of his hopes to someday support her in more lavish style. "Someday," he tells her, "you can cut the bread in slices as thick as a door if you want to. And you'll have beautiful clothes and you won't have to work no more." The daughter, who knows nothing of McBain's grandiose plans for building a new town, says with a look of blank confusion (and in close-up), "We gonna be rich, Pa?" Her look is so neutral and confused that it implies, without intending to, disbelief in the "crazy Irishman's" dream — another example of Leone's ability to express the maximum through the most minimal of facial gestures. The girl's close-up is effective in its innocent accusation, but McBain's reaction shot is even better. In close-up, we see him read his daughter's face. He sees his dreams are so distant to his daughter as to be incomprehensible to her. The hopeful fantasy on his face freezes and melts into embarrassment. He is conscious of making promises he may not be able to keep and of looking foolish in front of his daughter, who (and this is reinforced by her austere physiognomy) seems accustomed to a life of duty and privation. Catching himself, he drops his fantasy abruptly. "Who knows?" he answers his daughter, almost angrily, and skulks away.

This sequence is a good example of the way Leone would use close-ups to show people thinking. Leone was critical of the "frenetic pace" of certain Hollywood films from the 1940s and 1950s and inspired by the slow rhythms of Japanese cinema, like that of Ozu. "The sense of pondering a reply I could only find in Japanese cinema."[6] In this scene, the camera takes the time to record McBain "ponder a reply." Leone mixes allusive dialogue and close-ups to convey his meaning. The dialogue only hints at the meaning of their conversation, poetically in this case, through the metaphor of the bread slices. The implicit meaning of the words, and the most explicit meaning of the scene, is to be read in the two characters' eyes.

Although Leone is perhaps most famous for the close-ups in the climaxes of his film — Harmonica's flashback, for example, or his duel with Frank — the sequence that to my mind represents his most effective use of close-up is the epilogue of sorts to the film, that in which Harmonica and Jill say farewell to each other, while Cheyenne watches sadly. I have analyzed this sequence on a more shot-by-shot basis in my section on Jill's character. It is characterized by the scantiest of dialogue — three or four allusive lines, along the lines of "Well, I gotta go now" or "Yeah, me too." But it is a monumental sequence in terms of how much is conveyed through the close-ups of the three actors, none of whom seem to move a facial muscle. Most of the communication is entirely through eyes. Cardinale's mouth barely moves as close-ups reveal Jill's relief that Harmonica

**Fonda on the set of *Once Upon a Time in the West*.**

has not died, a relief that turns into hope that he will stay with her. That hope, in turn, transforms quietly into sadness when she looks into his eyes and realizes he will not. Bronson's face is so stony as to give the impression that it cannot express emotion and, for the most part, Leone capitalizes on that stoniness to create an effect of impassivity. Nevertheless, here we see Harmonica meet Jill's hopeful expression with the slightest hint of an almost mocking smile that makes it clear staying with her is not remotely possible. But if his mouth is slightly cruel, the almost completely flat expression in his eyes somehow manages to convey great pity and affection for Jill and regret at hurting her. Interspersed with this exchange are close-ups of Cheyenne's face, his most expressive in the film (though not most mobile). Cheyenne wears a hang-dog look that conveys, most of all, pity at the spectacle of a woman's affections spurned, though we assume also that Cheyenne pities himself because we know that, were he not mortally wounded, and had she loved him as much as she loves Harmonica, Cheyenne would have agreed to take Harmonica's place and settle down with Jill.

It is in close-ups like these that we strongly sense Leone's affinity with Robert Bresson who also had a reverential feel for what the camera ("wondrous machine") could record in the human eye. Bresson was keenly conscious of the way the eye could express itself in cinema in ways that it could not in other arts. Photography can give us close-ups of the eye as well, but not in movement. Only film can capture the movement of the eye — its glint or flash — and the trace of thought betokened by that movement. "The spark caught in his eye's pupil gives significance to his whole person," Bresson says of his actors. Bresson recognized, as many have, that the movie camera catches "physical movements that are inapprehensible by pencil, brush or pen" but he emphasizes also, and more than other film theorists, that the camera can also capture "certain states of soul recognizable by indices which it alone can reveal." The play of the eyes in close-ups represent one of those indices (involuntary movements of the mouth and hands are others) that reveal the agitation or movement of an actor's interior world. Film, Bresson felt, was made, not just of physical movements but of these "inner movements that are seen."[7]

## Respective Brands of Close-ups

Leone's use of close-ups is so frequent, varied and precise that each of the main characters has their own genre of close-up. For example, Fonda seems to have taken advantage of his close-ups to convey, through his eyes, a hunted animal look, a fear in Frank that stands in quiet contrast to his overall sadism and confidence of carriage.

Cheyenne's close-ups are the most philosophical. As mentioned early, the camera will often approach Cheyenne in close-up, or Cheyenne will step before the camera to create a close-up, at the end of certain scenes where Leone wanted to Cheyenne to deliver whatever aphorism he had chosen to finish off the scene. Cheyenne's close-ups then accent his perceptive nature and are used to support him in his role as the film's chorus, commenting on and interpreting the characters in the film. His emblematic emotion in close-up in his sequences with Jill is a puppy-dog look of sick love for this woman who reminds him of his mother. Cheyenne is surprised by his feelings for Jill. He is surprised by his desire for a life with her that, notorious gunslinger that he is, he could never have, particularly now in the waning days of his career. Cheyenne's close-ups express a wistful desire for a love that can never be.

Harmonica's close-ups, as I discussed in my chapter on his character, are repeatedly in profile. Leone films Harmonica entering a scene from the side, either left or right, and in profile, at least eight different times. Clint Eastwood noted that Leone often chose actors for their faces more than their acting ability and Bronson's performance substantiates that observation. With its rock hardness, its deep grooves and crevices, his face is closer to those of the many extras Leone chose for his films because of their picturesqueness. Leone does not seem as interested in drawing meaning from Bronson's face, hence the profile shots. These shots, which are most often arrival shots also, convey a sense of Harmonica as an active agent on the film, someone who acts on a scene, rather than reacts. He comes on the scene as a force of nature. Leone wields his profile like an ax.

Leone's writer, Serge Donati, felt that Jason Robards did not translate well onto the movie screen ("He hasn't got the eyes"). But many feel that Robards' character, Cheyenne, is the most successful in the film, and the closest to Leone's heart.

Harmonica also has frontal close-ups in those moments where he flashes back to Frank's murder of his brother. And here, as in so many of Jill's close-ups, Leone uses the close-up to convey reflection, as a portal to the thinking world. In the last close-up of Harmonica before Leone finally discloses the entirety of his memory of Frank's murder of his brother, Leone uses the tightest close-up of the film, a shot that closes in so tightly on Bronson's face that the screen finally fills up with just one of his eyes. The shot is Hitchcockian in its emphasis on the eye as the gateway to memory. But it should be noted that in Harmonica's frontal close-ups, Leone does not go for much more expression than he does in his profile close-ups. Bronson does not convey the meaning that Cardinale, Fonda, Robards or Woody Strode do, through slight glints of eye and curls of lip. His face remains passive and unemotive, a mask of sorts having more to do with the physical world, the landscape. Leone tended to shoot around Bronson's face, to treat it like part of the environment, rather than try to draw something from it, as he did his other actors' faces. About the only emotion that Bronson ever allows his character is a slight smile, one that usually surfaces when he is being threatened. The smile is his reaction to male combativeness and competitiveness, as though he were politely trying to hide the humor he finds in anyone challenging him.

Jill's close-ups are the most frequent and the most introspective. She is the most reflective character, not only in this film, but in Leone's entire oeuvre up to this point. Only Noodles in *Once Upon A Time in America* rivals her for the number of times she is filmed in thought. Her trademark close-ups are those in which the camera searches her face while she is lost in reflection —for example in the reveries occasioned by the train station clock or at McBain's when, on two separate occasions, her reflection in the mirror sends her on an inward journey.

Jill's close-ups are often interspersed with pan shots from her point of view, for instance when she first arrives in Flagstaff and surveys a town that hardly seems to notice her or when she arrives at McBain's and casts a sweeping glance at the long line of mourners who represents her macabre welcoming party. Leone often scans an environment from Jill's point of view, then gives us a reaction shot in close-up. She is the newcomer to the West and so is constantly in the position of trying to figure it out. She represents a useful point of view for us because we too are outsiders looking into a distant, foreign world.

Jill's reaction shots to this new and disturbing world are studiously neutral. It would certainly be difficult to find another film where Cardinale has given this quiet of a performance, and that is saying a great deal because a big part of Cardinale's allure is her ability to hold something back from the camera. The only close-up of a broadly smiling Jill is the first one, as she exits the train, when she still believes the West betokens a sunny future. That smile soon falls prey to the alienating bustle of an indifferent Flagstaff. We will not see her smile broadly again until the final scene of the film, when she brings water to the railway workers and even then not in close-up.

## Actors and Close-ups

Cardinale's performance in this film has long been underrated. There are several reasons why it has been. First, as is true of many of the greatest directors, Leone was not able to apply his great talent for authenticity to his leading lady's hair and makeup and so Cardinale's appearance is one of the few elements in the film that dates (in the pejorative sense of the word) the film as a "'60s movie." Moreover, the scene in which Harmonica strips Jill of all the white lace from her dark outfit provokes guffaws in the audience, and probably rightly so, as a fairly hackneyed and predictable pretext for exposing Cardinale's shoulders and bosom for the rest of the film. In fairness to Leone, justification is provided for the scene—Harmonica is making her a less easy target for Frank's assassins by removing the bright white lace. And there is symbolism as well. Harmonica is stripping her of her Eastern finery and transforming her from New Orleans prostitute to Western pioneer woman. Nevertheless, Cardinale's costume, along with the dubbed dialogue, are the elements in the film that most tempt critics to treat the film as kitsch.

But there is nothing kitschy about the delicate play of emotions recorded in Cardinale's face in her final scene with Harmonica. In

Claudia Cardinale in costume as Jill in *Once Upon a Time in the West.*

that scene, as in most of her scenes in the film, one is struck by the restraint of her performance and the variety of emotions that cross her face. Cardinale was one of the actors who felt most at home with Leone's technique and could also analyze it most lucidly. She liked Leone's habit of shooting lots of close-ups and found it easier to act with the camera very close. After many films, the camera, Cardinale says, "has become like a friend to me: the way it hums is familiar to me, and I can feel at once if it is set up well or not."[8] Cardinale's reference to the camera is a propos. Those who were most comfortable working with Leone were those who were most comfortable with a camera, film professionals like Cardinale, Fonda or Woody Strode, who most understood the relation of the camera to the actor, how little an actor needs to do before the camera, how they can count on the camera to record the smallest of their gestures. Those who struggled most with Leone's technique were actors who were less trusting of the camera, often actors trained in stage traditions, actors whose loud gestures overwhelmed Leone's very intimate camera.

Frayling notes, for example, that there were tensions between Leone and Gian Maria Volonte on the set of *For a Few Dollars More*, as Leone tried to quiet Volonte's performance.[9] And Leone sounds just like Hitchcock, who also waged a continuous war with stage actors, in the advice he gave to the stage-trained Romolo Valli on the set of *Fistful of Dynamite*. He tried to get Valli to forget the mannerisms he had learned in the theater: "I asked him to unlearn everything he'd learned so far."[10] This posturing of the great visuals-oriented director trying to encourage the stage actor (usually a Method actor) to "unlearn" his theatrical technique is very familiar. Hitchcock often spoke of getting his actors to "unlearn" their technique and bragged of his struggles with "Method actors." Paul Newman was one of his favorite targets. "I wasn't too happy with the way Paul Newman played it," he said of Newman's role in *Torn Curtain*. "As you know, he's a 'Method' actor, and he found it hard to just give me one of those neutral looks that I needed to cut from his point of view."[11]

Leone's favorite Method-acting whipping boy was Rod Steiger, with whom he struggled on the set of *Fistful of Dynamite*. Steiger, Leone said, "thought of the film as very serious and intellectual, and had a tendency to come in the style of Zapata or Pancho Villa."[12] His comments here are reminiscent of Hitchcock's on Ingrid Bergman, with whom he often struggled on the set, "Except for *Joan of Arc*, she could never conceive of anything that was grand enough; that's very foolish."[13] It is interesting to note that if screenwriters often mock film directors for not being intellectual enough, directors often take their revenge by teasing actors for being too intellectual. Leone often exaggerated his squabble with Steiger, turning their story, as Frayling says, "into a prize fight between the Maestro and the Actor's Studio."[14] Hitchcock did the same thing. Still, there is much to learn about Leone's cinema and the way he films actors in his advice to James Coburn on the set of *Fistful of Dynamite*. "The less you do in this film, the more you'll benefit," he told him. "Steiger grimaces," Leone complained, "He wants to eat the lens. If you do nothing, you will be the one to collect everything."[15] Leone stresses, as Cardinale does, the intimacy of his camera. Cardinale learned to be lulled by the hum of the camera into the quietest of gestures. Leone counseled against performances that devour the very quiet and observant film camera.

Leone recognized, as Robert Bresson did, that too often actors' "effort to render themselves more alive do just the opposite," that "the slightest crease" on the actor's face, "controlled by him and magnified by the lens, suggests the exaggeration of the kabuki." Leone looked for the same qualities in his actors that Bresson did: "no ostentation. Faculty of gathering into himself, of keeping, of not letting anything get out. A certain inward configuration common to them all. Eyes." Bresson here describes an approach to film acting in which there is a proportional relationship between the neutrality of the actor's general performance and its freshness, a proportional relationship between the restraint of the body and the expressiveness of the eyes. "Models," Bresson wrote, using the word he preferred for his actors, "mechanized outwardly. Intact, virgin within." The job of the director was to get past the actor's accumulation of technique and to strike into this virgin territory. Bresson felt that "the to-and-fro of the character in front of his nature forces the public to look for talent on his face, instead of the enigma peculiar to each living creature." He aimed to get past the talent on the actor's face. "Your camera passes through faces provided no mimicry (intentional or not intentional) gets in between." Like Bresson, Leone's direction of actors aimed to strip away imitative habits. He approached actors as he did the other aspects of his Western, as a restorer, returning them to their true quality.[16]

What is interesting is that Leone, though he often is noted for his "iconographic" way of choosing and shooting actors, selecting them for their faces rather than their acting and for shooting them to match his landscape, generally summoned great respect and affection from his actors. Here again, the parallel to Hitchcock is striking. Hitchcock is famous for referring to his actors as cattle and for telling them on the first day of shooting that storyboarding had been the really fun part of making the film and that the actual shooting, the time he would spend with the actors, was the most boring part. He too ruffled the feathers of him most self-serious actors. But in general, actors loved working with Hitchcock, as they did with Leone, because he made them look good, and not only good, but good in ways that were most distinctive to themselves. "Actors always loved Leone for his way of filming them," says Sergio Donati, "big close-ups, dramatic sense, and so on."[17] Mickey Knox too notes that Leone "was very good to his actors. You know that actors love close-ups."[18] As we have seen, both Woody Strode and Henry Fonda were ecstatic about their closeups in *Once Upon a Time*, with Strode effusing that he had never been granted such quality time in any of his previous films and with Fonda referring to Leone as "the best director I ever worked with in my life." Strode's cameo in particular is evidence of Leone's close-ups at their best — a microscopic study of menace and calm self-assurance.

And just as a close analysis of Hitchcock's career will reveal that, despite all his joking about actors as cattle, he did encourage his actors to improvise and play with their roles, so Leone's actors often emphasize that they felt very free working with him, despite his "iconographic" style of filming them. Eli Wallach said that Leone made the actor felt like he had some input into the film. Wallach felt he was able to be creative with Leone rather than simply "a puppet on a bunch of strings," an interesting comment since James Woods described Leone as "using actors like marionettes" in his films.[19] Donati describes Leone as "an actor's director" and notes that Leone understood that there was an exchange between what the actor and the film could give each other, referring again, I think, to the reward the camera bestows on understatement in film. Leone, Donati emphasizes, "knows how to get everything out of the actors; he does not try to squeeze the actor into a picture or vice versa."[20] This is a different kind of observation than we usually get on Leone and his actors. Here, the stress is not on Leone matching his actors to his landscape, "squeezing" them into his film. The emphasis is on his ability to draw something out of his actors, to expand their effect. Leone would actually give more attention to an actor's presence than the actors were used to. He would reflect on his appearance and how he could use that appearance (Woody Strode's bald head, Jack Elam's wandering eyes, Fonda's long legs and famous baby-blue eyes). He would study their faces in the most exacting of close-ups for the quietest expression of emotion, one that called forth the actor himself, not just his skills of mimicry.

## Montages of Close-ups

Leone's close-ups are noteworthy, not only for their frequency and unusual tightness, but also for the idiosyncratic way in which Leone arranges them. There are several scenes— Cheyenne's arrival at the wayside tavern, the auction for Jill's property, Harmonica's flashback — where Leone unleashes a barrage of decorative close-ups featuring the peripheral characters in the scene. The shots of people in the tavern reacting to the gunfire outside the tavern just before Cheyenne makes his arrival, for example, seem almost experimental in nature. Here we are treated to a series of lovingly etched portraits of the kind of faces one might have seen in the old West, each an interesting psychological study in itself — a nervous old woman, a man washing his feet, another old woman woken from a nap. Leone seems to take advantage of this tumultuous moment to exult a little in the multitudinous quality of the West, as he does in the sequence in which Jill descends from the train and, in searching for her ride, passes by the entire cultural and economic gamut of the West. The portraits in the inn are match-cut to lead into each other and follow one another nicely but there is almost no effort to link these portraits together spatially, or to let us know where these people have been, or are now, in relation to our principal agents in this scene: Harmonica, Cheyenne and Jill. There is a kind of frank artificiality, or intentional naïveté, to these shots, as there is in Leone's indifference to direct sound. The goal here is not realism but a stark expression of the styles and postures of the West, a magazine layout of sorts, the subject of which is Leone's fascination with the interesting mixture, the diverse "types" that one imagines would congregate in a dingy tavern of this sort in the most remote corner of the old West.

Similarly, in Harmonica's flashback we are treated to a frenzied montage of faces, as the sequence mounts in energy, moving towards the death of Harmonica's brother. The quick montage seems meant to match, in pacing, the excitement of thoughts we see reflected in Frank's gleeful expression as he watches his sadistic plan unfold. These close-ups of Frank, his various men, Harmonica and his brother are reminiscent of those from the saloon. They seem detached from any spatial continuity. Like the saloon shots, they are gorgeous and highly composed, though this time the study seems less like one of tavern culture in the remote West, and more one of the savage beauty of Southwest banditry. The images of toothless bandits and gleeful sadism come at us like a rapid succession of Caravaggios. Here too, there is little effort to tie in these close-ups to their background. The definition of space is more Cubist here than traditional, despite the classicism of the establishing shot, with fragments of the scene flashing by in a strange angularity, meant, perhaps to convey the twisted nature of the event and Frank's warped sensibility. This sequence comes closest to Frayling's summary of the way Leone edited his close-ups, "not as the traditional 'reaction shots' or 'reverse shots,' but as a series of portrait studies of faces ... Andalusian gypsy faces, scarred Italian actors, an American with two weeks of stubble. Gargoyles." As Frayling notes, these "portrait studies" are much closer to Sergei Eisenstein's cinema and his ideas on "faces as types" than they are to the Hollywood treatment of close-ups, which is to say closer to the traditions of art or independent cinema than those of Hollywood or the classic film style.

One is struck, not only in these more stark montages, but throughout the film, by the frankness and simplicity of Leone's close-ups. Leone worked hard to avoid the American tendency to use close-up shots simply as a means of conveying that dialogue was coming or simply in reaction shots. Leone did not like to use "a close-up to show that the character is about to say something important" or to indicate where two characters are in relation to each other during a conversation. His close-ups are more expressive than utilitarian. "I reacted against all that and so close-ups in my films are always the expression of an emotion. I'm very careful in this area."[21] Leone's close-ups are not subordinate to conventional editing techniques used to record dialogue. They have their own valor. Leone wanted his close-ups to have the impact and immediacy of paintings.

As we have seen, Leone avoids reducing dialogue to action and reaction shots by filming his dialogue in one shot that contains both people, one in the foreground and the other further back in the screen. He saves his close-ups for when he has something to say about what the person is thinking or feeling. When we get a close-up in Leone's film, it tends to be head-on. Jill, at the auction, for example, is the center of action, and often spoken to, and yet is filmed primarily in isolated close-ups that face the screen head-on. We lose something, when Leone shoots like this, in terms of getting a sense of where her close-ups figure into the spatial arrangement of the scene (although in this scene her position is well-established by far shots). But we gain something in never losing our sense of the intensity of Jill's feelings at this moment, or her immense sense of solitude. As much as Leone's cinema is characterized by a lovely *mise-en-scène* based on, and developing, the long-take and deep-focus vocabulary of Hollywood's screen masters, an equally important part of his cinema is characterized by a raw simplicity and liberating artificiality, which we see reflected in his indifference to direct sound and his emphasis on expressive close-ups over spatial continuity. In this respect, his cinema is less classical than it is modernist, close to the studied artificiality of Godard or the rich angular confusion of Cubist painting.

## Close-ups of Objects and Gestures

We should not ignore Leone's close-ups of objects. Cheyenne, for example, is often introduced not with a close-up of his face, but by a close-up of his boots, with the camera then tilting up or pulling back to reveal his entire figure. Cheyenne's boots open both the scene where Cheyenne and Harmonica unpack McBain's lumber and the one where Harmonica introduces the chained Cheyenne, whom he has just ransomed for $5,000, to the auction audience. Cheyenne's boots are also featured in close-up in the scene where he hides his gun in his boot and shoots one of Frank's men in the face on Morton's train. Boots, along with hats and guns, are one of the most essential ingredients in the uniform of the cowboy, so as usual Leone is taking advantage of items with iconographic weight for his visual schemes. Leone also features Frank's longer and more elegant black boots in a shot, from below, during his duel with Harmonica, one of Leone's trademark foreground/background contrasts, with Frank's legs dominating the right foreground (the shot cuts him off at the waist) and Harmonica's small figure tucked into the back left of the screen. Whereas Frank's boots suggest the classic gunslinger's finicky elegance, Cheyenne's weathered and dusty boots convey the endurance and weariness of a more "working class" brand of outlaw. They express nicely the stoic and fatigued nature of Cheyenne's character.

Woody Strode is first introduced to us via his boots as well. As Strode enters the train station, Leone films only his boots in close-up. Strode kicks the door shut and then settles firmly into place. Once Strode has taken on a rock-like stance, the camera travels up his leg, as it often does in Cheyenne's introductions, only a great deal more slowly than usual, taking the time to take full measure of the short-barreled rifle Strode's character wears in his holster like a pistol, pivoting slightly to the right to note his cartridge belt and then traveling up his shooting arm until the camera, from a low angle, rests on Strode's face, which stares ahead with the look of beatific calm Strode wears throughout this scene. It is the lengthiest introduction of this kind (from the boot up) in the film, the sole purpose of which seems to announce Strode's presence and to celebrate his iconographic status in the film.

Leone likes to introduce his cowboys by their hats as well as their boots. When Cheyenne makes his first appearance, at the doorway of the tavern where Jill and her driver have stopped for a drink, the door opens to reveal only a hat, which slowly lifts to reveal Cheyenne's face. Leone cherished the arrivals of his characters. He loved to draw out and dramatize their introductions to his scenes in any way he could. Here, the cowboy hat, elsewhere used as a framing device in his pictorial compositions, becomes a stage curtain, pulling back to dramatically introduce the character. Cheyenne's entrance is echoed, or matched, moments later when he hurls the lantern that hangs from a runner above the bar towards Harmonica, who is seated at the bar. The light that is dramatically shed on Harmonica reveals he too is hidden beneath his hat. He slowly lifts his face, as Cheyenne did, although this shot is even more dramatic, as the swinging light creates a shadow effect that comes and goes as Harmonica raises his face. These introductory shots of the two rivals in this scene are fitting, considering that this scene represents their first look at each other.

Of course, both of these shots reference the shot in Ford's *Stagecoach* when Ringo, in the course of the dusty and arduous journey, falls asleep under his hat. In this shot, Ringo's hat fills nearly the whole frame. Ringo lifts his face slowly until his face appears and he is able to return the adoring gaze of Dallas, his love interest in the film, and then drops again in fatigue, the hat filling the screen once more.

The menace of Frank's character is often conveyed by close-ups of objects or gestures, particularly close-ups of his hands and things that he holds. When Harmonica, spying on Frank's gang, steps down from the roof of Morton's train carriage, Leone treats us to a close-up of Harmonica's face. Frank then announces his presence by means of the long barrel of his gun that quietly intrudes on Bronson's close-up from the left. The shot is an exact match to the scene in *Stagecoach* in which, during the Apache attack on the stagecoach, Ford shows a weak and sickly Claire Trevor in close-up. The previous shot has indicated to us that her Southern gentleman protector, John Carradine's character, has saved one bullet to spend on her, rather than give her to the Indians alive. During Trevor's close-up, the barrel of Carradine's gun slowly enters the screen from the left, pointing at her ominously. There is something quite disturbing about these disembodied guns, appearing out of nowhere and in close-up. Both Ford's and Leone's shots are characterized by a gorgeous menace, though, as usual, Ford's has a more noble and mythic purpose.

Similarly, in the scene where Jill rummages frantically through McBain's trunk looking for the miniature train station sign that represents the visual key to McBain's dream of building a new town, Frank announces his presence, again from off-screen, and by means of an object that he protrudes into Jill's close-up. This time the object that enters the screen is not a gun, but something much more innocent, the very little toy train station sign for which Jill is searching. The contrast in this scene between the huge off-screen menace (Frank has come to kidnap and kill her) and the delicacy of the object (a carefully wrought miniature, a child's toy) is striking, typical again of Leone's tendency to often wrap his threats in the most delicate of packages.

Leone often sought to express Frank's menace in close-ups of quiet gestures. As Jill stretches out on Frank's bed, he tells her that he has learned about her past as a prostitute in New Orleans. "Wonderful invention, the telegraph," he says mockingly, mimicking the sound of the telegraph while tapping an imaginary telegraph machine on her bare back. Leone cuts to close-up to isolate the image of Frank maliciously tapping. It is a quiet but disturbing gesture that conveys both Frank's sexual desire and his potential for violence. The gesture emphasizes Frank's control over Jill as he essentially turns her into an object or machine that he controls. If Cheyenne is symbolized by close-ups of his boots (dirty, earthbound and fatigued), Frank seems to symbolized by close-ups of his dangerous and menacing hands.

The last close-up of his hands, though, signals Frank's undoing and his loss of power. Leone communicates, finally, that Frank has lost the duel to Harmonica through two close-ups: the first, a close-up of Fonda's face, wearing a hideously distorted expression, the second, a close-up of the gun in his hand blindly groping for the holster that it will never reach. It seems fitting that Leone would communicate Frank's demise through the same means that he often conveyed his menace, a close-up of his hands.

# TEN

# "A Rhythm He Believes In"*: Leone's Editing

## Long Take, Small Detail

Leone tended to construct his films as a series of large set pieces. Leone's editor Nino Baragli noted that when Leone had to cut scenes to shorten a film, he would invariably cut an entire sequence, never within a sequence. Leone was essentially a *mise-en-scène* director who arranged his film as a series of long sequences, each characterized by its own rhythm. This goes for his very musical sequences, where the images are timed to Ennio Morricone's soundtrack, but also for sequences where the rhythm is not dependent on music — the opening sequence, for example, which represents only a musical arrangement of sights and sounds, or the sequence at the desert tavern, the rhythm of which is determined by an interplay of sight, sounds, music and dialogue.

Within these sequences, with the exception of a few moments of frenzied montage at key moments of climax, the pace tends to be leisurely — lots of long takes, lots of highly choreographed *mise-en-scène*. Baragli felt that it was a greater challenge to cut at Leone's leisurely pace, then to cut faster paced films. Movies with fast editing, he felt, are more superficially exciting but more easily forgotten. Cutting at Leone's slow rhythms was more difficult because cuts in Leone's films were fewer and more significant, and therefore more perilous. His editors had to be adept at handling large, less flexible pieces of information. By comparison, Baragli said, cutting excited battle scenes was a simple chore.[1]

As Frayling has noted, Leone's tendency to conceive of films in large

*Serge Donati, quoted in de Fornari, p. 147.

154

blocks of sequences, inseparable within themselves, contributes to a final product more easily prone to errors in continuity. When Leone was forced by producers to cut *Once Upon a Time in the West,* he had to take out fairly large sequences that leave gaps in the final product. So, for example, Harmonica appears early in the film with the bruises from a beating by three deputies in a scene that we never see. Frank shows up at the saloon all gussied up for no apparent reason because a scene at a tonsorial parlor (*à la My Darling Clementine*) had been excised. These errors in continuity are relatively insignificant compared to those that existed after American producers cut the film. Among the scenes cut for American audiences (to shorten the film and make it more distributable in commercial theaters) was Cheyenne's four-minute death scene, so that the film audiences were left to deduce that Cheyenne, at the end of the film, must have been suffering from acute digestion problems.

Leone tended, in the spirit of his idol Charlie Chaplin, to shoot a great deal more film than was needed, so that he had as much flexibility as possible in piecing these long sequences together. Baragil recalls Leone "banging the clapper" as many as 18 times and of shooting 300,000 meters of footage, of which at least 200,000 would have to be edited. Leone shot a lot of footage, says Baragli, because he wanted to have a variety of means with which "to cover himself." There were a "thousand ways" to edit his film, says Baragli and the scene could change dramatically in the editing room.[2] Here, Leone reveals himself to be a much more intuitive director than, say, a Hitchcock, who not only storyboarded all of his scenes ahead of time, but had also more or less completely thought out the ideas and tone implied in his pictorial compositions. Leone would shoot and then later in the editing room fiddle with the tone, making fairly significant decisions at that point, such as whether a scene would be handled dramatically or ironically. Despite this improvisational approach to filming, Leone's final product reminds us of the work of meticulous planners like Hitchcock in its clean and polished veneer. As Dario Argento has observed, Leone's films "which seem so highly constructed are actually very instinctive."[3]

Tonino Valerii also remarks on Leone's tendency to "cover himself" through lots of shots and footage. He notes that among the "precious secrets" Leone learned from the Hollywood professionals at Cinecittà studios was to shoot all sorts of things that you might use later on. First Leone would shoot a master of every scene, then the details of the scene from different camera angles and with a variety of lenses. This kind of practice, Valerii notes, was characteristic of the silent film directors who, after shooting a scene, left it to the cameraman to shoot "a curtain blowing in the breeze, a grandfather clock ticking away, the remains of a banquet table, footsteps in the sand."[4]

This is a telling insight into Leone's art. First, it supports the sense we have, in watching a Leone film, that we are watching a species of silent film. The pleasure an audience takes in watching a Leone film is similar to that of a silent film audience. Leone lets the visuals speak for him and we spend a lot of time figuring out his movies through visual clues. There is a visual game playing in Leone's films, a call for an actively reading audience, that recalls the silent film era.

Valerii's comments also shed light on Leone's editing technique. What Valerri describes here is one of the most significant aspects of Leone's craft. Like silent film masters, Leone would not simply shoot a scene, but rather would break that scene down into a myriad of images, large and small, taking the time to record all sorts of concrete details that he would only decide later on how to use. This technique allows the filmmaker to continue to search for ways to express himself in the editing room and to find means of expression that are concrete — visual rather than verbal. Leone made the same demands on his editor that he did on his screenwriter, to work in an open-ended way, leaving open all sorts of possible scenarios and providing Leone with as much variety of material as possible from which to choose when it came to editing a sequence.

## An Orator of Images

But it would be inaccurate to suggest that Leone's editing style grows wholly out of the Hollywood tradition. Leone's editing is in part due to the lessons he learned from Hollywood masters, but at the same time Leone's editing is far too quirky, fragmented and off-balance to be described as classical. Baragli worked with Pasolini and Leone and he praises both for their willingness to sacrifice a smoothness in editing for the sake of emotional effect. Both directors had enough of the spirit of the French New Wave in them to court a certain messiness or disorder in their films. At one time, Nino Baragli, noted, it was taboo to cut from a long shot to close-up. But with Leone, he says, they did it all the time.[5] Leone loved to move abruptly from far-shots to close-ups and vice versa, without taking the time, as a Hollywood director would, to grade the shots in between, to temper the suddenness of the transition.

And just as he would often ignore conventional filmmaking rules of segueing from far shots to close-ups gradually, so his editing could be at one moment languorously slow and the next quick and violent, as, for example, when Harmonic's luxuriously drawn flashback gives way to the sudden shots of his duel with Frank. In moments like this, we have the impression of being jerked out of slow motion and into fast. As Luc Moullet writes, "In the wink of an eye several gun-loads of bullets are fired, but only after an unlikely ceremonial, five minutes long, articulated by countless close-ups contrary to narrative logic, where no action takes place. This rhythm is contradictory, as is the constant accumulation of vulgar with majestic elements."[6] Leone was fond of strong and immediate gestures. We see the same frankness and simplicity in his abrupt edits that we see in his close-ups. "It does not matter if sometimes there are some wrong cuts," says Baragli, "what counts is the feeling."[7] There is an Expressionist quality to Leone's editing. He is after an art form that jolts and he is willing for a cut to look messy if it has the effect of greater emotional resonance.

So, when Leone was arranging the bits of material that he had chosen so carefully from his great quantity of shots, he would often organize them using unconventional editing methods. He was often indifferent to linking them together in such a way that they conveyed clearly their spatial context. Sometimes it takes awhile in watching a scene in Leone films to understand exactly where all the figures are situated in relation to each other. This is true of the opening scene of *Once Upon a Time*, where the shot composition is often very classical and Fordian, but the layout of the shots, the editing and sequencing is quite modernist. This sequence is missing a few of the large-scale shots that we depend on to put all the disparate elements together in a general context. Rather, we are given a variety of fields of interest that we have to match in our mind, like a jigsaw puzzle, in order to determine how they fit together spatially.

The shots that frame Woody Strode, for example, are given to us in isolation from those involving Jack Elam and the fly on the porch. And both of these sequences are presented in isolation from the scenes inside the station that begin the sequence. But as we watch through a window from inside the train station and see Strode walk past the seated Elam, we are able to connect, spatially, where Strode, Elam and the train station are in respect to each other.

In another shot, we see Knuckles in the background of the screen to the right, and Elam looking at him in the left foreground, so that, by inference, we are able to put the separate sequences of each of these three cowboys, and the train station, together in one spatial area. But we have to work at it. Leone provides us with an architectural game of sorts, where we map coordinates and draw lines in our mind. A Cubist approach to space, it breaks it apart and half puts it together again for us, while expecting us to figure out the rest. It is the farthest thing possible from the work of those directors who like to let their camera sit and take in the surprising movements of the world in its wholeness. Leone is distant from the kind of open-ended, long-take direction which lets the world speak for itself. This is one reason he runs afoul of critics like David Thomson who have a bias for that kind of cinema. In these instances, Leone does not like to let the world breathe. He wants to get rid of accident, to carve his scene so it is molded around the actions, and follows the logic, of his figures. Hence, his figures tend to be revealed at the very spot where they are most gorgeously framed by the world that surrounds them.

It is more important to Leone that his images collide together in ways that are interesting, that they work off each other in such a way as to create drama or significance, than that they are placed smoothly or classically. He wants something more from the juxtaposition of his images than that they match nicely or explain where they are in relation to each other. Robert Bresson emphasized in his writings that there is "no absolute value in an image." He compared film images to words in a dictionary that "have no power and value except through their position and relation." Hence, just as Leone made sure that he filmed all sorts of things, seemingly insignificant things, or things he did not yet know the significance of, with an eye towards making use of them later in the editing process, so Bresson too reminded himself to "apply myself to insignificant (non-significant) things."[8] Later, in the editing process, he would find how to invest these things with meaning. Bresson was studiously neutral and confined himself as much as he could to quiet images. He felt if one image was too strong, it would overwhelm the others, distract the viewers from the general rhythm of the film. Leone probably had more of a taste for loud or photographic images, but he also shared Bresson's fondness for the quiet, seemingly insignificant object — the "curtain blowing in the breeze, a grandfather clock ticking away, the remains of a banquet table, footsteps in the sand," that placed in just the right spot or moment can absorb and express the scene's meaning. A shot of Cheyenne's boot becomes symbolic of his tough, weathered nature. A shot of a pheasant foreshadows the McBains' slaughter. A close-up of the toy train station becomes a touching child-like expression of McBain's childish dream of building a new world in the desert. A creaking windmill expresses the inexorability of fate for both Harmonica and the three men who wait for him at the railroad.

Bresson believed that these "insignificant" objects took on significance in relation to each other, that they were "transformed on contact." In film, he writes, one senses a "visible parlance of bodies, objects, houses, roads, trees, fields." As a director, you would not know how these images spoke to each other until you started colliding and arranging them together.

The film's climax. Not just a moment of revenge but one of shared destiny. By this point, Harmonica and Frank are almost without malice in their understanding of each other.

Images, he argued, "only release their phosphorus in aggregating." A director's style, his "flair," is a result of this "phosphorus" discharge, how you draw your images together; "Creation or invention confines itself to the ties you knot between the various bits of reality caught." In the end, Bresson writes of arriving at a kind of personal rhythm in a lay-out of sounds and images. "A sigh, a silence, a words, a sentence, a din, a hand, in repose, in movement, in profile, full face, an immense view, a restricted space…. Each thing exactly in its place: your only resources."[9]

This litany of the sequence at which a filmmaker might arrive is particularly close to what we find in Leone's sequences: silences, words spoken not so much for their meaning as for their rhythmic value, a close-up of a hand, a profile shot placed illogically next to a full face, an immense view placed illogically next to a restricted space, all sorts of surprising conjunctions of sounds and images, and images arrived at, not for their picturesqueness or their contribution to spatial clarity, but for their expressive power and for their surprise, the phosphorus they discharge next to one another. It is this aspect of his art that Leone referred to when he described himself as "a director of gestures and silences ... an orator of images."[10]

Think of the way Leone presents the final duel between Frank and Harmonica. Extraordinarily distant shots are suddenly conjoined to tight close-ups, scenes of stunning composition in depth shots give way to to flat profiles, elegant *mise-en-scène* is conjoined with absolute immobility. Bodies are broken into fragments—Harmonica's eye, Frank's boots. This way of filming represents a Cubist dissection of space, but since this is a film, not a painting, all of these contradictory points of view and fragments are not reassembled into one glittering heap, as they are in Picasso. Rather, they tumble one into the other in the sequential forward moving way of film, their power residing in how they lead into and follow one another, a kind of surprising and lyrical visual music, an "oratory of images."

Bresson and Leone saw filmmaking as an instinctual process in which you search for just the "right place" for your pieces of sound and image, search "to find a kinship between image, sound and silence. To give them an air of being glad to be together, of having chosen their place." To find this right place, Bresson suggests, is to find, or give yourself up to, a rhythm, to approach filmmaking as a form of music. Bresson urged the "omnipotence of rhythm," that, in the end, "nothing is durable but what is caught up in rhythms."[11]

Similarly, Dario Argento said that he learned from Leone that "films are time, rhythm."[12] Serge Donati too emphasizes the importance of rhythm when he describes Leone's Western as a kind of devotional hymn. Donati, as we have seen, felt that for Leone "the Western was a kind of religion; he invented a rhythm, a world in which he believed."[13] The interesting thing about Donati's comments here is that he describes rhythm as something you would believe in, as if it were not just a formal aspect of the film but something at its heart, something that contains, and expresses the essence of the film. This sense of the "indomitability of rhythm" explains why Leone can, at times, come off as so morally indifferent. He did not really care if the events he was describing were immediately optimistic or morally uplifting in themselves, but he was always careful that the rhythm that carried those events was dramatic and stirring. In Leone's films, the bad and good things that happen to people are just the surface phenomenon implying much deeper and more mysterious meanings operating below, and that can be more legitimately detected in the rhythm of the film than its content. One might describe Leone's goal in *Once Upon a Time in the West* as being to capture the rhythm of fate itself, which does not care if it operates fairly or kindly but, in Leone's cinema, always expresses itself with slow power and majesty.

Lee Van Cleef expresses quite simply the power of Leone's editing in his summary of the final shoot-out scene in *The Good, the Bad and the Ugly.* "He made that scene last, what, five minutes? And all we do is stand there and look at each other across this great circle, with the music blaring on the soundtrack. It's one of the most impressive scenes I've ever seen, let alone been involved in."[14] Leone would dissect a still subject ("all we do is stand there"), break it down, as if he were filming a painting. He would equip himself with a huge quantity of striking compositions and telling details from which he would choose his final ingredients. Then Leone would arrange those shots into a "durable" rhythm that, as Donati said, "he believed in deeply," a rhythm, that as we have seen is rich and mournful, invested with a Romantic sense of loss. The result was what Van Cleef described, scenes where nothing happens, and usually where there is little suspense as to the outcome, but which mesmerize audiences, and do so without the fast editing with which action films cheat. Leone's editing does not so much dazzle our eyes, as so many contemporary action films do, as it stirs our soul, in the manner of opera. There are some moments of quick montage in *Once Upon a Time* (the moment of Harmonica's brother's death, for example) but mostly the components Leone builds with are long and slow. The drama is in the clarity and sequencing of the shots. The final duels at the end of both *The Good, the Bad and the Ugly* and *Once Upon a Time* bring to mind Bresson's comments on "slow films in which everyone is galloping and gesticulating; swift films in which people hardly stir."[15] Leone specializes in swift films that hardly stir. The figures are immobile, but the audience's emotions run amok, through the drama of the images and the musical effect of their sequencing.

There is a point for many filmgoers where action films, contrary to their manic intent, become boring and that point is often at the moment of greatest climax, where the barrage of images simply fatigues us. Leone's intent is opposite to this. He knew that moments of greatest drama were also the most self-sufficient moments, the moments that required the least speed. In the party pieces of *Once Upon a Time*—the opening sequence, Jill's arrival in Flagstone and her meanderings around the McBain house, the desert tavern scene, the final duel and Harmonica's flashbacks—Leone follows Bresson's dictum to "be sure of having used to the full all that is communicated by immobility and silence."[16] Where others speed up, Leone slows down. Hence, his difficulty in getting *Once Upon a Time* in under three and a half hours. The more Leone cared for a scene, the more he recorded it at a ceremonial pace, slowing it down, deepening and extending it. The rhythm Leone follows is one of the slowest in the history of films that aimed for any commercial viability.

# The Dilation of Time

As many critics have noted, the slowness of Leone's rhythm has had the effect of giving the impression that time slows down, or dilates, in his films. The most famous and striking scenes in *Once Upon a Time* are those in which time seems to come to a near halt. In these scenes, regular time seems to be arrested and we go into a kind of time where seconds seem to last minutes and where quick exterior action gives way to a brooding interior feeling. For example, time comes to such a grinding halt in the opening sequence of the film that the sounds of buzzing flies, water dripping and the rusty windmill creaking seem to represent cataclysmic events. Killings in the film are almost always preceded by long bouts of ponderous reflection, and not just those described in the film's final duel and in Harmonica's flashback. Any murder of significance, that of McBain's daughter, for example, or later, that of his smallest son, Timmy, is preceded by an eerie moment where we seem to step out of time, where the characters look around as if they could sense the grim reaper themselves, or stare into each others' eyes as though they had as much time at their disposal as they needed to fathom the motives of their killer or the feelings of their victim. The sound of the cicada gives way to an eerie silence moments before McBain and his daughter are killed. This silence captures the puzzled attention of both McBain and his daughter as though they had a premonition of their death. Leone holds that silence as long as he can, the way a conductor holds a quiet note before a momentous part in a musical score. Moments like these, in which time seems suspended, are frequent in *Once Upon a Time.*

A kind of temporal vortex occurs in the film's finale. Time slows to a crawl as Harmonica and Frank circle each other in preparation for the duel. Leone seems to recognize that in moments of great drama and destiny, near-death moments for example, time often does seem to slow down. Perceptions clarify. And so here he slows the rhythms down to his trademark crawl so that he can register every tiny detail with hyper-clarity. It is in scenes like these that Leone seems most like a Surrealist, aiming for a slow dream-like effect that, nevertheless, expresses itself with vivid clarity.

Leone gradually introduces Harmonica's flashback during his duel with Frank, by gradually closing in on Harmonica's single eye. (Leone's films, like Surrealist paintings, are dominated by eyes and clocks.) Harmonica's eye represents a sort of portal into his interior consciousness, where we arrive at the final, complete version of the flashback that Leone has been teasing us with throughout the film. At this point, exterior time gives way to the peculiarity of dream time, and just as we often have the experience of having dreamed an elaborate scene in a second of conscious-ness, so the rapid burst of gunfire that follows Harmonica's lengthy vision of his brother's death makes it seems as if that vision transpired in only a few seconds of exterior time. Exterior time has frozen and we have entered into the logic of dream time now.

But, within the dream, time stops again, because as the camera pulls back to reveal the moment of Harmonica's brother's death, Leone extends the moment to incorporate a barrage of images communicating the brother's anger, Harmonica's despair, Frank's sadistic glee (mixed with strange tinges of affection), the indifferent laughter and cruelty of Frank's gang. Leone, in this scene, times the moment of hanging to match the moment when one of Frank's men bites into an apple, so that he might suggest the death from off-screen. But there are a good many images between the moment where the man opens his mouth to bite and finally does bite: a close-up of his brother, a close-up of Frank gleefully mesmerized by the spectacle he has created for himself, a close-up of Harmonica's eyes, another close-up of his brother, this time cursing Frank, another close-up of the weeping Har-monica. Only then does Harmonica's brother kick Harmonica away and Frank's man finish biting the apple. In this fashion, time is elongated in this dream which, in itself, already represents the cessation of time. Leone frames one dilation of time within another. He locates the resolution of his mystery in the most remote heart of the unconscious, in a moment where time slows, within a moment where time stops. We have the sense of having penetrated deeply into human consciousness, of having plucked the answer to our question from the deepest recesses of this character whose exterior is as granite-like and unfathomable as the Western exteri-ors that surround him.

Leone creates the effect of time stopping even in scenes where we know, logically, that it has not. For example, a great deal happens in the desert tavern scene. Cheyenne escapes in a shootout, bullies a bar patron and confronts both Jill and Harmonica for the first time. The scene is char-acterized by a sequence of long stare-downs. But when it is all over, Lionel Stander returns to his ebullient conversation about New Orleans with Jill as if nothing ever happened. The way Leone book-ends this long ominous sequence with Standers' comical dialogue, as though he had simply been frozen in time during the entire sequence, makes us feel as if this long sequence of stare-downs actually took place in the blink of an eye, as if, when Standers picks up his conversation again, we are just waking from a dream. Leone wants us to feel, in scenes like this, that time has stopped, that we have fallen into a dream. Harmonica and Cheyenne tend to bring their own mythic sense of time with them and this time has little to do with the more pedestrian time of the bartender's likes. Whenever they show up, things slow down and the air becomes heavy with portents. There is a duality about these cowboys. They are both in our world and outside it at the same time, and so this recurrent feeling in Leone's films that time is constantly slowing and speeding.

One of the essential paradoxes of Leone's cinema is that this director—so physical, so concrete, so determined to pursue an exterior verisimilitude in depicting the West, and so often criticized for the crudeness and violence of his Westerns—is, at the same time characterized by some of the most deeply felt moments of psychology, of interior feeling that Westerns have ever seen. Boorman is right when he praises Leone's cinema for de-psychologizing the Western, saving it from the chatter that degrades the quiet power of the genre. Nevertheless, Leone's cinema *is* deeply psychological. It specializes in showing people caught in reflection, and not just through close-ups, but through the careful use of an array of first person techniques that put us into the mind of a person caught in reverie. Leone is expert at giving us, not just the image, but the feel of reflection. When Jill looks at that train station clock in Flagstone, time, ironically, seems to stop. Jill realizes that something is wrong and this realization introduces a reflectiveness in her point of view that was absent moments before, when she was just a happy newcomer to the West. Now, as she turns her attention to Flagstone, Leone treats us to gorgeous sweeping pan shots of the town, set to the melancholy theme Morricone has written for Jill. The dominance of the music over actual sound makes us feel as though we are locked in Jill's head. We are strangely detached from all the bustle before us, which we see from a point of view of an increasing fear and alienation.

Jill's scenes at the McBain place are punctuated by these moments where time stands still, when she loses herself in reflection: fondling the objects in McBain's drawers, lying on her bed looking up through the lacy canopy or staring into mirrors while Morricone's soundtrack seems to give body to her thoughts. Morton, too, loses himself in contemplation of his Romantic water-scape and, viewing it with him through a fuzzy point-of-view shot, we feel we are falling into his interior world, his dream state. Cheyenne loses himself in the study of McBain's portrait, thinking about this man who is so different from him but who had managed to earn the affection of Jill, something to which Cheyenne is turning his mind. For a film that is so famous for its realistic grit, the new attention it gave to the concrete feel of the West, it is extraordinary how often it politely stops for people lost in reflection and how much it aims to capture the feeling of reverie.

# Translating the Invisible Wind

Despite his reputation for the loud gesture, Leone's editing can also be delicately allusive. If we are going to gauge Leone's rhythm, we must take into account the small ellipses that punctuate it, as small gaps of silence will punctuate a musical score. To cite just a small example, when Morton bribes Frank's men by dealing out $100 bills instead of playing cards, Leone resists the temptation to show us the bribe money right away and in doing so explain what is happening. Instead we watch Morton in a near shot, dealing the cards, but do not see his hands. Then we cut to Frank's men. They were laughing at Morton — they find the spectacle of the crippled businessman playing poker laughable — but their expressions change to ones of confusion as they look down at what Morton is dealing out. We watch their change in expression without understanding it, because we have not seen that Morton is dealing $100 bills. Leone primes us by leaving us, momentarily, in a state of confusion. When he cuts to a close-up of the bills, and when we finally understand that Morton is bribing the men, we experience a small but satisfying sense of discovery. Leone made us reflect a while before he let us know what was going on. He taxed us a bit, made us work for our pleasure. When we arrive at our understanding, we enjoy it a little more for it having been withheld from us. This scene is a small example of what Leone refers to when he says, "I'm always looking for the element of surprise. I work hard to sustain people's curiosity"[17] or of what Bresson means when he advises the film director to "draw the attention of the public (as we say that a chimney draws)." Leone elicits our curiosity by providing gaps in the given visual information — little holes or ellipsis that draw our attention the way smoke is drawn by the opening in a chimney.

Another small moment of gently humorous ellipticism occurs when Cheyenne is scampering around Morton's train carriage, systematically picking off Morton's men one by one. At one point, Leone shows him using the strap which is used to flush the train's toilet as a stirrup with which he hoists himself up and out through the bathroom window. The flushing sound adds a comic aspect to his clever maneuvers. When Cheyenne has dispatched all of Morton's men, we hear the flushing noise a second time as Cheyenne emerges triumphant from the bathroom, and we chuckle to ourselves, knowing, without having to be shown this time, how he managed to descend back into the train, his maneuver just a little bit funnier for having been communicated to us in shorthand.

Cheyenne's gently humorous nature seems particularly well-suited for Leone's moments of ellipticism. At the moment of gunfire in Frank and

Harmonica's duel, Leone cuts to a close-up of a shaving Cheyenne (he has been cleaning himself up for his last moments with Jill and his last moments of life). Cheyenne, in close-up, wears a gently annoyed expression as we see a bit of blood trickle down his cheek. We realize, without it having been shown us, that the gunfire of the duel jarred Cheyenne and caused him to nick himself. But the moment is more amusing for having been implied rather than actually shown. The scene is less crass because the emphasis is not on the physical comedy, the schtick, but the after-effect, Cheyenne's annoyance. (We have come by this time to sympathize with Cheyenne's frustrated search for good cup of coffee and a little rest.) The sequence testifies to Leone's gentle touch. And it shows how an audience takes pleasure in segueing scenes for themselves, in the little electrical charge that goes off in our brain when we have to put two scenes that were shown us together to understand a third scene that was not. These moments represent a curious kind of visual silence, as important to Leone in the rhythm of his images, as pauses and moments of silence are to the rhythm of his soundtrack.

Leone puts his allusive editing to more serious purpose as well. For example, it is his means for introducing Harmonica into the first scene of the film. We never actually see Harmonica arrive; the action of him stepping down from the train is too pedestrian for the first appearance of Leone's hero. He wants Harmonica to slip into the scene like an angel. So we watch with the villains as the train arrives. No one descends and the train starts to depart. The outlaws look at each other, confirming that no one has arrived, and then turn to leave. Only with the sound of Harmonica's harmonica, coupled with a surprised close-up of Jack Elam's character (another chance to register Elam's expression of cock-eyed lunacy), does Leone signify Harmonica's presence. Cut to a shot of the three cowboys with, as the train passes, Harmonica in the background playing the harmonica. By not showing the action of Harmonica's arrival, Leone makes the arrival more powerful. Leone's editing here parallels his advice to actors: By showing less, you can arrive at greater resonance in emotion.

Leone's editing becomes most careful and elliptical when he is dealing with violence. Despite Leone's great reputation for excessive violence, the vast majority of his scenes of violence are transcribed with care and subtlety. Leone criticized the violence in certain films, for example Peckinpah's later films and Coppola's *Apocalpyse Now,* "for not having been shot in a state of complete lucidness."[18] Lucidity could be cited as the hallmark for most of Leone's scenes of violence. For every violent scene that is rendered crudely or explicitly (for example, Frank's execution of the sniveling Wobbles, or Cheyenne's violent dispatching of Frank's men on the train), there tend to be three or four that are handled with a graceful delicacy and ellipticism. For example, Cheyenne's first escape, outside the desert tavern, involves the slaughter of a number of guards. However, this slaughter is conveyed to us through a wild assortment of sounds—gunshots, the whinnies of horses, men's groans—that is conjoined to an Eisensteinian montage of the frightened faces of the people in the tavern. The sounds are so wild as to almost play for comic effect. It as if Leone were referring here to a generic Western shoot-up. The sounds conjure comic scenes of violence, as if Yosemite Sam had just entered the film. Leone obviously had no interest in filming this violence. If anything, he seems most interested in the musical nature of the gunfight, the way this wild tumult of sounds introduces so nicely the close-up of Cheyenne as he comes through the door.

The murders of Timmy McBain and his sister, of Morton, Cheyenne and Frank, all take place off-screen and are communicated to us in a variety of allusive ways. Timmy's murder is communicated to us by a close-up of a gun (pointed directly at the camera) which then discharges, its harsh sound segueing to, and combining with, the harsh sound of the train whistle signaling the arrival of Jill's train in the next scene. We see, for a split second, Frank and Harmonica discharge their weapons in their duel, but the mortality of Frank's wound is suggested rather than shown through two close-ups, one a tight close-up of his hideously distorted face, the second of his gun searching errantly for its holster. We learn of Cheyenne's second violent bust-out from prison, this time from his confinement on the train, only through a quiet pan shot of the after-effects of the fight. This shot not only denies us the violence of the scene but taxes our reasoning skills by asking us to puzzle out what happened by examining the quiet remains of the event.

The moment of Cheyenne's death is registered in a close-up of Harmonica, who rests on his horse nearby. We know Cheyenne has died because we hear, off-screen, his last gasp. Also, Cheyenne's banjo theme allows itself to be interrupted for a moment, out of respect for the moment of death. We then pan with Harmonica over to Cheyenne's crumpled body in the back of the screen. The effect is as if the camera discreetly looked away so that Cheyenne could die in privacy and dignity, as he told Harmonica he wanted.

Similarly, as mentioned earlier, the actual moment of death for Harmonica's brother is conveyed implicitly by the gesture of one of Frank's men, lounging nearby, biting deeply into an apple. This is reminiscent of the shot from the big fight scene in *Shane* where the blow that Shane lands on his opponent is registered not by the image of the blow, but by the image of the nervously watching boy biting down on and breaking the candy cane.

The death of McBain's daughter is also handled particularly elegantly. Leone operated under the principle that the more we know or care about a character (Cheyenne, for example, or the McBain children), the more important it is to not show violence occurring to that character. The event is horrifying enough in itself. He saved his most explicit violence for characters we did not know or like very well, Wobbles, for example — a marginal bad guy, untrustworthy to the very end when he dies literally in the middle of betraying Cheyenne.

Leone intentionally confuses us in the way he conveys the death of Maureen McBain. Moments before the fatal shot rings out, we watch with McBain as a bevy of pigeons burst from their hiding and rise to the sky (an allusion to the massacre scene in *The Searchers*). We are looking at the birds in flight when we hear the shot, so we assume, as the reaction shot shows McBain does, that a hunter has just fired at the birds. (McBain and his son have just returned from hunting.) Only then do we see, from a great distance, McBain's daughter crumple to the ground and realize that the shot was meant for her. The violence of the scene is tempered both by the shooting taking place off-screen and by the filming of its effects from such a great distance. Leone manages to capture the sense of confusion and disbelief one might feel if one was actually witnessing the murder.

Not surprisingly, Leone's editing has elicited much comment for its more literal effects. He is often rightly appreciated for the Ford-like beauty of his match cuts. A shot of Knuckles in the left foreground watching the train in the distant right of the screen gives way to a shot of Jack Elam's character in left foreground, watching Knuckles in the distant right, occupying the same spot for Elam the train did for him. Critics, too, have often noted the clever, Welles-like segues in *Once Upon a Time*. The sound of Frank's gun firing as he kills Timmy McBain blends into the loud screech of Jill's train as it arrives at Flagstone. "You make good coffee at least," says Cheyenne, concluding his scene with Jill. "Not bad," says Morton beginning the next scene, a dialogue with Frank.

But Leone's greatest accomplishments in editing are in those moments where he follows Bresson's advice, "to translate the invisible wind by the water it sculpts in passing"[19] — in other words, to render an action by the effects of the action, rather than the action itself. The idea behind this kind of elliptical editing is that the more powerful (violent or dramatic) the action, the less a director has to do capitalize on that power. In these instances, the director's job is to quiet the scene, and in some cases, erase it entirely and render it only through its effects.

# ELEVEN

# The Leone-Morricone Soundtrack

## A More Serious Score

A great deal of the success of *Once Upon a Time in the West* is due to its soundtrack and Leone's fourth, and perhaps most successful, collaboration with composer Ennio Morricone. Leone and Morricone shared a rapport on what kind of music they felt would be interesting for the background of a Western from the outset of their collaboration. Both were hostile to the symphonic language of earlier Westerns which they found too rich and excessive.[1] Both felt Western soundtracks were too noisy — a busy conglomeration of symphonies, sound effects and chatter that made it impossible for the viewer to hear any element of the soundtrack distinctly. In their noisy clutter, the soundtracks did a disservice to the West, which Leone saw as majestic in its simplicity, spaciousness and silence. "The producers laid so much vocalizing on top of the gunshots and hoofbeats that they lost sight of what the Western stories were all about. All those voices!"[2]

In his interviews, Morricone often laments directors' unwillingness to simplify a soundtrack for the sake of the viewer. "A human being cannot decipher more than two different levels of sound at the same time. I'm not speaking of just music. Physically, the brain cannot receive more than two sounds at a time. If a director mixes in the general sound column the dialogue and the sound effects as well as the music, the human ear cannot distinguish the music. What one hears is a very confused noise." Leone's great talent, according to Morricone, was to "allow more time and more space for music than other directors did."[3] Rather than toppling sound, dialogue and music on top of each other, Leone separates each element and takes the time to make something of each element. He felt that every sound and every silence should have a "raison d'etre."[4] Leone slows down the Western soundtrack as he does the general pacing of the Western, taking time to listen to sounds, to silences, and to let the music play long enough that it could be heard and appreciated. Morricone felt that the music from Leone's films sold well for him in music stores, not because it was better music, but because the audience had actually been able to hear the music fully.

In their first three Westerns together, Leone and Morricone seemed to make it much more their goal to turn the Western soundtrack upside down, to approach it with an irreverent creativity. Morricone stresses that he and Leone shared an ironic view of the West, and that Leone, for all of his love the Western, "never really shared the American psychology, to which he manifestly preferred a more Italian reality — a down to earthiness."[5] Hence, the self-conscious, sometimes comic, very Italian flavor of Morricone's soundtracks, with their Sicilian guimbards and maranzanos. De Fornari feels that Morricone approaches the Western from a point of view that is even more "barbaric and amused" than Leone. He notes Morricone's love of "eccentric instrumentation," his recourse to anvils, bells, whistles, whips, shots, animal noises, his use of human voices as instruments and the way he would whirl all these devices into passages from Bach and Mozart.[6] There was never any attempt on Leone and Morricone's part to conceal their Italian approach to the West. Morricone's soundtrack with its eccentric instrumentation, its drawing from both classical and pop traditions, its wild mixture of references, rivals in its post-modernist feel Leone's own eclectic mixture of references to both American and European cinema.

Morricone's *Once Upon a Time in the West* soundtrack differs from those he wrote for the previous three Leone Westerns. In this film, Leone tones down Morricone's irony and barbarism. There is still that distinct mix of eccentric instrumentation (wailing harmonicas, steel guitars, glockenspiels), Goffredo Alessandroni's clear whistle and Edda dell'Orso's lush soprano voice, used as an instrument rather than a vehicle for words. But as Frayling notes, the music of this film has a slower tempo. It is more stately and the instrumentation varies less. This film seems to move to the rhythms of Morricone's soundtrack, whereas in the earlier films, Morricone's soundtrack seemed to interrupt the film in order to tease the film and establish ironies. "This time," Frayling writes, there was "no 'sproing' of the maranzano, no grunting chorus, no whipcracks, pistol shots or bird cries to punctuate the driving rhythms." Leone wanted to distance himself from the riotous effects of earlier films with this soundtrack, which

Frayling feels resembles that of a 1940s Hollywood score.[7] He was after something much more epic and dignified in this film, less ironic and earthy, more ceremonial and magisterial. I am not sure I have ever heard a 1940s film that sounded like this one but the soundtrack here does represent a more classical approach to film music in its careful laying out of motifs and its careful development of those motifs through reiteration and variation.

## Operatic

*Once Upon a Time in the West* is the most operatic of Leone's "horse operas." Obviously, it is operatic in that the characters are each assigned a theme or motif that accompanies them throughout the film and is as carefully varied and developed as the characters themselves. Jill, for example, gets the expansive main title theme voiced, wordlessly, by Edda dell'Orso, which seems to express such sympathy for her dashed hopes in arriving in Flagstone and to express Cheyenne's and Harmonica's sympathy for her plight.

If the soundtrack sympathizes with Jill, it pities Morton with the gentle, Impressionist piece that accompanies his scenes. This piece has a paradoxical quality, expressing the touching dream imprisoned within the crippled soul of the capitalist. Cheyenne gets an ambling, good-humored piece, the most Italian of the bunch, a banjo and saloon piano tune that takes its time and expresses Cheyenne's warmth, comedy and philosophical world weariness. The piece is so slow-moving that it stops at times and provides Leone with some of his most effective confusions of language and music.

The party piece of the soundtrack, which Leone and Morricone called "As a Judgment," is the theme shared by Frank and Harmonica. It is a haunting and dramatic dirge with its roots in the deguello tradition of mournful Mexican marches that Leone had inherited from Hawks' *Rio Bravo*, played in trumpet and steel guitar, and introduced by the four notes of wailing harmonica with which the character Harmonica always enters a scene. This piece provides the background for the three most impressively musical scenes in the film — the McBain massacre, Harmonica's flashback and the duel between Frank and Harmonica. That the theme is shared by Harmonica and Frank suggests that their fates are so conjoined that they cannot be separated into distinct musical themes.

This theme has several sections. It is introduced by the wailing of Harmonica's notes. It moves to a seesawing horn section that idles in anticipation of the three huge amplified guitar chords that dramatically mark the piece as music of justice and retribution. These chords are carefully timed to the action, sounding out, for example, just as Timmy McBain reaches the door and sees his slaughtered family, when Harmonica appears for his duel with Frank, and when Frank jams his harmonica into Harmonica's mouth in the flashback. Then this declamatory, or judgmental, section of the theme segues into the majestic march which really represents the body of the theme. This section is so lyrical and moving that it is often at odds with the violence it scores (for example, the spectacle of Frank and his men towering over the little boy they are going to kill). Leone's musical themes often question, or complicate, his visuals rather than simply supporting or reinforcing them.

The film is not only operatic in its use of music as motif. Its highly ritualized and ceremonial feel and its culmination with epic deaths also mark it as operatic. Peter Bonadello notes that "the settling of accounts in Leone's work takes on a symbolic function, a ritual act which concludes a narrative cycle and employs music in a manner similar to that of grand opera, where death is often linked to spectacular aria accompaniments."[8] This operatic quality of deaths set to spectacular arias is most distinct in *Once Upon a Time*, where the presence of death so permeates the entire film. In this film, death scenes are extended further, enacted with greater ceremony, and accompanied by more extensive musical themes than in his earlier films. Marcia Landy wrote that in Leone's films, as in opera, "there is also a union between verbal and gestural language and the music,"[9] and *Once Upon a Time* contains Leone's greatest innovations in the movement of bodies and camera to music and his most creative interplay of music and spoken language.

## Music on the Set

One of the most famous means by which Leone achieved his particularly operatic quality of slow, ritualistic movement timed to epic music was by playing the music to the actors on the set as they moved through their scenes. We sense this technique when we watch Frank and his men emerge from the sagebrush after slaughtering the McBains. Their majestic approach to the little boy who is the sole survivor of the slaughter is carefully paced to the music. James Woods talks about the almost childish pleasure he took in acting to music on Leone's set during the filming of *Once Upon a Time in America*. "You always imagine, as an actor, walking down a dirt road with a shotgun next to Bill Holden at the end of *The*

*Wild Bunch* and having that music playing. Of course, it never happens when you're an actor; you're walking down, and there's people gawking, and the guys are tripping over the cables. But when you're there with Leone, it's just like in the movies. You're sitting, looking at the other guy, and there's a hundred guys on violins playing. You go, 'This is exactly like I thought it was gonna be. This is why I became an actor.'"[10] Frayling notes that while Woods and DeNiro were troubled by Leone's propensity for post-synchronized sound, and convinced him to shoot more in direct sound than he ever had before, by the end of shooting they came to enjoy shooting Leone's way more and more. Acting to music allows actors to experience a heightened sense of drama while they act and the camera to capture that drama.

And what the camera captures is not simply dramatic movement to music, as in the scene where Fonda emerges so elegantly from the sagebrush. Claudia Cardinale recalls how, during the making of *Once Upon a Time in the West*, Leone would play the music Morricone had written for her character and how this helped her to concentrate, to "remove myself from the real world."[11] As Cardinale describes it here, Leone's camera is not capturing movement to music here, but introspection occasioned by music. Leone uses music to deepen our sense, during close-ups, of that character's interior world. He often spoke of how he used music to trigger the flashbacks in his films and he also emphasized that these flashbacks took him "to the rock-bottom of my character."[12] So Leone's themes introduce us to the deepest parts of his character. Leone had a strong sense of the connection between music and the interior world. This sense permeates his script, where music often leads characters to reflection and memories. And it guides his direction of actors. He uses music to unlock an interiority, to get actors to gaze within themselves and reveal, for his hungry close-up camera, not an acting technique, but the real workings of an actor's interior world.

And Leone did not just use music to help the actors. Serge Donati remembers that when Leone played the music for the McBain funeral scene, the entire crew was crying real, "even the grips, the tough guys were crying."[13] Leone intended the music to have an effect on everyone on his set, not just his actors. Leone recalls playing music on the set of *Once Upon a Time* in order to help the chief camera operator find "the softness necessary to make tracking shots, as if he was playing a violin."[14] And Morricone recalls that Leone measured the speed of the crane shot when Claudia Cardinale leaves the station, to fit the "musical crescendo" of her theme, which is playing at the time.[15] Leone's goal was to get his camera operator to move to the music, to trace the music in his camera movements. He wanted to implant the rhythms of Morricone's music in all the essential movements of the film.

Even Leone himself was dependent on the inspiration of the music. He felt music should be written before filming so that it could be integrated into the story at script stage, and so that the he could "conjure up mental images of its impact in advance."[16] Among all filmmakers, Leone is distinct in how much he centered his filmmaking around his musical score. Morricone's music leads him to the film's images. It guides the hand of his camera operator. Actors move in rhythm to it and the camera capture the actors' introspection occasioned by it.

## Introspection Set to Music

Each of the principal characters in *Once Upon a Time* not only has his own theme, but his own way of relating to that theme and to the music of the soundtrack. Harmonica is the one character whose music is internal to, or built into, the action of the film. The harmonica that he plays at certain dramatic moments within the action of the film trips off the "As a Judgment" theme. These moments represent a collision between music that exists within the dramatic framework of the film, and music that scores that drama from the outside. Frank and Harmonica are the dancers in the film, their scenes highly choreographed to their theme, though Harmonica's movements are much more limited, while Leone tends to celebrate the majesty of Henry Fonda's elegant stride matched to the score. Cheyenne's theme interweaves with his dialogue. Jill's theme usually accompanies moments of introspection.

Jill is introduced to us in an elaborate sequence set to music in which she does not say a word. Leone chooses to communicate his ideas about Jill here through her sometimes sad, sometimes soaring, theme, accompanied by close-ups and first-person tracking shots. She acts out her emotions to the soundtrack, as in a silent film. We watch Jill emerge from the train with a sense of exuberance and excitement as she surveys the extraordinary bustle of the town and looks excitedly for McBain. Leone accompanies these initial moments with a free-flying saloon piano piece with slide whistle accompaniment, which Morricone entitled "Bad Orchestra," the pejorative title perhaps a reference to the clichéd nature of this saloon piano piece. As Jill begins to worry about why no one has come to pick her up, the saloon piece dies away and we hear for the first time Jill's theme, first its forlorn, echoing introduction, then the sad but soaring vocals of Edda dell'Orso, which seem to give body both to Jill's sense of foreboding

Three of the principal stars of *Once Upon a Time in the West* at the time of shooting: (left to right) Bronson, Cardinale and Jason Robards.

and our knowledge of the sad fate that awaits her. The beginning of this theme is matched to a close-up of Jill. Jill's melancholy theme is always paired with images of her slipping into dreaminess or reflection.

Many of Jill's scenes represent this kind of introspection set to music. Leone is famous for his elaborately choreographed scenes, set to operatic music and expressed dramatically through elegant, flying pans. But is it underestimated how often, and how well, he films moments of stillness and thought set to music, how important it was to him to capture the movement of thought to music as well as the movement of bodies. After the funeral, when Jill tears apart McBain's house looking for clues to the motive for McBain's murder, she is surprised by her image in the mirror. She appears startled by the sight of herself in the throes of greed. As she stops to regard herself in the mirror, Jill's theme picks up gently. She seems to become instantly fatigued and to realize several things at once — that her dream of domestic security has been dashed, that she is alone again, that she has been turned upon herself yet again in a desperate search for financial gain. She goes to lie down on her bed and closes her eyes just at the moment that the last forlorn note of the stilted, echoing piano introduction to her theme sounds. As she does, Edda dell'Orso's soaring portion of the song takes off and one has the sense that Jill has let go of reality for a bit and is lost now in dreams. Leone shoots her from above her bed, tracking through the lacy, black design of her bed's canopy. The camera tracks down on her as she opens her eyes and begins to think again, though the camera never passes the curtain of lace. Through the use of a zoom shot, she is in close-up, but still with the lacy, black material shrouding her face, suggesting a widow's veil, and creating a strange mask of shadows. The lace casts an effect on Jill's face that is both sad and dreamy and gives perfect visual expression to the dreamy, melancholic theme.

The next morning, Jill will be trapped into introspection by a mirror again. This time she is downstairs and has just been looking out the window to see if Harmonica is there. He had appeared outside her door last night; at this point in the film she still perceives him as a threat. As she walks from the window, Harmonica's theme quietly plays, suggesting both his presence outside the house and within Jill's thoughts (she has heard him play the theme twice now). As she passes by the mirror, she is again caught by surprise at her image. This time, she is taken aback by how disheveled she is. She appears momentarily depressed at her situation, but then, after a moment, smiles to herself, as if she has regained a sense of humor about herself now that daylight has arrived. She grooms herself a bit and now seems mildly satisfied with herself. As she bends down to pick up her valise, we realize she has resolved to leave Sweetwater. All of this introspection occurs to a quiet version of Harmonica's "As a Judgment" theme, reminding us that, though she thinks she is going to leave, Harmonica, who is just around the corner, plans for her to stay ("It's not time to leave" are his first words to her) and realize McBain's dream of building Sweetwater.

The only other character in the film who is as introspective as Jill —

and whose scenes also are of introspection set to music — is Morton. Morton has a scene that is similar to Jill's mirror scenes when Frank has left him on the train, guarded by several of Frank's men, who are playing poker. Morton hobbles up to a lavishly framed and distinctly Romantic painting of a stormy ocean scene. Morton had already expressed his intense desire to see the Pacific Ocean and to realize his dream of a trans-continental railway earlier in a fairly expository dialogue with Frank. In this wordless scene, we sense that Morton's desire to reach the Pacific is a kind of rich, internal obsession — a mystical dream of sorts. As Morton stares at the painting, his theme announces itself, the only one in the soundtrack as plaintive as Jill's. Morton's theme also introduces itself by forlorn and stiffly articulated chords on the piano, before dissolving in an Impressionistic piece, the film's least melodic theme, with a dreamy and melancholy feel. Leone's camera, from Morton's point of view, tracks in on the painting so that the scene becomes one of waves and music. Leone's camera gets so close that the picture starts to blur, and this blurriness, combined with the sound of waves, serves to disconnect us from our external surroundings and to give us the impression of being entirely within Morton's consciousness. Leone seems to want to break into Morton's consciousness here as he did Jill's when he filmed her through the black gauze that seemed to represent the veil of consciousness. We are wholly in Morton's dream world when suddenly Leone interjects the sound of Frank's crude men playing poker, at which point we are jerked back to reality. Leone cuts to a severe close-up of Morton's eyes which express an aesthete's frustration with being shocked from his reverie by barbarians. Morton decides at that moment of irritation to do something about his situation. In the next scene, he will offer a bribe to Frank's men for Frank's murder.

# Jill and Cheyenne

All of the characters in this film have an occasional scene where they think to music. After Jill blasts Cheyenne with her speech about how unafraid she is of him, even of the prospect of rape, and then walks away, slamming his coffee pot on the table before him, Leone follows with a close-up of Cheyenne. Cheyenne's loping theme starts up with this close-up. When Leone wants to convey his actors' thoughts, he does not have him speak, he plays his theme. As Cheyenne stares at the coffee pot, we have to deduce his thoughts, but it is not that difficult to do. Cheyenne is taken with Jill. We know from dialogue, moments later, that Jill reminds him of his mother, who was also a prostitute and also a strong woman.

Cheyenne almost looks surprised by his thoughts and his humorously laconic theme embodies that surprise in a bemused fashion. Leone is very subtle in the way he delineates character. He was very careful to keep his script spare. His heroes tend to express themselves in brief aphorisms. Beyond that, to get to know them you have to look at their eyes, both in dialogues, and in scenes like this one, of introspection set to music. In these moments, their music expresses their thoughts and gives body to the deepest parts of their character.

A similar moment occurs in the second phase of Jill and Cheyenne's conversation, after we have traveled to Frank and Morton's discussion on the train, and then back to Jill and Cheyenne. Now they are no longer adversaries but coffee buddies sitting at Jill's table. They have quickly warmed to each other. Jill confesses to Cheyenne all the hopes she had wrapped into marrying McBain ("You say to yourself, 'Why not?' I wouldn't even mind giving him a half dozen children"); Cheyenne watches with an expression halfway between neutrality and puppy-dog adoration. He continues to be stunned by his feelings for Jill. Robards' performance is singular in how much devotion he expresses towards Jill with so little facial movement — but Leone's close-ups make this kind of subtlety in acting possible. The music behind this second phase of their dialogue is no longer Cheyenne's joking theme (more fitting for their initial jockeying for power) but Jill's plaintive theme, which expresses both her vulnerability and Cheyenne's affection for her. Jill leaves the table after a little eulogy over McBain's picture ("God rest your soul, Brett McBain, even if he's gonna have a job pulling you out of the Devil's grip") and the camera moves to contemplate Cheyenne left to think things over again, only this time to Jill's theme, not his. When he had been left to stare at the coffee pot earlier, the announcement of his theme, with its comic pathos, suggested the initial surprising feeling he had for Jill. Now, after this more personal conversation, the music and the emotions have deepened. Cheyenne picks up McBain's picture and studies it with great concentration. Through Jill's eyes, McBain seems more interesting, enviable. Cheyenne seems to be thinking, as gunslingers often do in Westerns, about whether he could ever be a McBain, that is, settle down with Jill and develop a homestead. Again, he appears almost befuddled by his thoughts. He places the picture face-down on the counter as if putting McBain and his dreams (and Jill's) to mournful rest before getting up and taking a wistful parting from Jill. They will not get to talk to each other again until the end of the film. At that point, any dreams of homesteading will be dashed finally by a bullet to his stomach.

# Jill and Harmonica's Final Sequence

This mournful affection of Cheyenne for Jill is particularly well stated in the final scene in which Harmonica and Cheyenne part from Jill. Leone is justifiably lauded for his more elaborate and baroque scenes of music and choreography but it has not been noted nearly enough how virtuosic is this final assemblage of close-ups, and thoughts, set to music. One critic has referred to those shots, in which Leone's characters stare at each other while the music plays, as "stared arias," operatic crescendos of emotions, which are played to music but in which barely a facial music twitches. Leone's camera comes in so close in these scenes as to capture ephemeral flashes in the eyes.

The dramatic music played in these scenes has two effects. It inspires thought in the actors (who are, of course, listening to it) that the camera then captures, a kind of rendering-forth of thought in material form. It also suggests deep caverns of feeling to the viewer that are a rich substitute for dialogue. Leone often spoke about how he wanted music to be another character in his films. In these scenes, it is the character of the person being filmed, expressing what words cannot and what proud faces will not. It represents a luxurious, operatic contrast to the characters' stern exterior neutrality. In scenes like this, Leone gives us a very complete picture of the human species, the wild articulations of its soul as well as the stern neutrality behind which it hides that wildness. He simultaneously takes advantage of film's great capacity for mechanical reproduction of objective reality, and of music's rich emotive expression of subjective feeling.

This sequence really begins as the door creaks open to reveal that Harmonica has survived his duel with Frank. His arrival is timed with the introduction of Jill's theme, telling us that this sequence will be very much about her. The door casts a shadow on Jill as we hear the quiet bass strings that introduce her theme. Her expression, shot in tight close-up (as nearly all the shots in this sequence are) changes from fear (she did not know whether it would be Harmonica or Frank who walked through the door) to happiness when she finds it is Harmonica, and finally to fear and concern as she sees from his face that he does not plan to stay with her — three distinct emotions that delicately flit over Claudia Cardinale's nearly immobile face, and which could only be registered in the tightest of close-ups, given how little she lets on about her emotions here. Harmonica, filmed in a near shot, says "Now I gotta go," fulfilling Cheyenne's prediction that he would not stay long. Bronson reads the line as if it were a line of poetry with descending meter that finishes hard on the word *go*. As he says this,

Jill gasps and the majestic soprano section of Jill's theme commences, giving soaring expression to Jill's great sadness.

The music continues to be timed to the dialogue. Harmonica turns away from Jill and Leone shoots him in profile (as he so often chose to shoot Harmonica's close-ups). Opening the door, Harmonica surveys the tumult of Sweetwater under construction and says, "It's gonna be a beautiful town, Sweetwater," signaling at least some pleasure in having helped Jill settle this community, some semblance of a Fordian feel for the beauty of the new West. As Harmonica says this, Jill's theme is momentarily interrupted by a horn interlude before gathering into the most orchestrally sweeping expression of that theme. This large-scale and least intimate section of Jill's theme has also been used as the backdrop to Jill's first view of the tumult of Flagstone when she first arrived at the beginning of the film. Leone and Morricone obviously meant this passage in Jill's theme to give expression to the building of the new West, something with which Jill (alone of the four principal characters) is connected.

Harmonica's optimistic comments on her community revive her hopes that he might settle there with her. "I hope you'll come back someday," she says with a childlike hopefulness. As she says this, the most emotional refrain of the theme breaks out again, in rapturous strings. The music is suitable for this moment where Jill comes closest to expressing her love for Harmonica. Leone cuts to a close-up of Harmonica staring back at Jill and saying nothing, his expression slightly sardonic, as if he were scolding here for entertaining childish fantasies, but also expressive of deep sympathy for her. Leone cuts to Jill's face, where the hopeful expression that accompanied her words gently withers and is replaced with the hurtful realization (again) that he has no intention of returning to her. "Someday," he says, the tone in which he speaks this word undercutting its meaning and making the unlikeliness of his return painfully apparent.

In between these shots, Leone interjects close-ups of Cheyenne, whose gaze is fixed on Jill's, and whose expression is similar to the one he wore in Jill's kitchen, those same deeply sympathetic eyes set within the neutral, even ironic canvas of his face. The only difference here is that Cheyenne's face tilts a little more sadly, and the eyes are a touch sadder, as he witnesses, and can do nothing to help, Jill in her moment of greatest sadness and humiliation. Cheyenne is the one character who thinks about Jill most and knows her best. He knows where she came from (like his mother), what she had hoped for, how those hopes were dashed. He sees all too clearly her love for Harmonica and feels it acutely. His gaze reflects sadness and sympathy for her and for himself. He would like to have her love but comes in second place to Harmonica. And even if she did turn her gaze to him in this final scene (as there are hints that she might), Cheyenne would not be able to take advantage of such happiness, bearing as he does a mortal wound.

There is a three-part round robin of feelings expressed in this scene: Jill's love for Harmonica, Harmonica's sympathy for Jill, Cheyenne's love and sympathy for Jill. These feelings are expressed with the smallest recourse to words and with little recourse to movement. There are no pans. Not only are the actors' bodies still, but their faces are close to still as well. The bulk of the meaning is expressed through "stared arias"— through something in the actors' eyes that is both inspired by and choreographed to the music. This still alchemy is as great a part of Leone's filmic accomplishment, and as powerful an example of the magic he could work with his musical themes, as any of his most baroque action sequence.

## Music and Movement

If Leone's "stared arias" are often underappreciated, the same cannot be said for his celebrated *mise-en-scène*, characterized by careful choreography, set in precise rhythm to music, captured in elegant pans and tracking shots which themselves move in measure to the music, and all of which is edited with an emphasis on the slow and ceremonial.

Not that Leone was always slow and ceremonial. He could be quicker and more intense in the rhythm of his editing if he felt the drama of the event definitely deserved that approach. For example, just before the death of Harmonica's brother in his flashback, Leone treats us to a manic, jagged montage of all the faces on the scene: Frank, Harmonica, Harmonica's brother, each of the five members in Frank's gang. The pace of the montage is fast and each of the images is posed and stylistic, often with disregard to spatial continuity. The montage here is reminiscent of the montage of Tippi Hedren's reaction shots to the gas station explosion in *The Birds*, almost a homage to the stylish montage of silent films.

But these instances of rigid or rapid editing are much more rare than Leone's extended scenes, characterized by the elegant movement of body, camera and music, and they tend to be reserved only for moments of intense drama such as when Frank and Harmonica finally confront each other, or when Harmonica's secret is revealed. Leone was a director of slow tempos, just the opposite of directors who speed up their filmmaking at moments of heightened drama. Leone tended to take a deep breath just at that point in the film where most directors were losing theirs.

Frank and his men, for example, emerge from the sagebrush after massacring the McBain family with the stately leisure of gods. One man steps out first and takes a position to the left, another steps out and takes his stance at the right. A human portal formed, Fonda emerges with a measured stride that moves slowly to the "As a Judgment" theme. Leone's films are lauded for their balletic quality, but Leone's dances are so slow they are virtually marches. Critics who compare his films to religious ceremonies and talk about their liturgical quality seem more on target. Even the massacre of the McBains is choreographed with such patience and gravity as to take on a sacred quality.

But of course the actor's dance with the soundtrack in Leone's films is really a three-way dance because the camera is also moving in measure to both the actor and the music. As we know, Leone wanted the camera operator as well as the actors to remain sensitive to the rhythms of Morricone's score. The effect of three different types of movement (music, actor, camera) at one time can be dizzying, comparable to what we might feel when watching and listening to a terzet in the climax of an opera where three different motifs are battling for attention and overwhelming us in our inability to fully grasp all three at the same time. Film has the same kinetic quality of music, to always be just slipping outside our grasp, and Leone made it his task to accentuate the excruciating musical pleasure in film as much as he could.

Cheyenne is often introduced in a three-way conjunction of actor, music and camera movement. When he first arrives at Jill's house, Leone's camera hides behind the door that Jill has just opened, registering her surprise at finding Cheyenne in her doorway. Then, as the door opens the rest of the way (seemingly on in its own creaky volition) to the left, the camera swings around it to the right, typical of the way Leone liked his camera to move in the opposite direction of the object being filmed. These dual, sweeping motions come to a halt when, the door fully open, Cheyenne's face fills the screen. And as the motion of the door and camera arrest, the movement of the music begins, and Cheyenne's theme is articulated in the darker intonations used earlier in the film when he is still perceived as a threat.

Similarly, when Harmonica dramatically introduces the captive Cheyenne to the auction audience, Leone's introduces Cheyenne to us with his typical triple mixture of movements. As Cheyenne moves to the spot on the landing he will share with Harmonica, Leone's camera travels from his boots up his body. Cheyenne hits his spot just as the camera finds his face. And at that moment, his theme song announces itself to the hushed cries of "Cheyenne!" among the crowd. Moments like these are not the loudest or most extended in *Once Upon a Time in the West* but they are among the most pleasureful, and the pleasure resides, first, in being moved in three directions—by the actor, the camera and the music—at one time and, then, in the resolution of all three of these movements in one carefully moment of unity. This technique is often used to register a moment of arrival or departure, or one in which Leone has primed us for one of his characters, usually Cheyenne, to deliver one of Leone's trademark, carefully wrought aphorisms.

## Jill's Arrival in Flagstone

Jill's arrival in Flagstone is represented in a series of elegant pan and crane shots that are not only literally timed to the music but which in their gentle stride match the mood of the scene. Jill arrives to a saloon stomp with slide whistle that matches her exuberant smile as she leans out of the train looking for her new family and life. The saloon stomp fades into the background as she wanders around the town a bit, trying to get her bearings. These shots are not really choreographed to the music. The music is meant to express the bustle and excitement of the new world that Jill is discovering. This music fades as she looks at a clock on the wall and for the first time seems to realize that something is wrong, that no one has come to greet her at the train. Leone interjects the sound of whistling wind although Jill is in the midst of the bustle of the town. This is a subjective use of sound, meant only to express her sudden sense of isolation. Out of this desolate silence emerges the first stiff, echoing chord of the piano piece that introduces Jill's theme. This is the point where Leone begins to set Jill's thoughts and movements to music. Jill paces next to her valises until the portion of her theme where Edda dell'Orso's voice introduces the main haunting theme. She seems to be waiting for the central motif of her theme music to begin; only when it does will she pick up her valises and begin her lonely march through town. The moment is very similar to the one during Frank and Harmonica's duel, where Frank waits to drop his coat and start his walk around Harmonica until the central motif of his theme begins.

Jill picking up her valise and starting to walk is one of those moments in Leone where the gesture is small but feels large. It is a touching moment because she moves with such purpose but the music that accompanies her is languorously sad. We see Jill's determination, but through the music we sense her apprehension. This is typical of the way in which Leone reveals, through music, things about his characters that their faces hide from us.

Moreover, it is not only Jill and the music that are moving together. As Jill picks up her valise, the camera seems to wake up too and tracks her from in front. Jill's porters jump to attention also, picking up her remaining luggage and following her from about the same discreet distance that we precede her. The speed of the tracking camera and Jill's march match the sad rhythm of her theme, as Frank's march up to Timmy McBain matched his. In both cases, the actors are moving to the music they are hearing. Tracking in front of Jill, rather than shooting from the side, the camera records her face, and growing fear and confusion, as she plunges into this frightening new world. The porters are an ingenious touch. Following in her wake, they give her a regal presence, as did Frank's men, moving in *his* wake. But the porters also seem to dog Jill. A confused person wandering through a new town is all the more confused when two servants follow her haphazard path. We see the porters' faces and postures with this tracking shot and even they, despite their inferior position, seem to have an intuitive sense of the woman's abandonment. They are concerned for her, as we are.

We track Jill from in front of her until we arrive at the train office; Leone's camera, as it so often does, moves aside discreetly to the right and watches as she enters the office through a door. Then, the camera moves to a window just to the right of the door and films her inside the train station. There has been no cut. After she has spoken with train officials, she heads out a door on the other side of the station. The building now bars us from her. The camera solves this problem by traveling above the station, over the roof (carefully constructed in shaggy wooden tiles for a verisimilitude that we appreciate in close-up) before finding her again, a small figure now amidst the turbulent crowds of the bustling crowd on the other side of the station. The camera is timed to arrive at its expansive view of the town just as Jill's theme reaches its expansive section, mentioned earlier, that Leone and Morricone time to Leone's larger vision of the West under construction. It is a Fordian shot, meant to express an awe at the vast enterprise of starting a civilization out West. This same portion of Jill's theme will serve as background when Harmonica surveys the huge bustle of Sweetwater being built. The melancholy melody of the theme returns as we spy Jill and the porters, small figures now in a fast crowd shot from high above. The melody adds a measure of sympathy for the small woman lost in this crowd.

This finishes the 85-second track and crane shot that marks Jill's arrival in the town and the film. But the music continues. A cut takes us out into the streets of Flagstone, where a majestic wagon guided by white horses sweeps by to the cadences of the music. In its dust and wake, Jill's carriage enters from the left, moves to the camera, then sweeps to the right and moves away. The camera dances with the wagon, tracking its arrival as it approaches the camera, moving back as it gets close, and then following after it when it speeds away. As we have seen, Leone liked this kind of shot, where the object in motion and camera are both making sweeping gestures that move in time to the music, meet at a central point and then separate dramatically. Cheyenne's march to the train that will take him to maximum security prison is shot very similarly, with the camera moving back as Cheyenne passes by, and then tracking him from behind. The camera's movement in shots like these is both elegant and obsequious, and we feel like a courtier bowing before a passing prince. We have in these tracking shots a sense of watching majesty, of getting out of the way of an important figure who does not notice us but whom we follow with fascination.

The final pans set to music in Jill's arrival sequence are from Jill's point of view on the wagon which drives her through town. The first of these pans is to the left of the wagon, the second one to the right. The pans follows the pace of the wagon (which, of course, follows the rhythm of the soundtrack). The images are again of the hustle and bustle of this town, of people, more in profile now, who seem to take no notice of Jill. It is a horizontally moving tableau of a town that is rich and vibrant in its energy but also indifferent to Jill's presence. Whereas the earlier crowd shots as Jill disembarked from the train incorporated street sounds and made us feel as though we were in the midst of a crowd, these first-person pan shots from the carriage are just music and image. Ever since Jill's music began, we have had the sense of being locked inside her head, distant, and a little alienated from the surrounding environment. Wind swirls dust around the town's inhabitants in these shots, and this, combined with the sound vacuum, gives the pans an eerie, dream-like quality. Jill's alienated sensibility here is at odds with the typical feel of Westerns, particularly at those points when they show the exuberant feel of the new Western community. One is reminded of the ways Terence Malick, in *Days of Heaven,* could communicate the extraordinary beauty of Midwestern farm harvests using the cold, alienated point of view of migrant workers who had no stake in the bounty.

These tracking shots set to music, studded as they are with close-ups and reaction shots, establish a kind of sad and increasingly deepening interiority in Jill that will be reinforced by the scenes of contemplation at the McBain house. We spend a lot of time watching Jill think, watching her take in her situation. And when she thinks, Leone plays her theme, as if the music were more eloquent in expressing her feelings than any words could be. The elegant tracking shots in her arrival at Flagstone are appropriate for a sequence which has to be characterized by movement (she is on a carriage) and which aims to visually capture the sweeping nature of a huge community. But the pans are not just utilitarian. They have an aesthetic payoff. Timed to Jill's theme and to Claudia Cardinale's elegant carriage, they are expressive of her elegance and dignity even in the midst of fear and confusion. And in their sweep they take in and convey the feeling of a town that is both disturbing and alienating in its vast bustle. The pans here, like the music, represent an ode to both Jill and the West, whose marriage will resolve this film. Jill had hoped to find a husband at the train station. What she found was the West. Disturbing as its images are to her, she was meant to get off here. At the outset of this film, she is an outsider intimidated by this strange, new world. By the end of the film, like a softer version of *Johnny Guitar*'s Vienna, she will own it.

# Frank and Harmonica's Duel

The duel between Harmonica and Frank and Harmonica's flashback represent probably Leone's most extended ballet, or choreography of body and camera movement to music. Here, as in the scene in which Fonda is introduced, the camera and the actors are considerate, the camera often moving only after the actors have stopped moving and vice versa. The duel begins with an image of Frank in the back of the screen to the left, as the "As a Judgment" theme begins with the seesaw introduction that anticipates those first massive guitar chords that are its most dramatic announcement. As Harmonica enters the frame in close-up from the right, the first guitar chord sounds. The second guitar chord is matched to a point-of-view shot from Frank's perspective, the third matched to a point-of-view shot from Harmonica's position.

After this rapid montage introduction, the camera and the actors start to move. Harmonica, in the foreground, moves to his left. Frank, in the background, follows. But the camera pulls back. As happens so often in Leone's films, a double movement occurs with the actors moving away from us, and the camera, rather than following them, moving in the opposite direction, back and away, as if to give them room and to provide an epic sweep to an important scene.

Harmonica arrives at a spot and stops (he is very certain of where he wants to be, whereas Frank ranges all over in this scene). Frank stops too. Leone cuts to a distant shot of Harmonica. The camera pans to the right to find Frank. This pan signifies that we will now move to Frank's rhythms. Leone cuts to a shot of the lower half of Frank's body. Conspicuous is the coat he has taken off in the heat and which he holds to his side, ready to drop to the ground. Both the camera and the music wait for Frank to drop that coat like race cars wait for the drop of the flag at the outset of a race. Just at the moment Frank drops his coat, the most expansive and dramatic part of the "As a Judgment" theme begins. Frank waits a moment and then starts to stride in time to the music, carving an arc around the perfectly still Harmonica. Leone traces this arc with several pans, some point-of-view shots (both far and close) from Harmonica's perspective of Frank moving, and other point-of-view shots from Frank's perspective of the still Harmonica. But all of these shots pan according to the movements of Frank's body. This is the most dramatic moment in the duel, representing Frank's march to Golgotha, the moment where he is finally going to figure out who Harmonica is and what role Harmonica plays in his destiny. The close-ups reveal Harmonica's sphinx-like neutrality and a look of intense, nervous curiosity on Frank's part.

Frank arrives at the spot that he will choose for the duel as the deguello portion of the "As a Judgment" portion of the theme finishes. The only scene that has matched this one for majesty and drama is the one in which Frank emerged from the sagebrush with his men, the day he murdered the McBains. Both sequences are comprised of the same components: Morricone's dramatic score, Fonda's majestic stride in time to that score, and Leone's carving up of the scene in pans and tracking shots also set to Morricone's music.

As Frank reaches his spot, the music recedes in volume and starts to wind down and disappear. Only now that Frank has arrived at his spot does Harmonica choose to move. This is typical of Leone's tendency to break down the components of a film that other directors layer on top of each other, to pull them out one by one, and give them to us in linear sequence. An actor's movement gives way to a camera movement or another actor's movement. Leone approaches his images as he approaches his sounds, always careful not to inundate our eye or ear, to make sure each of his sounds and images has the space and leisure to breathe and echo dramatically.

A far shot of Harmonica to the left side of our screen pans with him as he moves to the right. A ramrod-still Frank appears on the right. The duelists have now taken their positions opposite each other in classic Western duel fashion and what follows is a series of exchanged close-ups that will lead to the flashback. This exchange of close-ups represents an interlude of silence between the two times Leone will play his central theme music here in the film's climax (once for Frank's march, another time for Harmonica's flashback). It is striking that Leone's film culminates with two musical crescendos. After pulling out all the stops on the "As a Judgment" theme during the duel scene, playing it with its most full orchestration and in accompaniment to highly choreographed scenes of crescendo-like drama, he takes a breather for a moment and does it all over again in the flashback scene. But we are not likely to complain of repetition or dissipated drama because both the confrontation between Frank and Harmonica and the revelation of Harmonica's past have both been so carefully introduced and so long anticipated that they both warrant their own climax. Multiple endings have become *de rigueur* in contemporary action films that are dependent on impressing increasingly jaundiced audiences with the multiplicity of plot twists. But what Leone does here is different. These are back-to-back set pieces or ceremonies, two elaborate rituals, both expressing the power, majesty and inescapability of fate.

During the exchange of close-ups between Frank and Harmonica as they ready to draw, Leone zeroes in on Harmonica's left eye and transports us back to his childhood memory of Frank. Harmonica's flashback has been introduced by echoing sounds of his harmonica, but the musical section begins when Frank sticks the harmonica in the child Harmonica's mouth. This action is timed to the first slamming guitar chord of "As a Judgment," as is Timmy McBain's arrival on the porch during the massacre and Harmonica's appearance in profile at the outset of his duel with Frank.

Next begins the one key pan shot set to music in this sequence. Leone pans out, gradually revealing, in a steady rhythm set to the theme, the elaborately composed image of the brother's execution. This is a simpler shot than Leone's other pans to music, as the *mise-en-scène* is fixed like a Renaissance painting. The actors barely budge. All the drama is in the camera as it slowly reveals the careful composition of the scene. The dance here is strictly between the camera and the soundtrack.

Once the camera has pulled back far enough to show the full glory of the scene, it stops and Leone cuts to a close-up of the sweating Harmonica with his brother's boots resting on his shoulders. Leone times the dramatic deguellos or march section of "As a Judgment" (the same section Frank marches to in his duel) to a tracking shot up Harmonica's brother's body. After that, the sequence is not so much musical in its camera movement as it is in its editing, as Leone unleashes an unusually furious montage of close-ups set to the climax of the theme, which I analyze in my chapter on the rhythm of Leone's editing. The music ebbs as Harmonica falls to the dusty ground, with the harmonica in his mouth, finishing with the same haunting harmonica echoes with which it began. Suddenly, reality intrudes with the gunshots of the duel. In Leone's films, when the music dies the dream ends, and we are shocked back into the much less gorgeous, much more banal world of exterior time.

# TWELVE

# The Music of Sound
# and Dialogue

## Sound

The movement of music, actor and camera represent the core ingredients of Leone's musical scenes. That said, Leone also weaves dialogue and sound into the rhythm or musicality of his films. One of the ironies of Leone's cinema is that his soundtrack dissuades many viewers from taking him seriously because its post-synchronized sound and dubbing remind them of the B-film dubbing they have seen in Godzilla movies and other cheap imports. And yet a cursory look at any of Leone's Westerns, and especially *Once Upon a Time in the West*, reveals that Leone's soundtracks were a labor of love.

Many different voices testify to Leone's concern with, and labor over, his soundtrack. His wife Carla notes that, while Leone did not have a good ear for music and sang out of tune, he was "hyper-sensitive to everyday sounds."[1] Dario Argento recalls first meeting Leone in the mixing studio where he was trying out different falcon cries for the a valley shot in *The Good, the Bad and the Ugly*. "He tried many but none of them satisfied him."[2] Serge Donati recalls the care Leone took to get the right sound from his Winchester revolvers in *Fistful of Dollars*, when, of course, there were plenty of archival sources for gunshots. Leone sent a man to a remote valley near Rome where there were few competing sounds and he came back with a variety of echoing ricochet sounds. "It wasn't electronic," Donati says, "It was recorded in a natural setting, because he wanted air and atmosphere."[3] Leone interested himself in the texture of his sounds. And he did not seem to care so much whether they were plausible or naturalistic sounds as whether they were interesting and had an expressive quality.

189

The gunshots, particularly in his early films, are almost ludicrously expressive. Like the dubbing, they tend to provoke grins in the audience. But they represent the highly charged quality of sound Leone sought and, as Donati emphasizes, they are the real thing, not tampered with electronically.

Clint Eastwood remembers how important sound was to Leone — "about 40 percent of the film," he estimated. Leone, Eastwood says, liked "a very operatic score, a lot of trumpets, and then all of a sudden, 'Ka-pow!' He'll shut it off and let the horses snort and all that sort of thing. It's very effective."[4] Leone liked to mix sounds with music and with silence and he liked to vary the tempo, aurally as he did visually, with languorous portions of silence or music shot through with sudden interruptions and then a return to silence and duration. Morton's dreamy contemplation of his Romantic seascape set to the Impressionistic score that represents his theme is rudely and abruptly interrupted by the crass sounds of Frank's men playing poker. Leone likes to contrast interior sound, often characterized by music, and exterior sound, characterized by the more pedestrian sounds of the real world. The slow, majestic music that scores Harmonica's flashback gives way suddenly to the gunfire exchange between Frank and Harmonica. Then Leone's world goes quite quiet. We watch Frank die to the sound of distant, quiet clanging — the sound of the men working on the railroad. The quotidian nature of the sounds contrasts with the drama of the moment. Frank does not get the mythic send-off Harmonica's brother does. He dies in the light of the day, with the most routine sounds in his ears. Of course, the sounds here are not completely incidental, as there is some irony in Frank dying to the sound of the railroad being built. The McBains were supposed to be buried under these train tracks, not him.

## Sound and Music

Morricone denied the influence of avant-garde composers like John Cage on his innovative mixtures of sound and music, but he does admit to Leone's influence: "Sergio's films did suggest to me a certain way of thinking; the insertion of everyday sounds into this body of Westerns seemed to give new life to these film compositions."[5] Leone and Morricone were in accord in seeing the value of "internal music," music that was rooted in, or suggested by, sounds within the film. The central theme of the *For a Few Dollars More* grows out of the delicate chime of Mortimer's pocket watch and in *Once Upon a Time* the central theme finds its origins in the mysterious wailing of Harmonica's harmonica. The division between sound in the film and the musical score soundtrack is bridged by these internal segues. They tend to make the soundtrack less superimposed, more organic, something that breathes with the force of the film.

But Leone works his soundtrack around the rhythms of his film's natural sounds in a variety of ways besides the use of "internal music." Cheyenne's first entrance in the film, at the roadside tavern at which Jill and Sam stop, is instructive of how Leone mixes sound and music. The conversation between Lionel Stander's bartender and Jill is interrupted by an outrageous cacophony of noises: horse whinnies and snorts, a chaotic beating of horse hooves, gun shots and a variety of men's groans and cries. A silent pause follows and then the door to the bar opens. Cheyenne enter backwards, turns and (as the camera finds his face) we hear the first chord of the more ominous variation on Cheyenne's theme.

The use of sound is distinctive here in two ways. First, the sounds are comically exaggerated. They summon images of unimaginable chaos, which is much more Leone's intention than in providing a realistic aural summary of a gunfight. Over and over, Leone's soundtrack tests the patience of the viewer wed to naturalism. Leone's sounds, like his choreographed *mise-en-scène*, his stylized dialogue, his extravagant close-ups, are more expressive than realistic. Secondly, the sounds outside the bar, combined with the music that follows, represent a dramatic introduction to Cheyenne's appearance and his theme. Leone gave thought to the rhythm of sound and how it fit into, or dramatized, the rhythm of his music. Cheyenne's entrance represents a sequence of three aural components. First, there is a collage of wild gunfight sounds. Then, we hear a suspenseful bit of orchestration, something in the nature of what Bernard Herrmann would do for Hitchcock, as we stare at the swinging doors through which Cheyenne will soon enter. Finally, we are given the first notes (in the entire film, this being our introduction to Cheyenne) of Cheyenne's theme as he comes through the doors, backwards with his head down, turns around and slowly lifts his face from under his cowboy hat until it meets his waiting close-up. The sound effects that describe Cheyenne's wild escape then are not as important for their representation of an event, as they are for the role they play in the three-part rhythm of Cheyenne's introduction.

There is a similar (though less comic) interplay of sound and music in the scenes depicting the McBain massacre. It is tempting to see the musical portion of this sequence, one of the film's most striking, as beginning, when the music does, as Timmy McBain arrives at the door to see his family murdered in the yard. Actually, Leone starts building the rhythm of this musical sequence long before the first notes of music. I would cite its beginning at the point where McBain has just read Jill's letter out loud to his son, and lost himself in a romantic reverie for a moment. He snaps himself out of this reverie and goes to the well to get a drink of water (presumably because of how the letter has overcome him). Leone than treats us to a series of sounds that lead up to the massive steel guitar chords that will introduce the musical segment of this scene. The sounds are given in linear sequence following the Leone-Morricone dictum that the viewer can really only concentrate on one or two sounds at a time. The sound of the locusts buzzing and McBain's daughter humming "Danny Boy" establish a peaceful mood that is disturbed by the sudden silence of the locusts. McBain suspects there is a hidden cause to the silence. And as he gazes over the scrubby land, the creak of the well pulley resounds nervously and is then replaced by the empty sound of the wind blowing through the silence. The heavy thudding of birds' wings breaks the tense silence. McBain's daughter is moved by the sight. McBain is confused, as he still wonders what is causing the locusts' and the birds' behavior. A shot rings out. McBain thinks it comes from a hunter (he is still watching the birds) but the shot has actually felled his daughter. As McBain realizes this, Leone zooms into a close-up of McBain's mouth as he yells, in panic, his daughter's name, "Maureen!"

At this point, the soundtrack shifts into high gear: McBain's running steps, more gunshots, the galloping sounds of frightened horses and then, most strangely, but also most pointedly, the amplified gobble of turkeys timed to coincide with the shots that finally fell McBain. Leone was fond of using the sound of loud turkey gobbles at moments to jar the viewer. Presumably, the sound provided him an opportunity to jolt his audience while staying consistent to his rural locales. But he also simply seems drawn to the comically chaotic quality of the sound. We have already heard turkey gobbles during moments of violence in the opening sequence at the Cattle Corners railway station. There, the sound is particularly incongruous, considering the scene is an interior one.

After this sequence of frenzied sounds, Leone pauses a moment to let us absorb the massacre we have just witnessed and then cuts to inside the McBain home for a tracking shot from Timmy McBain's perspective as he runs to the door to see what happened. The shot of the door, until it opens, is dark and formless so we hear more than we see at this point. What we hear, right on the heels of the turkey gobble, is the sprinting steps of a young boy. The movement of the steps corresponds to the movement of the tracking shot, from the boy's point of view, as it approaches the door. As the door opens, the sound of anxious steps comes to a halt, the camera slams into position, and the first of the powerful guitar chords that introduce "As a Judgment" resounds. The music has begun, but it really has

had a three-part introduction: the peaceful sounds of the picnic preparation, the chaotic sounds of the slaughter, and the single, isolated sound of
Timmy's steps, the percussion of which leads in perfect rhythm to the
music.

This sequence closes with a mixture of sound and music as well. Frank
decides to kill Timmy just as the "As a Judgment" theme, which had already
quieted, comes to a halt. As we look at a close-up of Frank's gun, the theme
concludes with its final note, the sound of a church bell, a sound obviously artificially introduced into the scene, there being no church nearby.
We have hardly heard the bell before we hear the gunshot, which quickly
overlaps with the screeching sound of the train coming into Flagstaff in
the next scene, which will describe Jill's arrival. The screech of the train
definitively ends the aural rhythm of the McBain slaughter but it should
be noted that this rhythm began before, and finished after, its musical
component.

Morton's death is also notable for its interesting mixture of sound and
music. When Frank finds the wounded Morton crawling on the ground
towards the mud puddle that must serve as a substitute in his final moments
for his dreamed-of Pacific Ocean, we hear the sound of water trickling.
The sound does not correspond to the image, because the puddle is stagnant. Rather, this trickling sound is the poor cousin to the sound of waves
that Leone has previously associated with Morton as he stared at his
Romantic ocean painting. Morton's lovely, impressionistic theme, which
seems to sympathize with the mystical vastness of this shriveled capitalist's dream, briefly sounds, as does the sound of ocean waves just as he
dies. The sound of the waves is a melancholy reminder that Morton did
not make it to the Pacific. As he dies, bells sound out, as they do in Timmy's
death, only here they clang like ocean buoys rather than intone like a church
bell. This clanging sound bridges us to the next scene and turns out to be
the sound of men striking railway ties with their sledgehammer as they build
the railroad that will cut through another man's dream, Brett McBain's town
of Sweetwater. McBain's dream, of course, can only be realized at the expense
of Morton's.

The sound of a bell ringing is something of a morbid leitmotif in this
film. The deaths of Timmy McBain, Morton and Cheyenne are all accompanied by various permutations of bells ringing. Harmonica's flashback
clues us into why that is. Harmonica's brother, we see in his flashback, was
hanged by Frank, by a noose tied to a bell. As Harmonica lands in the dust,
the sound of a bell rings out from off-screen (mixed in with the wild tumult
of music and noise in this sequence) signifying his brother's death. So, the
sound of bells ringing is associated with death throughout this film. Every

time the bells ring, they seem to both hearken back to Frank's original crime (particularly in the case of Timmy McBain, his second act of unspeakable cruelty to a child) and to look forward to his punishment. The bells seem mostly to toll for Frank. With every death caused by him and the railway with which he has aligned himself, the noose tightens around his own neck, and he finds himself that much closer to his own demise.

## Opening Sequence

Of course, Leone's greatest accomplishment in a musical use of natural, everyday sound has to be the opening sequence of the film, which has no dependence on music whatsoever and which discovers a rhythm built wholly of everyday sounds. Morricone referred to this music-less sequence as "the best music I've ever composed."

In fact, *Once Upon a Time in the West* begins, not with conventional theme music, but with a sound: the creak of the door to the railroad office that Woody Strode opens. That noise is quickly followed by the sound of the train clerk's chalk on the schedule board and the sound of boots on the floorboards. From that point on, we are treated to a veritable flood of sounds.

These sounds fall into several categories. First, there are conventional background sounds, pulled from the generic studio archive of sounds: the wind blowing, a dog whining, birds singing, a rooster crowing. But interspersed with these conventional background noises are more specific sounds, carefully tended. Each of the three outlaws is given his own signature noise, just as each of our main characters in the film will be given their own musical theme. Leone is nothing if not precise. The character referred to as Knuckles in the credits cracks his knuckles. Jack Elam's villain is pestered by a buzzing fly. Water drops echo on Woody Strode's head and hat after he positions himself under the train water well. Leone attends so carefully to these sounds as to even vary their timbre. The splat of the water on Strode's head is different than the sound the water makes (richer and deeper) when it falls on his hat. Jack Elam takes the time to enjoy the more cavernous buzzing the fly makes when he has trapped it inside the barrel of his gun. These minute variations in sound are not as insignificant as they seem. They testify to Leone's ardent desire to slow down time. He is aiming at a languorousness typical of those moments when our apertures are most open, when we have slowed down so much as to be able to perceive the world in its most minute transformations. He is taking advantage of film's ability to magnify the world for us both visually and aurally.

Layered on top of the background sounds and the three sounds of the gunmen is a third track of sound, the endless refrain of the creaky wind-mill that will run throughout nearly the entire opening sequence. Loud noises (the telegraph, the train, gunshots) will try to assert themselves over and against the quiet and monotonously repetitive sound of the wheel but they will all be defeated. They pass as suddenly as they arrive and the creaky wheel asserts its dominance again. Just in this interplay of sounds, we can see a central theme of this film, the reassertion of ancient time against the progress (telegraph and train) and bombast (gunfire) of man. Men have as much chance of making a lasting presence or of changing the world as these noises do of supplanting the wheel. Leone may concede the victory temporarily to the train and progress in this film but the film's slow pac-ing, its attentiveness to the antique rhythms of the world, attest to an unal-terable movement in the world that, in the end, no human accomplishment can alter.

After establishing the three key sounds (fly buzzing, knuckles crack-ing, water dripping), Leone increases the montage between the three char-acters to a speed that is rapid enough to pick up a rhythm or interplay between the three noises and which communicates that we are arriving at a climax soon: the arrival of the train. The train's arrival here is just one of many moments in this sequence where Leone interrupts the general quiet with loud noises that jolt or surprise us. Leone delights in shifting abruptly the rhythm of his natural sounds here. Elam's character grabs the old man's shoulder with a thud just as turkeys gobble wildly (the same sound effect that registers McBain's death). The quiet of the telegraph office is inter-rupted by the highly amplified sound of the iron door closing on the old man as Jack Elam locks him away. The door comes to a close with a ridicu-lously amplified crash that makes us jump (and is also timed to the film's first credit, "A Film by Sergio Leone"). The quiet interplay of the fly buzz-ing and Elam trying to blow the fly away (without moving a muscle) is interrupted by the huge echoing thud of the barrel of Elam's gun against the wood as he traps the fly. The quiet (and the windmill) reassert themselves again before the train whistle is heard in the distance. Leone, however, cuts quickly to a close-up of the train, and as he does, gives us an uncomfort-ably amplified shriek of the train. Leone likes to lull us to sleep with the leisure of a Sunday afternoon and then fiendishly jolt us awake with noises that are exaggerated in their amplification. This sequencing of sounds is emblematic of his cinema as well, which testifies to human mortality in two distinct ways—first, in its careful attention to the antique rhythm of time, next to which we are inconsequential; and secondly, in its emphasis on how quickly tragedy strikes, how suddenly and violently are lives are

lost or ruined. Of the noises that mar the silence of Leone's West, two stand
out by their repeated use in this film: the loud report of a gun, and the
shrill whistle of the train. The former is from the antique West that Leone
loves, the later from the modern, civilized one he laments. Both the train
and the gun, however, represent affronts to our desire for peace and security. Both represent our doom.

## Dialogue and Music

Leone was also very effective in weaving his music together with his
dialogue. Hitchcock said that "dialogue should simply be a sound among
other sounds, something that comes out of the mouths of people"[6] and
Leone too felt that dialogue was important not only for the ideas it expresses
but for its musical relationship to the rest of the soundtrack. Leone's dialogue is musical to begin with, particularly in this film — spare, aphoristic, often as much poetry as screenplay. Leone was anxious to simplify and
aggrandize the dialogue of the Western, which he felt had become too psychological and introspective. Hence, the hard, tight aphorisms or the lines
that seem almost written in meter and which Leon's most ardent devotees
love to memorize and repeat — lines like "Can you shoot, or can you only
play?" or "Inside the duster were three men, inside the men three bullets."
This is a rather stylized way for a cowboy to talk, the verbal equivalent to
the stylish way the cowboys move in Leone's films: cowboy poetry and outlaw ballet.

Leone's language has then already the spare, musical feel of poetry.
But he accentuates the musicality of his language even more by his careful interweaving of that language with the rest of his soundtrack, particularly his music. Dialogue often assumes a lordly place in Leone's sequences.
A long musical section will introduce a single, chiseled aphoristic line of
dialogue or a brief, highly stylized exchange, meant to represent, musically,
the finish of the scene. The gorgeous *mise-en-scène* of the sequence in
which the captive Cheyenne is led across town to the train that will take
him to prison, finishes with two of Cheyenne's men framing the ticket
window, dwarfing the wizened vendor behind the window. "Two tickets.
One way only," says one of Cheyenne's men, in his best bandito drawl.
"Mmmm," grunts the other menacingly, closing out the scene. The drawn-
out sequence of the McBain massacre is timed to finish with Frank's menacing line, "Well, since you called me by my name." Lines like this are
effective both for literary and musical reasons. They are elliptical enough
that we have to piece together the speaker's meaning. When Frank says,

"Since you called me by name," he means he intends to kill the child. When Cheyenne's man says "One way only," he means that Cheyenne's escape is assured. This literary effectiveness is then dramatized by their musical positioning. These lines come on the heels of, or rather represent the culmination of, an extended musical introduction of great drama and beauty. They sit in a privileged spot.

The same is true of Frank's one line in Harmonica's flashback, "Keep your loving brother happy." In a sense, the entire film has been an introduction to this line, with its many teasing images of the young Frank walking in a blur towards the camera and its extended introduction to the duel. In this single line, Leone explains the reason for Harmonica's revenge and the significance of the harmonica, reason enough to find it a fairly dramatic line. But the line, spoken as Frank jams the harmonica into the young Harmonica's mouth, is also musically timed (as is Timmy McBain's arrival at the doorway) to the first of three massive chords, played on highly amplified electric guitar, that represent the judgment part of the "As a Judgment" theme. After Frank jams the harmonica in the boy's mouth, the camera pans back in slow timing to the majestic theme, to reveal the lavishly decorated *mise-en-scène* of Harmonica's brother's death. Frank's line is a pivotal one, at once the resolution of a mystery and the introduction to one of Leone's most expansive tableaux. It has a highly significant meaning in terms of its words. It explains the film's central mystery to us. But its greater significance lies in its place, the musical spot it occupies in the rhythm of the scene.

Leone is careful to make his dialogue more poetic and aphoristic and to mix it with music, when the situation is dramatic enough to earn that kind of stylish touch. For example, the first time Frank and Harmonica speak (when Harmonica is tied up on the train), Harmonica catches Frank's attention by saying, "Your friends have a high mortality rate, Frank. First three then two." (As we have seen, Harmonica, spokesman for the inexorability of fate, has a tendency to express himself in the pure language of numbers.) As Frank leans into Harmonica, Leone plays a very quiet version of "As a Judgment," the theme that yokes Frank and Harmonica together. While the music plays, the language becomes even more terse and weighted with meaning. "So you're the man who makes appointments," Frank says, perhaps already understanding that Harmonica represents his final judgment or appointment. "And you're the one who doesn't keep them," responds Harmonica, alluding to Frank's foolish belief that he can escape his fate. Harmonica's words disturb Frank and he asks, with a quiet panic in his eyes, "Who are you?" Harmonica responds by listing, slowly and with great ceremony, the names of men Frank has killed, again emphasizing that he represents Frank's fate catching up with him. After each name, Leone distorts the musical theme to which this conversation is arranged in such a way as to convey Frank's panic before this man who knows his past so well. This kind of scene represents a dance of dialogue to music.

## Cheyenne's Music and Dialogue

Leone reserves many of his cleverest mixtures of music and language for the scenes with Cheyenne. In many ways the entire film is paced to Cheyenne's theme. Jill's theme and the "As a Judgment" theme that ties together Frank and Harmonica story represent the dramatic and lyrical expostulations of the film. But it is to Cheyenne's theme — calm, humorous, melancholy — that Leone returns to when his fits of drama have spent themselves. Though the film reaches its final crescendo when Edda del'-Orso's voice soars over the epic image of Jill bringing water to the railroad workers, the film actually finishes with Cheyenne's theme, as the camera pans away from Jill at the well to reveal to us, far in the distant hills, Harmonica taking Cheyenne's body away for burial.

Time after time, Leone turns to Cheyenne and his theme to finish off scenes and sequences. "He not only plays, he can shoot," Cheyenne says, completing the scene where Harmonica dispatches Frank's assassins at Jill's well. "But sonsabitches, yeah," he says to Harmonica, who has just turned him in for bounty money, the crowning line to the lengthy auction sequence. Leone not only gives Cheyenne some of the film's best lines, the most allusive and epigrammatic, he also gives those lines privileged position. They finish scenes and sequences, and they do so in a highly dramatized way. Cheyenne's theme will sound, the camera will pan towards him (often traveling the length of his body, from his boot to his face), he will step into the camera (usually a close-up) and only when all three of these movements (camera, actor and music) have conjoined will he utter his line. This kind of flourish invests Cheyenne's line with an oracular quality. "You don't understand, Jill," Cheyenne says, trying to explain Harmonica to her. "People like that have something inside them." As he says this, he steps up to the left of a post in Jill's kitchen, and the camera pans over and up to meet his face as he steps into a close-up. "Something to do with death." Cheyenne may be the most light-hearted of the characters in the film, but it is to him, the philosopher-outlaw, that Leone turns when he wants to anchor a scene with a certain gravitas. Cheyenne always finishes things with a bang, for example, when he says goodbye to Jill by comparing her to his mother, "the biggest whore in Almeda and the greatest woman I've ever known. Whoever my father was, for an hour or a month, he must have been a happy man."

Because Cheyenne, with his loping theme and his measured bits of wisdom, is so important to the rhythm of *Once Upon a Time*, his dialogue tends to be more closely interwoven with the film's music than that of any other character. When Jill asks Cheyenne what Harmonica "is waiting for out there" as Harmonica whittles on a piece of wood, Cheyenne utters one of his typical epigrams, meant to close out the scene. "He's whittling on a piece of wood," he tells Jill. As he says this, the "As a Judgment" theme gathers quietly in orchestral form. As Cheyenne approaches his point, the music moves towards a climax also. "I got a feeling when he stops whittling," Cheyenne says, portentously, "something's going to happen." As he says this, Leone cuts to a gorgeous telephoto far-shot of Frank riding on his horse into Sweetwater, the up-and-down rhythm of his horse matched to a particularly slow, Bach-like march version of the "As a Judgment" theme. It is one of the film's most stirring cuts and it is so because Cheyenne's line, already a nicely chiseled epigram, is dramatized by the music. First the line and the music gather, together, towards Frank's appearance. Secondly, the very dramatic line ("something is going to happen") is timed to introduce both image and music of corresponding drama.

Cheyenne's dialogue and music work so closely in league with each other that sometimes the music will step aside so that whatever Cheyenne is saying or doing can be more clearly articulated. For example, after Jill delivers her eloquent tirade to Cheyenne upon his first visit (the gist of which is that she is not afraid of him or his men, not even of the prospect of rape or murder), she slams down the coffee that he has forced her to make him. As she walks away, the camera rests on Cheyenne as he stares at the coffee pot before and reflects on what he just saw. His theme song begins, as it does in Leone's films, when people lose themselves in thought, and he wants to express musically the general tenor of their thoughts. The theme, however, does not get much of a chance to develop. Just before it reaches the end of its first bar, Leone stops it, to give room for Cheyenne's deep sigh. It is not at all a natural moment for cutting the music. "Do you make good coffee at least?" Cheyenne asks in frustration. The sigh Leone makes room for by stopping the soundtrack is the articulation of Cheyenne's concession to Jill. "All right," he seems to say, "I'll settle for a cup of coffee."

Another example of the way Leone interrupts Cheyenne's theme when he wants to accentuate Cheyenne's thoughts occurs when Jill and Cheyenne are watching the railroad workers, while they wait for Harmonica and Frank to duel. "You know what I would do if I was you?" Cheyenne tells

Jill (in a near shot from the point of view of the window he is looking out of). "I'd go down and give those boys a drink." At this point, Jill approaches the window, stands next to Cheyenne and looks out the window with him, pondering his words as if they were quite significant in meaning. She seems to be contemplating, for the first time, the role that awaits her once Cheyenne and Harmonica leave. "You can't imagine how happy it makes a man to see a woman like you," says Cheyenne wistfully, "just to look at her." Cheyenne's advice gets more wry ("and if one of them should pat your behind...") before Leone makes the surprising decision to cut the musical theme that has heretofore been accompanying the dialogue, so that Cheyenne's next line ("just make believe it's nothing") can resonate in silence. After this one line, the music recommences, though only long enough for Cheyenne to express the epigram to these sentiments, "They earned it," the words to which the music and the scene finishes. As usual, Cheyenne gets the final word in this scene and, as usual, Leone chooses to resolve his scene in accordance to the tired, world-weary rhythms of Cheyenne's theme.

This scene represents a fairly specific dance between soundtrack and dialogue. If Leone cut the music so that one line of dialogue ("just make believe it's nothing") would be amplified, then it must have been an important line to him, and, indeed, it is a line that is pregnant with meaning. Cheyenne, as we have seen, was attracted enough to Jill to fantasize some about settling down with her. But this dream is lost to him, both because he is too much the gunslinger to ever settle down, and because he has been wounded mortally. He feels Jill's beauty, and all that is lost to him acutely in this scene and seems to transpose his feelings on to the men he leaves behind, encouraging Jill to take care of them and treat them with patience. It the same kind of attitude *he* would have appreciated from this woman the film has made clear he sees as a mother figure of sorts. But by advising Jill to "make believe it's nothing," he is also telling Jill to be strong and keep a sense of humor in the lonely life that lies ahead of her.

The line will be repeated at the end of the long sequence in which Harmonica takes leave of Jill and Cheyenne. As Jill stares longingly at the doorway through which Harmonica has just departed, Cheyenne comes up from behind her and surprises her by patting her on the behind. "Just make believe it's nothing," he reminds her. Now the words seem to pertain more to Jill than to the men of the railway. Cheyenne is advising Jill here to let her feelings for Harmonica go. It is as important to take her own feelings lightly.

In moments like these, the Leone-Donati script, by virtue of its suggestiveness and allusiveness, seems to express meanings beyond the scene at hand. Here, the tired Cheyenne seems to suggest that the best approach to love is to not expect too much or to be too judgmental of others. It is a sentiment, in Leone's mind, worthy of its own framing and so the soundtrack steps aside just long enough for the line to echo and find its resonance. What is the best way to deal with loss? Just make believe "it's nothing."

Leone pointedly interrupts Cheyenne's theme music one final time — at the moment of his death. He interrupts the theme, which is accompanying Cheyenne's death throes, just long enough to record the sound (Cheyenne is off-screen) of Cheyenne's body falling to the ground and a moment of silence after. Then he once more picks up the theme, but again only briefly, here only to register one final note. No need to explain the interruption here. The cessation of the music represents the cessation of Cheyenne's life. The interruption occurring before the finish of the tune captures the randomness of death, though Leone insists on finishing on providing the theme's last note out of respect to Cheyenne. Here, Leone provides a small ellipsis in the soundtrack that provides both a quiet place for Cheyenne to die and for us to pay our respects.

Cheyenne's slow, loping theme reflects his calm, tired, humorous and philosophical personality. The theme has a slow doggedness to it. It keeps getting interrupted and then returning, right to the end when it sounds the film's final moments. Frank and Harmonica's story is the most dramatic in the film. The greatest amount of sympathy for a character is poured out through Jill's theme. But the film's dramatic themes are couched in the laconic rhythms of Cheyenne's theme. It was with Cheyenne's roguish charm that Leone most identified. It is often under-emphasized, especially by those critics who fault or praise Leone for his operatic bombast, that this film, in the long run, is paced to the loping, world-weary rhythms of Cheyenne.

# Chapter Notes

## One. Defending Leone

1. Bill Krohn, "La Planète Leone," *Cahiers du Cinéma* 422 (July-August 1989): 11. (Translation mine.)

2. Christopher Frayling, *Sergio Leone: Something to Do with Death* (London: Faber and Faber, 2000), 181–82.

3. Mario Patry, "Il était une fois dans l'Ouest: 25 ans après le choc," *Sequences* 166 (September-October, 1993), 65. (Translation mine.)

4. Frayling, *Something to Do,* 332.

5. Frayling, *Something to Do,* 181.

6. Frayling, *Something to Do,* 293.

7. Frayling, *Something to Do,* 294.

8. Cenk Kiral, "An Exclusive Interview with Mickey Knox," on Kiral's website, *FistfulofLeone.com*, April 9, 1998, p. 2.

9. Bernardo Bertolucci, "Once Upon a Time in Italy," *Film Comment* 25 (July-August, 1984), 78.

10. Cenk Kiral, "The Good, the Bad, and Luciano Vincenzoni," interview with Vincenzoni on Kiral's website, *FistfulofLeone.com*, September 1998, 15.

11. This film was originally given the ludicrous title in English of *Duck You Sucker.* The best title of the film, closest to Leone's intentions, is the French title, *Il était une fois une révolution,* or *Once Upon a Time in the Revolution.* This title allows us to reflect on the film as part of a trilogy of fairy tales (the others are *Once Upon a Time in the West* and *Once Upon a Time in America*).

12. D. Nicholls, "Once Upon a Time in Italy," *Sight and Sound* 50, no. 1 (Winter 1980-81), 49.

13. Frayling, *Something to Do,* 77.

14. Cenk Kiral interview with Vincenzoni, p. 15.

15. Frayling, *Something to Do,* 476.

16. Bertolucci, "Once Upon a Time in Italy," 78.

17. Cenk Kiral interview with Vincenzoni, 15.

18. Cenk Kiral interveiw with Vincenzoni, 14.

19. Cenk Kiral interview with Christopher Frayling, on Kiral's website, *Fistfulof Leone.com,* May 17, 2002, 7.

20. John Boorman, *Money into Light–A Diary* (London: Faber and Faber, 1985), 22–23.

21. Gian Lhassa, *Seul au monde dans le Western Italien* (Mariembourg: Grand Angle, 1983), 201–14.

22. Oreste De Fornari, *Sergio Leone: The Great Italian Dream of Legendary America* (Rome: Gremese, 1997), 147.

23. Sergio Leone, "Il était une fois…," *Cahiers du Cinéma* 422 (July-August, 1989), 18.

24. De Fornari, *Sergio Leone,* 143.

25. Frayling, *Something to Do,* 154.

26. Leone, "Il était une fois," 18.

27. Patry, "Il était une fois," 65.

28. Patry, "Il était une fois," 65.

29. Frayling, *Something to Do,* 194.

30. Cenk Kiral interview with Mickey Knox, 15.

31. De Fornari, *Sergio Leone,* 136.

32. Luc Moullet, "Who Betrayed the

Italian Cinema," in Oreste De Fornari, *Sergio Leone: The Great Italian Dream of Legendary America* (Rome: Gremese, 1997), 7.

    33. Boorman, *Money into Light*, 23.

## Two. *Once Upon a Time in the West:* The Meta-Western

    1. Oreste De Fornari, *Sergio Leone: The Great Italian Dream of Legendary America* (Rome: Gramese, 1997), 9.

    2. Christopher Frayling, *Sergio Leone: Something to Do with Death* (London: Faber and Faber, 2000), 492.

    3. Frayling, *Something to Do*, 300.

    4. John Boorman, *Money into Light — A Diary* (London: Faber and Faber, 1985), 22–23.

    5. Mario Patry, "Il était une fois dans l'Ouest: 25 ans après le choc," *Sequences* 166 (September-October, 1993), 66. (Translation mine.)

    6. Christopher Frayling, *Spaghetti Westerns: Cowboys and Europeans from Karl May to Sergio Leone* (New York: St. Martin's Press, 1981), 194.

    7. Thompson, "Leonesque," 26–30.

    8. Frayling, *Something to Do*, 300.

    9. Patry, "Il était une fois dans l'Ouest," 65. (Translation mine.)

    10. Frayling, *Something to Do*, 321.

    11. Frayling, *Something to Do*, 109.

    12. Noel Simsolo, *Conversations avec Sergio Leone* (Paris: Stock, 1987), 112–14.

    13. Frayling, *Something to Do*, 138.

    14. Patry, "Il était une fois dans l'Ouest," 65.

    15. Frayling, *Something to Do*, 488.

    16. De Fornari, *Sergio Leone*, 139.

    17. Frayling, *Something to Do*, 253.

    18. Frayling, *Something to Do*, 255–56.

    19. Frayling, *Spaghetti Westerns*, 147–150.

    20. Bill Krohn, "La Planète Leone," *Cahiers du Cinéma* 422 (July-August, 1989), 13.

    21. Mario Patry, "Il était une fois ... Sergio Leone," *Sequences* 207 (March-April, 2000), 24.

    22. Frayling, *Something to Do*, 265.

    23. De Fornari, *Sergio Leone*, 7.

    24. Frayling, *Something to Do*, 47.

    25. Frayling, *Something to Do*, 256.

    26. Frayling, *Something to Do*, 255.

    27. Frayling, *Something to Do*, 255.

    28. Robert C. Cumbrow, *Once Upon a Time: The Films of Sergio Leone* (Metuchen, New Jersey: Scarecrow Press, 1987) 65.

    29. Stuart Kaminsky, "The Grotesque West of Sergio Leone," *Take One* 3, vol. 9 (January-February 1972), 26.

    30. Kaminsky, "The Grotesque West," 28.

    31. Sergio Leone, "Il était une fois...," *Cahiers du Cinéma* 422 (July-August, 1989), 19.

    32. Leone, "Il était une fois...," 19.

    33. Gilles Lambert, *Les bons, les sales, les méchants et les propres de Sergio Leone* (Paris: Solar, 1976), 56–58.

    34. Frayling, *Something to Do*, 181.

## Three. Ford and *Once Upon a Time in the West*

    1. Christopher Frayling, *Something to Do with Death* (London: Faber and Faber, 2000), 266.

    2. Sergio Leone, "John Ford," *Cahiers du Cinéma* 422 (July-August, 1989), 14–15.

    3. Leone, "John Ford," 14–15.

    4. Frayling, *Something to Do*.

    5. Edward Buscombe and Roberta E. Pearson, "John Ford and Monument Valley," in *Back in the Saddle Again: New Essays on the Western* (London: British Film Institute, 1998), 160–67.

    6. Leone, "John Ford," 14–15.

    7. Frayling, *Something to Do*, 260.

    8. Frayling, *Something to Do*, 306.

    9. Oreste De Fornari, *Sergio Leone: The Great Italian Dream of Legendary America* (Rome: Gremese, 1997), 21.

    10. Sergio Leone, "John Ford," 14–15.

    11. Sergio Leone, "John Ford," 14–15.

    12. Frayling, *Something to Do*, 258.

    13. Frayling, *Something to Do*, 321.

    14. Robert C. Cumbow, *Once Upon a Time: The Films of Sergio Leone* (Metuchen, New Jersey: Scarecrow Press, 1987), 66.

    15. Cenk Kiral, "An Exclusive Interview

with Mickey Knox," published on Kiral's website, *FistfulofLeone.com,* April 19, 1998.
16. De Fornari, *Sergio Leone,* 142.
17. De Fornari, *Sergio Leone,* 76.
18. Frayling, *Something to Do,* 269.
19. De Fornari, *Sergio Leone,* 19.
20. Frayling, *Something to Do,* 271.
21. Woody Strode, *Goal Dust* (New York: Madison Books, 1990), 233–37.
22. Cenk Kiral, "An Exclusive Interview with Mickey Knox"
23. Frayling, *Something to Do,* 342.

# Four. Harmonica and Cheyenee

1. Robert Cumbow, *Once Upon a Time: The Films of Sergio Leone* (Metuchen, New Jersey: Scarecrow Press, 1987), 71.
2. Christopher Frayling, *Sergio Leone: Something to Do with Death* (London: Faber and Faber, 2000), 274.
3. Oreste De Fornari, *Sergio Leone: The Great Italian Dream of Legendary America* (Rome: Gremese, 1997), 156.
4. Cumbow, *Once Upon a Time,* 77.
5. De Fornari, 147.
6. Noel Simsolo, *Conversations avec Sergio Leone* (Paris: Stock, 1987), 131–32.
7. Stuart Kaminsky, "The Grotesque West of Sergio Leone," *Take One* 3, vol. 9. (January-February, 1972), 28.
8. Frayling, *Something to Do,* 276.
9. Simsolo, 146–47.
10. D. Nicholls, "Once Upon a Time in Italy," *Sight and Sound* 50, no. 1 (Winter 1980-81), 48.
11. De Fornari, *Sergio Leone,* 73.
12. De Fornari, *Sergio Leone,* 19.

# Five. Jill

1. Christopher Frayling, *Sergio Leone: Something to Do with Death* (London: Faber and Faber, 2000), 261.
2. Frayling, *Something to Do,* 263.
3. Robert Cumbow, *Once Upon a Time: The Films of Sergio Leone* (Metuchen, New Jersey: Scarecrow Press, 1987), 72.
4. Noel Simsolo, "Notes sur le westerns

de Sergio Leone," *Image et Son: Revue de Cinéma* 275 (September, 1973), p. 34.
5. Christopher Frayling, *Spaghetti Westerns: Cowboys and Europeans from Karl May to Sergio Leone* (New York: St. Martin's Press, 1981), 202.
6. Frayling, *Spaghetti Westerns,* 129–30.
7. Frayling, *Something to Do,* 261.
8. Frayling, *Something to Do,* 261.
9. Frayling, *Something to Do,* 263.
10. Marcia Landy, "'Which Way Is America?' Americanism and the Italian Western," *Boundary* 2 (Spring 1996), 53.
11. D. Nicholls, "Once Upon a Time in Italy," *Sight and Sound* 50, vol. 1 (Winter 1980-81), 48.
12. Frayling, *Something to Do,* 263–64.

# Six. Morton and the Politics of *Once Upon a Time in the West*

1. Oreste De Fornari, *Sergio Leone: The Great Italian Dream of Legendary America* (Rome: Gremese, 1997), 79.
2. De Fornari, *Sergio Leone,* 23.
3. Noel Simsolo, *Conversations avec Sergio Leone* (Paris: Stock, 1987), 149.
4. Christopher Frayling, *Sergio Leone: Something to Do with Death* (London: Faber and Faber, 2000), 305.
5. De Fornari, *Sergio Leone,* 22–23.
6. Noel Simsolo, "Sergio Leone," "Il était une fois en Amérique," *La Revue du Cinéma,* no. 395, (June 1984), 56.
7. Sergio Leone, "Il était une fois," *Cahiers du Cinéma,* no. 422 (July-August, 1989), 19.
8. Frayling, *Something to Do,* 332, 306.
9. Frayling, *Something to Do,* 205, 306.
10. Frayling, *Something to Do,* 23.
11. Christopher Frayling, *Spaghetti Westerns: Cowboys and Europeans from Karl May to Sergio Leone* (New York: St. Martin's Press, 1981), 65.
12. Cenk Kiral, "More than a Fistful of Interview with Professor Christopher Frayling on Sergio Leone," article from Kiral's website *FistfulofLeone.com,* 3.
13. Sergio Leone, "I'm a Director of Ges-

tures and Silences," *American Film*, no. 14 (September, 1989), 31.

14. Leone, "Director of Gestures," 31.

15. Frayling, *Something to Do*, 24.

16. D. Nicholls, "Once Upon a Time in Italy," *Sight and Sound* 50, no. 1 (Winter 1980-81), 49.

17. Frayling, *Something to Do*, 251.

18. Nicholls, "Once Upon a Time in Italy," 48.

19. Frayling, *Spaghetti Westerns*, 195.

20. Frayling, *Something to Do*, 351.

21. Nicholls, "Once Upon a Time in Italy," 47, 49.

22. Nicholls, "Once Upon a Time in Italy," 47.

## Seven. A Neo-Realist Fairy Tale, Leone's Set Design

1. Oreste De Fornari, *Sergio Leone: The Great Italian Dream of Legendary America* (Rome: Gremese, 1997), 160.

2. Robert Bresson, *Notes on the Cinematographer* (London: Quartet Books, 1986), 86.

3. Christopher Frayling, *Sergio Leone: Something to Do with Death* (London: Faber and Faber, 2000), 232.

4. Frayling, *Something to Do*, 290–91.

5. Pete Hamill, "Once Upon a Time in America," *American Film* 54 (June, 1984), 20–29; Frayling, *Something to Do*, 456.

6. Gilles Lambert, *Les bons, les sales, les méchants et les propres de Sergio Leone* (Paris: Solar, 1976), 12–13.

7. Cenk Kiral, "An Exclusive Interview with Mickey Knox," published on Kiral's website, *FistfulofLeone.com*, 13.

8. Frayling, *Something to Do*, 354.

9. Oreste De Fornari, *Sergio Leone*, 143.

10. Noel Simsolo, "Sergio Leone Talks," *Take One* 3, no. 9 (January-February, 1972), 31.

11. De Fornari, *Sergio Leone*, 143.

12. Frayling, *Something to Do*, 292.

13. Kiral, Knox Interview, 13.

14. Frayling, *Something to Do*, 286, 289.

15. Christopher Frayling, *Spaghetti Westerns: Cowboys and Europeans from Karl May to Sergio Leone* (New York: St. Martin's Press, 1981), 59–60.

16. Frayling, *Something to Do*, 190, 158, 143.

17. De Fornari, *Sergio Leone*, 21.

18. Frayling, *Something to Do*, 289.

19. De Fornari, *Sergio Leonei, 160*.

20. Frayling, *Something to Do*, 289.

21. Frayling, *Something to Do*, 192.

22. Frayling, *Something to Do*, 287.

23. Simsolo, "Sergio Leone Talks," 31.

24. Frayling, *Spaghetti Westerns*, 212.

## Eight. Composition

1. Noel Simsolo, "Sergio Leone Talks," *Take One* 3, no. 9 (January-February, 1972), 30.

2. Christopher Frayling, *Sergio Leone: Something to Do with Death* (London: Faber and Faber, 2000), 234.

3. Oreste De Fornari, *Sergio Leone: The Great Italian Dream of Legendary America* (Rome: Gremese, 1997), 145.

4. Jonathen Rosenbaum, ed., *This Is Orson Welles: Orson Welles and Peter Bogdanovich* (New York: Harper Collins, 1992), 203.

## Nine. Leone's Close-Ups

1. Christopher Frayling, *Sergio Leone: Something to Do with Death* (London: Faber and Faber, 2000), 267.

2. Oreste De Fornari, *Sergio Leone: The Great Italian Dream of Legendary America* (Rome: Gremese, 1997), 155.

3. Robert Bresson, *Notes on the Cinematographer* (New York: Quartet Books, 1986), 12.

4. Guy Braucourt, "Interview with Sergio Leone," *Cinema* 69, (November, 1969), 86–90.

5. Frayling, *Something to Do*, 237.

6. Noel Simsolo, *Conversations avec Sergio Leone* (Paris: Stock, 1987), 144–45.

7. Bresson, *Notes*, 12, 82, 97, 112.

8. De Fornari, *Sergio Leone*, 143.

9. Frayling, *Something to Do*, 194.

10. Simsolo, 155.

11. François Truffaut, *Hitchcock* (New York: Touchstone, 1983), 313.

12. Noel Simsolo, "Sergio Leone Talks," *Take One* 3, no. 9 (January-February, 1972), 27–28.

13. Truffaut, *Hitchcock*, 189.

14. Frayling, *Something to Do*, 342.

15. Simsolo, 158.

16. Bresson, *Notes*, 17, 33, 73–74, 77.

17. Cenk Kiral, "Face to Face with Sergio Donati," published on Kiral's website *FistfulofLeone.com*, January 1999, 7.

18. Cenk Kiral, "An Exclusive Interview with Mickey Knox," published on Kiral's website *FistfulofLeone.com*, April 1998, 6.

19. Frayling, *Something to Do*, 224, 442.

20. De Fornari, *Sergio Leone*, 147.

21. Simsolo, "Leone Talks," 29–30.

## Ten. "A Rhythm He Believes In": Leone's Editing

1. Oreste De Fornari, *Sergio Leone: The Great Italian Dream of Legendary America* (Rome: Gremese, 1997), 136.

2. De Fornari, *Sergio Leone*, 136.

3. De Fornari, *Sergio Leone*, 135.

4. De Fornari, *Sergio Leone*, 156.

5. De Fornari, *Sergio Leone*, 136.

6. Luc Moullet, "Who Betrayed the Italian Cinema," in De Fornari, *Sergio Leone*, 7.

7. De Fornari, *Sergio Leone*, 136.

8. Robert Bresson, *Notes on the Cinematographer* (New York: Quartet Press, 1986), 10–11, 21.

9. Bresson, *Notes*, 14, 26, 64, 65, 82.

10. Sergio Leone, "I'm a Director of Gestures and Silences," *American Film* 14 (September 1989), 31.

11. Bresson, *Notes*, 48, 58.

12. De Fornari, *Sergio Leone*, 135.

13. De Fornari, *Sergio Leone*, 147.

14. Christopher Frayling, *Sergio Leone: Something to Do with Death* (London: Faber and Faber, 2000), 238.

15. Bresson, *Notes*, 80.

16. Bresson, *Notes*, 20.

17. Noel Simsolo, *Conversations avec Sergio Leone* (Paris: Stock, 1987), 112–14.

18. De Fornari, *Sergio Leone*, 21.

19. Bresson, *Notes*, 67.

## Eleven. The Leone-Morricone Soundtrack

1. Oreste De Fornari, *Sergio Leone: The Great Italian Dream of Legendary America* (Rome: Gremese, 1997), 154.

2. Christopher Frayling, *Sergio Leone: Something to Do with Death* (London: Faber and Faber, 2000), 154.

3. Jon Burlingame and Gary Crowdus, "Music at the Service of Cinema: An Interview with Ennio Morricone," *Cineaste* 12, no. 1–2 (1995), 77.

4. Frayling, *Something to Do*, 155.

5. Frayling, *Something to Do*, 155.

6. De Fornari, *Sergio Leone*, 154.

7. Frayling, *Something to Do*, 155.

8. Peter Bondanella, *Italian Cinema: From Neorealism to the Present* (New York: Ungar Press, 1983), 258.

9. Marcia Landy, "'Which Way Is America?' Americanism and the Italian Western," *Boundary* 2 (Spring, 1996), 51.

10. "Interview with James Woods," *American Film* (May, 1990), 51–53.

11. De Fornari, *Sergio Leone*, 143.

12. Frayling, *Something to Do*, 197.

13. Frayling, *Something to Do*, 280.

14. Frayling, *Something to Do*, 428.

15. De Fornari, *Sergio Leone*, 154.

16. Frayling, *Something to Do*, 155.

## Twelve. The Music of Sound and Dialogue

1. Christopher Frayling, *Sergio Leone: Something to Do with Death* (London: Faber and Faber, 2000), 109.

2. Frayling, *Something to Do*, 238.

3. Frayling, *Something to Do*, 150.

4. Frayling, *Something to Do*, 150.

5. Frayling, *Something to Do*, 157.

6. François Truffaut, *Hitchcock* (New York: Simon and Schuster, 1985), 222.

# Bibliography

Bertolucci, Bernardo. "Once Upon a Time in Italy," *Film Comment* 25, no. 77–78, July-August 1984.

Bogdanovich, Peter. "Two Beeg Green Eyes," *New York*, no. 6, November 26, 1973.

Bondanella, Peter. *Italian Cinema: From Neorealism to the Present.* New York: Frederick Ungar Publishing, 1983.

Braucourt, Guy. "Interview with Sergio Leone," *Cinema* 69, November 1969.

Burlingame, Jon, and Gary Crowdus. "An Interview with Ennio Morricone," *Cineaste* 21, no. 1–2, 1995.

Carlson, Michael. *Sergio Leone.* North Pomfret, Vermont: Pocket Essentials, 2001.

Chaput, Luc. "*Once Upon a Time in the West*: Western Opera," *Sequences,* no. 203, July-August 1999.

Ciment, Michel. "Il était une fois dans l'Ouest." *Positif,* no. 110, November, 1969.

Cumbow, Robert C. *Once Upon a Time: The Films of Sergio Leone.* Metuchen, New Jersey: Scarecrow Press, 1987.

Daney, Serge. "Il était une fois dans l'Oeust," *Cahiers du Cinéma,* no. 216, October 1969.

De Fornari, Oreste. *Sergio Leone: The Great Italian Dream of Legendary America.* Rome: Gremese International, 1997.

Frayling, Christopher. *Sergio Leone: Something to Do with Death.* London: Faber and Faber, 2000.

_____. *Spaghetti Westerns: Cowboys and Europeans from Karl May to Sergio Leone.* London: Routledge and Kegan Paul, 1981.

Grugeu, Gerard. "Entretien avec Eric Kahane," *24 Images,* no. 65, February-March 1993.

Hughes, Howard. *Spaghetti Westerns.* North Pomfret, Vermont: Pocket Essentials, 2001.

Kaminsky, Stuart. "The Grotesque West of Sergio Leone," *Take One* 3, no. 9, January-February 1972.

_____. "The Italian Western Beyond Leone," *The Velvet Light Trap,* no. 12, 1974.

Krohn, Bill. "La Planète Krohn," *Cahiers du Cinéma,* no. 422, July-August 1989.

Lambert, Gilles. *Les bons, les sales, les méchants et les propres de Sergio Leone.* Paris: Solar, 1976.

Landy, Marcia. "'Which Way Is America?' Americanism and the Italian Western," *Borders 2,* Spring 1996.

Leone, Sergio. "Ill était une fois…," *Cahiers du Cinéma,* no. 422, July-August 1989.

_____. "I'm a Director of Gestures and Silences," *American Film,* no. 14, 1989.

_____. "John Ford," *Cahiers du Cinéma,* no. 422, July-August 1989.

Leutrat, Jean-Louis, and Suzanne Liandrat-Guigues. "John Ford and Monument Valley." In Edward Buscombe and Roberta E. Pearson, eds., *Back in the Saddle Again: New Essays on the Western.* London: British Film Institute, 1998.

Lhassa, Gian. *Seul au monde dans le Western Italien.* Mariembourg: Grand Angle, 1983.

Lomenzo, Elaine. "A Fable for Adults," *Film Comment,* August 1984.

Mardore, Michael. "Il était une fois dans l'Ouest," *Le Nouvel Observateur,* August 1969.

Nicholls, David. "Once Upon a Time in

Italy," *Sight and Sound* 50, no. 1, Winter 1980-81.

Patry, Mario. "Il était une fois dans l'Ouest: 25 ans après le choc," *Sequences*, no. 166, September-October 1993.

_____. "Il était une fois...Sergio," *Sequences*, no. 207, March-April 2000.

Pierre, Sylvie. "Il était une fois dans l'Ouest." *Cahiers du Cinéma* no. 218, March 1970.

Simsolo, Noel. *Conversations avec Sergio Leone*. Paris: Stock, 1987.

_____. "Notes sur les westerns de Sergio Leone," *La Revue de Cinéma*, no. 275, September 1973.

_____. "Sergio Leone," *La Revue du Cinéma*, no. 395, June 1984.

_____. "Sergio Leone Talks," *Take One* 3, no. 9, May 1973.

Staig, Lawrence, and Tony Williams. *The Italian Western*. London: Futura Publications, 1975.

Strode, Woody. *Goal Dust*. New York: Madison Books, 1990.

Thomson, David. "Leonesque," *American Film*, no. 14, September 1989.

Weisser, Thomas. *Spaghetti Westerns — The Good, the Bad and the Violent*. Jefferson, North Carolina: McFarland, 1992.

# Index